The 'BrainCanDo' Handbook
Teaching and Learning

The 'BrainCanDo' Handbook of Teaching and Learning provides teachers and school leaders with a concise summary of how some of the latest research in educational neuroscience and psychology can improve learning outcomes. It aims to create a mechanism through which our growing understanding of the brain can be applied in the world of education. Subjects covered include memory, social development, mindsets and character.

Written by practising teachers working in collaboration with researchers, the chapters provide a toolkit of practical ideas which incorporate evidence from psychology and neuroscience into teaching practice with the aim of improving educational outcomes for all. By increasing both teachers' and pupils' understanding of the developing brain, 'BrainCanDo' aims to improve cognitive performance and attainment, foster a love of learning and enable a healthy and productive approach to personal development.

This book will appeal to educators, primarily those working in secondary schools, but also those within higher and primary school education. It will also be of interest to students of education, professionals looking to enhance their teaching and researchers working in the fields of education, psychology and neuroscience.

Julia Harrington is headmistress at Queen Anne's School and founder and chief executive officer of BrainCanDo. She has featured in and been interviewed by publications and media outlets including the *Times*, the *Telegraph*, the *Guardian* and the BBC.

Jonathan Beale is researcher-in-residence at Eton College, a research fellow for BrainCanDo and head of public speaking at Queen Anne's School. He is the co-editor of two books for Routledge: *Wittgenstein and Scientism* (2017) and *Wittgenstein and Contemporary Moral Philosophy* (forthcoming – 2022). He has published articles on philosophy and education in journals and media outlets, including the *New York Times*.

Amy Fancourt is head of psychology at Queen Anne's School and director of research for BrainCanDo. She has published articles on psychology and education in journals, including *Nature Scientific Reports, Frontiers, Psychomusicology, Impact* and *Mind, Brain and Education*, and in media outlets, including the *Times*.

Catherine Lutz is training and development manager for BrainCanDo and a PhD candidate in psychology at the University of Essex, writing a doctoral thesis on the theme of the motivational role of pregame speeches in relation to elite athletic performance.

The 'BrainCanDo' Handbook of Teaching and Learning

Practical Strategies to Bring Psychology and Neuroscience into the Classroom

Edited by Julia Harrington, Jonathan Beale, Amy Fancourt and Catherine Lutz

Routledge
Taylor & Francis Group

LONDON AND NEW YORK

First published 2021
by Routledge
2 Park Square, Milton Park, Abingdon, Oxon OX14 4RN

and by Routledge
52 Vanderbilt Avenue, New York, NY 10017

Routledge is an imprint of the Taylor & Francis Group, an informa business

British Library Cataloguing-in-Publication Data
A catalogue record for this book is available from the British Library

Library of Congress Cataloging-in-Publication Data
Names: Harrington, Julia (Headmistress), editor.
Title: The 'BrainCanDo' handbook of teaching and learning : practical strategies to bring psychology and neuroscience into the classroom / Julia Harrington, Jonathan Beale, Amy Fancourt and Catherine Lutz.
Other titles: 'Brain Can Do' handbook of teaching and learning
Description: Abingdon, Oxon ; New York, NY : Routldge, 2021. | Includes bibliographical references and index. |
Identifiers: LCCN 2020008574 | ISBN 9780367187033 (hardback) | ISBN 9780367187057 (paperback) | ISBN 9780429197741 (ebook)
Subjects: LCSH: Educational psychology. | Cognitive neuroscience. | Academic achievement–Psychological aspects. | Brain–Growth.
Classification: LCC LB1051 .B4784 2021 | DDC 370.15–dc23
LC record available at https://lccn.loc.gov/2020008574

ISBN: 978-0-367-18703-3 (hbk)
ISBN: 978-0-367-18705-7 (pbk)
ISBN: 978-0-429-19774-1 (ebk)

Typeset in Bembo and Helvetica
by Integra Software Services Pvt. Ltd.

Contents

Editors

Julia Harrington is headmistress at Queen Anne's School and founder and chief executive officer of BrainCanDo. She has featured in and been interviewed by publications and media outlets including the *Times*, the *Telegraph*, the *Guardian* and the BBC. She joined Queen Anne's School as headmistress in 2006 and founded BrainCanDo in 2013. Prior to joining Queen Anne's, she was deputy head at Prior Field's School (2003–6), where she also taught history and government and politics. Before training as a teacher, she worked for the Independent Television Companies Association and trained as a psychodynamic counsellor.

Jonathan Beale is researcher-in-residence at Eton College, a research fellow for BrainCanDo and head of public speaking at Queen Anne's School. He is also a visiting research fellow at the University of Hertfordshire and a fellow of the Royal Society of Arts. He is the co-editor of two books for Routledge: *Wittgenstein and Scientism* (2017) and *Wittgenstein and Contemporary Moral Philosophy* (2022). He has published articles on philosophy and education in academic journals and media outlets, including the *New York Times*. He taught in the Department of Religion and Philosophy at Queen Anne's from 2015 to 2019, the final two years of which he was head of department. He has lectured at the University of Reading and from 2011 to 2013 he was a fellow in philosophy at Harvard University.

Amy Fancourt is head of psychology at Queen Anne's School and the director of research for BrainCanDo. She has published articles on psychology and education in journals including *Nature Scientific Reports*, *Frontiers*, *Psychomusicology*, *Impact* and *Mind, Brain and Education*, and in media outlets including the *Times*. Prior to joining Queen Anne's in 2014, she lectured at Goldsmiths, University of London, for five years, where she completed a PhD in psychology in 2013. Throughout her doctoral studies and in her role for BrainCanDo, Amy has worked to facilitate collaborative research partnerships with leading universities exploring the impact of active musical engagement over adolescence, the role of social networks in motivation contagion and the impact of a later school start time on well-being and cognition.

Catherine Lutz is the training and development manager for BrainCanDo and a PhD candidate in sport and exercise psychology at the University of Essex, writing a doctoral thesis on the motivational role of pre-game speeches in relation to elite athletic performance. Catherine has developed a series of resources for schools and delivers INSET training to staff and pupils in a range of primary and secondary educational settings on areas such as managing performance under pressure and the social brain. Prior to beginning her PhD, Catherine completed an MSc in clinical mental health counselling and an MSc in sport and exercise psychology. She has played professional basketball for six years. She currently plays competitively for the Essex Rebels of the Women's British Basketball League and was recently named an ambassador for Basketball England's All Girls Campaign promoting participation in basketball and a healthy lifestyle.

Contributors

Victoria Bagnall is a co-founder of Connections in Mind. Victoria is a teacher and pioneer in the field of executive functioning. As a dyslexic who overcame her executive function challenges to achieve her dream of studying geography at the University of Cambridge, she knows first-hand how difficult it is to grow up with executive function deficits. Victoria's teaching career started in the geography classroom but quickly moved into SEND support, and subsequently she pursued work as a tutor and coach, working one-on-one with children with executive function challenges. She now works with people of all ages and backgrounds to improve their executive function skills so that they can flourish. Victoria regularly speaks at conferences and delivers training to teachers, education leaders and corporates.

Annie Brookman–Byrne is deputy editor of the British Psychological Society's magazine *The Psychologist*. She regularly writes about the science of learning for the Jacobs Foundation's Blog on Learning and Development (BOLD). Prior to her current post, she was an educational neuroscience researcher at Birkbeck, University of London, completing her MSc, PhD and postdoctoral research in the Centre for Educational Neuroscience (2014–19).

Joseph O. L. Buckingham is a research executive at the communications research agency Edelman Intelligence. He previously worked at the UCL Clinical Psychopharmacology Unit and holds a PhD in social psychology from Queen Mary, University of London. His research interests include social identity, motivation, psychophysiology, stress and addiction.

Sarah A. Buckingham is an artist, psychotherapist, clinical hypnotherapist and independent research consultant. She is also trained as an early-years educator (Froebel). She holds a PhD in social psychology from London South Bank University and is particularly interested in non-conscious behavioural change, social identity and addiction.

Laura Burgess is a postdoctoral researcher in psychology at the University of Reading. Her doctoral thesis was on the theme of motivation contagion within schools, looking at similarities between friends both in observable behaviour and in brain activation. Following the submission of her thesis, she is now undertaking a postdoctoral research fellow position at the University of Reading, where she continues to work in the field of contagion in the classroom, as well as beginning a psychology teaching position at Queen Anne's School.

Iroise Dumontheil is a reader in cognitive neuroscience in the Department of Psychological Sciences, Birkbeck, University of London. She obtained a PhD from the University of Paris VI and then was a postdoctoral researcher in labs in London, Cambridge and Stockholm. She is a member of Centre for Educational Neuroscience at the University of London. In 2015 she received the British Psychological Society Spearman Medal and in 2017 the British Neuropsychological Society Elizabeth Warrington Prize. She studies the typical development of social cognition and cognitive control and cognitive predictors of academic achievement using functional and structural neuroimaging, behavioural and genetic data. She is interested in the impact of cognitive training, from computerised games to mindfulness meditation practice, as well as the potential implications of neuroscience research for education.

Laurie Faith is a seventeen-year veteran teacher. She is currently finishing a PhD in developmental psychology at the Ontario Institute for Studies in Education at the University of Toronto. After having begun the 'Activated Learning' teaching movement, she now provides research support and engages in collaborative inquiry with the many educators using it.

Peter Harrison is a postdoctoral researcher at the Computational Auditory Perception Research Group at the Max Planck Institute for Empirical Aesthetics. Previously, he studied at the University of Cambridge, Goldsmiths, University of London and Queen Mary University of London. He is particularly interested in computational approaches to cognitive science and how they can help us understand auditory perception, musical aesthetics and statistical cognition. In 2018 he was awarded the Jon Rasbash Prize for Quantitative Social Science at the ESRC Research Methods Festival.

Bettina Hohnen is a senior clinical teaching fellow at UCL, teaching on the MSc in Child and Adolescent Mental Health. She received her PhD from UCL and her doctorate in clinical psychology from the University of Kent. She has specialist training in paediatric neuropsychology and expertise in the area of neurodiversity. She has recently co-authored the book, *The Incredible Teenage Brain: Everything You Need to Unlock Your Teen's Potential,* with Jane Gilmour and Tara Murphy, published by JKP. She works therapeutically with young people, parents and teachers and is passionate about translating findings from neuroscience and psychology for the lay audience to ultimately support mental health and well-being in children and young people.

Joni Holmes is head of the Centre for Attention Learning and Memory at the Medical Research Council's Cognition and Brain Sciences Unit, University of Cambridge. She has a PhD in psychology, awarded by the University of Durham in 2005, and has held numerous postdoctoral and lectureship positions. Her research focuses on the causes and remediation of specific learning difficulties. She runs a research clinic for children with difficulties in attention, learning and memory that aims to illuminate the cognitive, neural and genetic underpinnings of learning difficulties.

Frances Le Cornu Knight is a lecturer in neuroscience and director of the BSc in psychology of education program at the University of Bristol. Following completion of an MSc in cognitive and clinical neuroscience and a PhD in developmental neuroscience, her research now centres on the consequences of poor sleep through childhood and adolescence, specifically focusing on mental health and attention capacity outcomes. She has enjoyed working with BrainCanDo since 2017, researching the beneficial effects of delaying the school start time for older adolescents.

Iro Konstantinou is head of research programmes at the Tony Little Centre for Innovation and Research in Learning at Eton College, where she oversees various research projects on character and pedagogical developments. She also edits the *Eton Journal for Research and Innovation in Education*. She oversees the Leadership Institute, an initiative between the London Academy of Excellence and Eton College. She works for Pearson, where she develops higher education modules in research methods and researches interventions to improve well-being in student transitions to higher education and is the manager of the Knowledge Transfer Partnership initiatives. She is also conducting research into character skills that are needed in the workplace and beyond and how these can be fostered within higher education. She is also a research fellow at BrainCanDo, leading a project on resilience in year nine pupils across state and independent schools.

Gill Little is deputy head for teaching and learning at Queen Anne's School. Having taught for over thirty years, she has a wealth of educational experience. The first fifteen years of her career were spent teaching geography at Henley College, a tertiary college where she was the subject leader for ten years. In 2002, she became head of geography at Queen Anne's School; she led the department until 2010. During that time, she developed a tracking and monitoring scheme that was rolled out through the school. She was promoted to assistant head (academic) in 2008 and further promoted to director of teaching and learning, when she further developed the tracking and monitoring scheme and undertook wider responsibilities for teaching and learning. In 2017, she became deputy head for teaching and learning.

Imogen Moore-Shelley is a co-founder of Connections in Mind and director of the Connections in Mind Foundation. She is a cognitive psychologist interested in how we can support children to strengthen their executive function skills. She is currently completing a PhD at the University of Cambridge, exploring this topic within mainstream classrooms. She has worked in executive function coaching, special educational needs, parental mental health, the early years and as a youth worker and a community organiser and is dedicated to finding ways to ensure that all children flourish.

Daniel Müllensiefen is a professor in psychology and co-director of the MSc programme in music, mind and brain at Goldsmiths, University of London. His main field of research is music psychology, and in recent years, he has focused on individual differences in musical abilities. Daniel has worked with BrainCanDo since 2015 on a long-term collaborative project exploring the impact of active musical participation on adolescent development.

Kou Murayama is a professor at the University of Reading. His research focuses on human motivation in educational settings. He has published more than 100 research articles and 30 book chapters. He is a winner of multiple early career awards, such as the F. J. McGuigan Early Investigator Prize from the American Psychological Foundation and the Transforming Education Through Neuroscience Award from the Learning and the Brain Foundation.

Jonnie Noakes is director of teaching and learning at Eton College and director of Eton's Tony Little Centre for Innovation and Research in Learning. He is an expert in character education, with two decades of experience in teaching emotional intelligence and a deep knowledge of boarding education. As an English teacher, he has led two departments concurrently at Eton and at the London Academy of Excellence and has published fourteen texts on contemporary novels for A-level and undergraduate level. He is a governor or trustee of several state and independent schools, a director of BrainCanDo, an editorial board member of the Chartered College of Teaching's journal *Impact* and a member of the global research committee of the International Boys' School Coalition.

Patricia Riddell is professor of applied neuroscience at the University of Reading. She has taught in psychology departments in both the United States and the United Kingdom, and her teaching and research cover a wide range of areas of psychology, including developmental psychology and neuroscience. One of her main interests is in the ways in which neuroscience can be applied in the real world, supporting and extending our understanding of human behaviour. This includes considering how the teenage brain affects creation of leadership skills and collaborating with Queen Anne's School on research into contagion within the classroom.

Michael S. C. Thomas is a professor of cognitive neuroscience at Birkbeck, University of London. He has been director of the University of London Centre for Educational Neuroscience since 2010. He has authored over 120 scientific papers, books and chapters. The focus of his research laboratory is the use of multidisciplinary methods to understand the brain and cognitive bases of cognitive variability, including intelligence and developmental disorders. Within educational neuroscience, his work includes understanding the role of inhibitory control in children's science and math learning, investigating the influence of mobile phone use on adolescent brain development, linking findings on sensitive periods in brain development to their educational implications and building links between genetics, environment and education in children's developmental outcomes. He recently created a resource giving an introduction to how the brain works for teachers and parents (www.howthebrainworks.science).

Foreword

Michael S. C. Thomas

In 2018, I was fortune enough to be invited to give a talk at the BrainCanDo conference entitled, 'Pathways from Neuroscience to the Classroom', held at Queen Anne's School, where I discussed the relevance of neuroscience research to the classroom. BrainCanDo aims to develop an educational approach informed by the latest evidence in educational neuroscience and psychology. What impressed me most at that conference, and also in this volume, is the commitment of BrainCanDo to leverage the latest research in the learning sciences into practical strategies to improve teaching. As the audience politely listened to my description of new cognitive neuroscience research on the adolescent brain, I could sense their growing impatience: 'Yes, this is all very nice, but how is this going to be relevant to what teachers *do* in the classroom, and to their students' lives both inside and outside school?'

The recent interest in mining educational neuroscience and psychological research for methods to improve educational outcomes belies the difficulty of translating research findings into classroom practice. For example, even with its 125-year history of studying learning, psychology still struggles to properly inform teaching practices – techniques can persist in the classroom despite a large body of evidence indicating a lack of effect (such as underlining/highlighting/rereading texts as methods to improve learning).[1] Effective translation crucially relies on a dialogue between educators and researchers: on the one hand, to turn an understanding of how the mind works into techniques to improve learning and, on the other hand, to enable educators to move the research agenda onto issues that are most pressing in schools today. This dialogue is something BrainCanDo does really well, and this volume gives many excellent examples of how researchers and educators are fruitfully interacting. Moreover, it suggests where a scientific approach to learning finds its limits, such as in Jonathan Beale's cautionary chapter on the perils of scientism (Chapter 1).

Should we focus more on the mind or the brain? As a proponent of educational neuroscience, I would argue that you can't talk about mind and brain separately.[2] The way the brain operates constrains the way the mind works. That is, the mind

1

could have worked in lots of ways (which artificial intelligence is now showing us). The way it *actually* works depends on what the brain can do, conditioned by its biology and that, in turn, by its evolutionary history. For example, the brain stores knowledge in the strength of the connections between neurons. This means that processing pathways tend to be content specific; they are not general purpose, dealing with lots of different types of content. You'll find a region of the brain for vision, one for audition, one for sensing the body, one for smell, not a general 'perception' mechanism.

Does this matter? Take working memory, which many advocate as a key capacity underlying academic success. Amy Fancourt and Joni Holmes (Chapter 4) argue that working memory is not a part of the brain but a faculty of the mind, a theoretical concept that is used to explain how active memory works. In the brain, it is carried out by lots of different regions, each 'keeping in mind' different types of content. How good these disparate systems are in an individual tends to correlate, giving the appearance of a unified single mechanism from the psychological perspective. When a child is held back in his or her academic progress because he or she has 'poor working memory', one might think the lesson is to give the child some activity that improves his or her working memory. But the shock finding of psychologists in this field is that training children on tasks that improve working memory, such as keeping numbers in mind or keeping track of the objects they have seen, does not improve the children's academic performance. It only improves their ability to ... keep numbers in mind or keep track of the objects they've seen. This is what you'd expect from the neuroscience perspective – you have only improved the working memory capacity of the particular circuits used in the training task because there is no *general* working memory mechanism.

The narrow lesson from neuroscience in this case is that if you want to improve some cognitive capacity, it needs to be embedded in the (educational) content in which it is typically used, not abstracted out into some kind of brain-training computer game. In this volume, this lesson is picked up in chapters that consider improving executive function skills (Laurie Faith, Bettina Hohnen, Victoria Bagnall and Imogen Moore-Shelley, Chapter 7) and techniques to enhance the learning of counterintuitive concepts in mathematics and science (Annie Brookman-Byrne and Iroise Dumontheil, Chapter 10). The broad lesson is that understanding how the brain does things helps us understand the effects of training on behavioural change, the bread and butter of education.

The preceding example suggests that the contribution of neuroscience to education will largely comprise improvements in psychological theories of learning. However, there may also be direct implications of neuroscience for education, by virtue of thinking about the brain as a biological organ that has certain metabolic needs – for nutrition, for energy, to consolidate changes to its structure, to avoid the harmful effect of chronic exposure to stress hormones. This direct route produces a parallel avenue of dialogue that can be thought of in terms of 'brain health', of optimising the condition of each child's brain for learning when he or she enters the classroom. Brain health draws focus to factors such as nutrition, physical fitness, stress reduction and sleep.[3]

Educational neuroscience is relatively new compared to the psychology of learning, and it is perhaps more controversial. Certainly, most of neuroscience research is not relevant to education (it is too low level, such as the role of ion channels in producing neuronal action potentials), and most of education research is not relevant to neuroscience (it concerns social, cultural and economic factors, such as designing curricula and determining organisational structures). No neuroscience data will ever be 'classroom ready' without an extensive process of translation into and testing of practical techniques and strategies. And there are distractions, such as the misunderstandings found in neuromyths and the influence of commercial organisations seeking profits from training packages with neuroscience window dressing. However, some resistance to educational neuroscience runs deeper: principled arguments that the sort of thing that neuroscience does *can never* be relevant to education. I won't go into those arguments here (see my contretemps with Daugherty and Robey, for a flavour of the lively debate[4]) other than to suggest that this resistance is more about academic turf wars (arguing about who has the right to do research in a given area) than being solution focused (i.e. getting a crack team of people together with different expertise to investigate the area and come up with solutions). For me, it's an argument not to be settled on philosophical principles but on actual outcomes: can neuroscience contribute to educational improvements?

Two great things about this book

What most sets this volume apart from others in the field is its focus on adolescence. It is noticeable how the educational neuroscience and psychological research taken to be of translational interest to education differs with the age of the child. For early-years education, the interest is in basic sensorimotor skills, oral language development, behavioural regulation and socioemotional development – skills that contribute to school readiness. For primary school age, the focus shifts to core cognitive skills underlying academic abilities, such as numeracy, literacy and reasoning, the limits imposed by the development of skills of cognitive control and more sophisticated socio-emotional skills involved in peer group formation and dynamics. Consider, then, the topics addressed in a volume aimed at secondary school: character development, gratitude, motivation, mindset, metacognition, regulation of sleep and extended musical training (Chapters 3, 5, 6, 7, 8, 9 and 11). The focus has shifted again, beyond core skills to children's understanding of their own learning and their motivations to learn. The individual must learn where he or she needs to put in effort to achieve his or her goals and indeed to decide what those goals are – *who they are as individuals.*

Despite the welcome openness of BrainCanDo to neuroscience, many of the chapters in this volume focus on psychological approaches. This is because there is still much we do not understand about how the brain achieves more sophisticated skills around metacognition, motivation and planning and decision making, as well as the interaction of these skills with peer group influence. (See Sarah-Jayne Blakemore's excellent recent book, *Inventing Ourselves: The Secret Life of the Teenage Brain*, for an overview of current knowledge.[5]) Sarah Buckingham and Joe Buckingham present the fascinating example of gratitude, a powerful socially embedded pathway to improving life satisfaction (Chapter 9). Adults whose brains were scanned while they experienced gratitude showed notably increased activation in two brain areas, the medial prefrontal cortex and the anterior cingulate cortex. Cognitive neuroscientists proposed that feelings of gratitude may involve the medial prefrontal cortex's processes of gauging subjective value and of considering the mental states of other people. This gives us an inkling of the processes that may be involved in gratitude, but only that – let alone insights into the best way to harness gratitude to improve life satisfaction.

Perhaps the most important contribution of neuroscience to understanding adolescence is to lay bare exactly how long many of these sophisticated skills take to develop, revealed by evidence that brain circuits can still be found to be changing into the late teens and early twenties. This has even been shown for levels of verbal and nonverbal intelligence.[6] The extended developmental trajectory means that we need to shape educational environments across the same time span to provide the best outcomes for each individual as he or she reaches adulthood.

The second crucial strength of this volume is how it encourages a culture of research – that at all levels of education, teaching should be informed by evidence. Gill Little gives examples of ways this can be achieved, such as generating a 'Teacher Handbook' and convening regular 'Learning Study Groups' for teachers (Chapter 2). An evidence-informed approach is no shortcut, however, because with so many influences on a child's development, causal pathways can be complex and tricky to unpick. Does reduced sleep in adolescence cause poorer mental health, or is a difficulty in sleeping a sign of worsening mental health? (See Frances Le Cornu Knight, Chapter 8.) Does success at learning a musical instrument cause improved academic outcomes, or are they both the result of a character trait to work hard and persist with practice? (See Daniel Müllensiefen and Peter Harrison, Chapter 11.) These kinds of questions cannot be resolved in large correlational studies. They need longitudinal studies and well-controlled intervention studies, supported by experimental studies showing the viability of the causal mechanisms these effects purport to exploit. Determining what works can be tricky, when educational outcomes may be the result of so many small influences, each hard to assess in isolation (a problem not readily rectified by the use of large-scale randomised controlled trials).

While not a shortcut, an evidence-informed approach holds the best hope for progress in education, through a gradual accumulation of knowledge of what works and for whom. I imagine a teaching profession suffused by a culture of research, where teachers will be empowered by an understanding of why effective teaching methods work. They will have the autonomy to vary teaching methods according to the context of their classroom and of the particular children in front of them, knowing what features of the methods can be varied at no cost and which must be retained as they carry the causal power. They will be less prone to be distracted by faddish approaches (even those supported by brain images!), more reluctant to rely on anecdotal evidence to confirm pet theories or reject disfavoured hypotheses. But teachers will also understand that evidence-based mechanistic accounts of learning in individual children are only a small part of the educational picture. Crucially, however useful, such accounts do not determine the values that our educational systems embody and reflect. These are quite rightly an issue for society, not to be reduced to the workings of single minds and brains.

Notes

1 Roediger, H. L. (2013). Applying cognitive psychology to education: translational educational science. *Psychological Science in the Public Interest, 14,* 1–3.
2 Thomas, M. S. C., Ansari, D., and Knowland, V. C. P. (2019). Annual research review: Educational neuroscience: progress and prospects. *Journal of Child Psychology and Psychiatry, 60(4),* 477–492. doi:10.1111/jcpp.12973.
3 Thomas, M. S. C., Mareschal, D., and Dumontheil, I. (2020). *Educational Neuroscience: Development across the Lifespan.* London: Psychology Press.
4 Dougherty, D. R., and Robey, A. (2018). Neuroscience and education: a bridge astray? *Current Directions in Psychological Sciences, 27,* 401–6. doi:10.1177/0963721418794495; Thomas, M. S. C. (2019). Response to Dougherty and Robey on neuroscience and education: enough bridge metaphors – interdisciplinary research offers the best hope for progress. *Current Directions in Psychological Science, 28(4),* 337–40. doi:10.1177/0963721419838252.
5 Blakemore, S.-J. (2018). *Inventing Ourselves: The Secret Life of the Teenage Brain.* New York: Doubleday.
6 Ramsden, S., Richardson, F. M., Josse, G., et al. (2011). Verbal and non-verbal intelligence changes in the teenage brain. *Nature, 479,* 113–16. doi:10.1038/.nature10514

References

Blakemore, S.-J. (2018). *Inventing Ourselves: The Secret Life of the Teenage Brain.* New York: Doubleday.
Dougherty, D. R., and Robey, A. (2018). Neuroscience and education: A bridge astray? *Current Directions in Psychological Sciences, 27,* 401–6. doi:10.1177/0963721418794495.
Ramsden, S., Richardson, F. M., Josse, G., et al. (2011). Verbal and non-verbal intelligence changes in the teenage brain. *Nature, 479,* 113–16. doi:10.1038/nature10514.

Roediger, H. L. (2013). Applying cognitive psychology to education: translational educational science. *Psychological Science in the Public Interest, 14*, 1–3.

Thomas, M. S. C. (2019). Response to Dougherty and Robey on neuroscience and education: enough bridge metaphors – interdisciplinary research offers the best hope for progress. *Current Directions in Psychological Science, 28*(4), 337–40. doi:10.1177/0963721419838252.

Thomas, M. S. C., Ansari, D., and Knowland, V. C. P. (2019). Annual research review: Educational neuroscience: progress and prospects. *Journal of Child Psychology and Psychiatry, 60*(4), 477–92. doi:10.1111/jcpp.12973.

Thomas, M. S. C., Mareschal, D., and Dumontheil, I. (2020). *Educational Neuroscience: Development across the Lifespan.* London: Psychology Press.

Introduction: The 'BrainCanDo' approach to teaching and learning

Julia Harrington, Jonathan Beale, Amy Fancourt and Catherine Lutz

This book outlines some of the latest research in educational neuroscience and psychology and offers practical strategies for its application in secondary schools. It covers some of the research undertaken over the past seven years at BrainCanDo, an educational neuroscience and psychology research centre based at Queen Anne's School, Caversham, United Kingdom, which engages in collaborative research with several universities. BrainCanDo aims to develop an educational approach informed by the latest evidence in educational neuroscience and psychology to provide educators with practical strategies to improve their teaching which are informed by state-of-the-art research.

This book reflects that aim. It provides an overview of some of the latest research concerning themes such as motivation, memory, sleep, well-being and social development alongside practical suggestions for how such research can inform teaching and learning. It also aims to address controversies concerning the application of educational neuroscience and psychology in teaching, covering issues such as neuromyths and scepticism about the applicability of neuroscience to practical settings, addressed from philosophical perspectives. Our hope is that by using the research and strategies offered in this book, teachers will be better equipped to enhance teaching and learning.

Educational neuroscience and psychology

Increasingly rapid advancements in neuroscience have provided us with far greater knowledge of the way the brain is organised, how information is processed and how the developmental changes that take place in the brain during adolescence influence behaviour. Growing research in educational neuroscience and psychology has provided us with new ways to apply our growing body of knowledge in educational contexts, giving us more resources for improving education on the basis of the latest scientific research. This has direct and indirect applications for the educational sector, which we can use to help students to flourish in terms of their learning, mental health, and cognitive and emotional development.

One route to improving teaching and learning is through a more robust engagement with such research. A more thorough understanding of areas such as adolescent brain development and how an adolescent learns to regulate emotions can, if channelled through viable practical, pedagogical strategies, help teachers to employ the most effective methods to improve the quality of teaching and learning.

Students, their parents and teachers understand that while adolescence can be an incredibly challenging time in a young person's life, it is also an incredibly exciting stage. During this period, the brain is going through rapid change, where new neural pathways are formed and an adolescent's character is shaped. Offering an education that is well informed by our growing understanding of this period of life can helps us to provide the best education possible for adolescents.

We know much more about the development of the adolescent brain than we did twenty years ago, and some of this knowledge can be used to improve teaching and learning. Although psychology has played a prominent role in pedagogy for a long time, there is now far more that we understand from educational neuroscience and psychology, especially cognitive psychology, that can help us make teaching and learning more effective.

What is BrainCanDo?

BrainCanDo is an educational neuroscience and psychology research centre based at Queen Anne's School. The centre takes an evidence-informed approach to improving teaching and learning by conducting research in collaboration with university experts and applying research in the classroom.

Since its inception seven years ago, BrainCanDo has brought together researchers and teachers to evaluate the practical effectiveness of research in educational neuroscience and psychology. By applying research through contemporary teaching and learning methods, and by increasing teachers' and pupils' understanding of the ways in which adolescents learn, BrainCanDo aims to provide educators with the skills and knowledge to apply research in educational contexts with the goal of improving the teaching and learning experience for all.

BrainCanDo is a collaborative endeavour involving partnerships with several universities, organisations and schools. Projects have been undertaken in collaboration with researchers at the universities of Oxford, Bristol, Reading and Sheffield Hallam, University College London, and Goldsmiths and Birkbeck,

University of London. BrainCanDo is a charitable company supported by the United Westminster and Grey Coat Foundation, a foundation of five secondary schools in the south-east of England. Several areas of research are conducted with these schools. The foundation consists of two state schools in London, the Grey Coat Hospital and Westminster City; one independent school in London, Emanuel; and two independent schools in south-east England, Sutton Valence and Queen Anne's. BrainCanDo has also worked with several other local secondary schools. We offer any interested schools the opportunity to work with us and to access the resources we regularly produce.

Collaborative research

With our research partners we have engaged in several projects, the research for which has been conducted at Queen Anne's and some of the schools mentioned earlier. Our collaborative projects aim to illustrate the practical effectiveness of our research in educational settings. Our most recent research projects include the following:

- A project with Dr Laura Burgess, Professor Kou Murayama and Professor Patricia Riddell, of the University of Reading, on motivational contagion in social networks. This project spanned three years and used functional magnetic resonance imaging (fMRI) brain scanning alongside social network survey data to map the neural correlates of the impact peer networks have on motivation.
- A project with Dr Frances Le Cornu Knight, of the University of Bristol, investigating the impact of a later school start time on attention and impulse control in girls aged 16–17.
- A project with Professor Daniel Müllensiefen, of Goldsmiths, University of London, on the impact of music and other co-curricular pursuits on personal development and academic outcomes during adolescence.
- A project with Dr Sarah Buckingham exploring the impact of gratitude on subjective well-being and social cohesion in school.

All of these researchers have contributed chapters to this book on the areas of collaborative research mentioned above.

Research output and applications of research

BrainCanDo has produced several practical resources for teachers, including a teacher's handbook, a teacher's toolkit and a revision guide. We have disseminated our research widely, through publications in academic journals such as *Frontiers* and *Mind, Brain, Education*; in teaching publications such as *Impact: Journal of the Chartered College of Teaching* and the *TES*; and in media outlets including the *Times*, the BBC, the *Guardian*, the *Independent* and the *Huffington Post*. We have also hosted several conferences and we offer INSET services to schools.

Sceptical worries and controversies

Scientism

Perhaps the greatest obstacle facing educational neuroscience and psychology is how to bridge the gap between neuroscience and psychology, on the one hand, and the practical application of findings from those fields in education, on the other – in other words, how we cross the bridge between theory and practice. At BrainCanDo, we do our best to carefully cross this bridge by trying to provide clear links between scientific evidence and educational applications.

Crossing this bridge too hastily can lead to 'scientism', which Jonathan Beale defines in his chapter as 'excessive belief in the power or value of science' (Chapter 1). Scientism can be manifested in educational neuroscience by, for example, dogmatically assuming that methods or findings from neuroscience and psychology can be immediately or straightforwardly applied in educational contexts. In educational neuroscience and psychology, scientism concerns the practical limits of these fields. Beale's chapter aims to address this issue by offering practical advice on how to engage with educational neuroscience and psychology without being scientistic.

In Gill Little's chapter (Chapter 2), examples are given of the ways that a secondary school has sought to bridge the gap between theory and practice through the introduction and encouragement of a school-wide culture of evidence-informed practice. Little describes the valuable role that learning study groups have played as like-minded teaching professionals come together regularly to share ideas and to reflect on the application of research in their own teaching practice. We also read how school initiatives such as focusing on the importance of gratitude can be a useful way to bring a school community on board with the application of neuroscience and psychology research in education.

Our philosophy concerning the relationship between theory and practice can be illustrated by the following analogy Beale employs in his chapter (Chapter 1) concerning the relation between musicianship and music theory. One can be an outstanding musician with little or no formal education in music theory. But it is *extremely likely* that music theory will improve even the best of musicians, and the *best musical education* includes music theory as a component. Moreover, the *most equipped* musicians will be well educated in music theory. To apply that analogy to educational neuroscience and psychology: while knowledge of educational neuroscience and psychology is not *necessary* to be an outstanding teacher, it undoubtedly has the potential to be useful, and the *most equipped* teachers possess the knowledge yielded by those fields.

Neuromyths

One of the challenges we have faced when applying research from neuroscience and psychology in the classroom has stemmed from the proliferation of supposed 'neuroeducation' programmes and interventions that have a dubious scientific underpinning. Such dubious interventions and programmes have been given the name 'neuromyths'. Pervasive neuromyths can make it difficult to separate applications with a strong scientific evidence base from those with less secure scientific foundations. For example, people tend to believe that we only use around 10% of our brains. This neuromyth has become so popularised that it is often considered a fact, even though there is no scientific evidence to support it.

We need to be careful and discerning consumers of educational research. One of the central aims of BrainCanDo has been to debunk some of the most prevalent neuromyths – for example, that girls are not neurologically wired to be risk-takers – and replace them with genuine evidence from neuroscience and psychology that has the potential to improve teaching and learning. We want to see genuine scientific evidence used effectively not only within the classroom but also within education generally.

Overview of chapters

This book consists of eleven chapters exploring themes in or relating to educational neuroscience and psychology. Several chapters outline the respective research area under discussion followed by an outline of practical examples of ways that our understanding of the adolescent brain can inform educational policy and practice.

The chapters are divided into five sections. The first section, 'Controversies and Applications' includes two chapters, the first of which (Chapter 1) addresses some controversies surrounding educational neuroscience and psychology; the second (Chapter 2) outlines the ways in which research from BrainCanDo has been applied at Queen Anne's School with the aim of improving teaching and learning. We have put these chapters in the same section because the main controversies surrounding educational neuroscience and psychology concern their application – that is, how to move from research in these fields to its application in practical settings, such as the classroom – in other words, how to cross the gap between theory and practice.

In Chapter 1, Beale discusses the greatest problem facing educational neuroscience and psychology: how to move from scientific evidence to its practical application in education. Beale argues that making this move too hastily leaves educational neuroscience and psychology open to the accusation of scientism. Beale offers an account of scientism and offers suggestions on how to avoid scientism when applying theories or evidence from neuroscience and psychology in education.

In Chapter 2, Little shares the ways in which Queen Anne's has attempted to bridge the gap between educational neuroscience and educational practice. From the introduction of resources such as a 'Teacher Handbook', disseminated to all teaching staff, through to the facilitation of research meeting groups for teachers engaged in research, Little offers those in school leadership a range of strategies to support the introduction of an evidence-informed teaching and learning culture in their own educational contexts.

The second section, 'Becoming a Successful Learner' includes two chapters, the first of which is on character education and the second of which is on the role of working memory in learning. In Chapter 3, Iro Konstantinou and Jonnie Noakes argue that in order for schools to equip pupils with the abilities required to become engaged citizens who can thrive in a diverse society, character education needs to be embedded within a school's curriculum, co-curriculum and wider culture. They outline several evidence-informed practices that can foster some of the character skills and traits that may equip pupils for a changing world, based upon research studies they have conducted at Eton College's Tony Little Centre for Innovation and Research in Learning.

In Chapter 4, Amy Fancourt and Joni Holmes explore the research surrounding the development of working memory and consider the extent to which working memory underpins many aspects of learning. Fancourt and Holmes highlight the nature of individual differences in working memory capacity and the need for teachers to recognise pupils who may have lower working memory capacity than others. The chapter concludes with a review of research investigating ways to use this knowledge of working memory to effectively support all learners in the classroom.

The three chapters in the third and longest section, 'Motivation', approach the theme of motivation through three psychological concepts, each of which is important in education: motivational contagion, mindset and executive functioning. In Chapter 5, Laura Burgess, Patricia Riddell and Kou Murayama provide practical guidelines on how to harness the advantages of motivational contagion in the classroom, drawing on their research at the University of Reading concerning this psychological phenomenon. This chapter begins with a review of the current literature explaining the impact of social influence on behaviour and particularly the role of contagion in academic motivation. The authors explore the mechanisms underlying the transfer of attitude and motivation from teacher to pupil and from pupil to pupil within the context of the classroom. The chapter finishes with practical recommendations on how teachers can use this knowledge to foster greater levels of academic motivation in their pupils.

In Chapter 6, Catherine Lutz explores the relationship between motivation and mindsets, drawing on her research in sports psychology at the University of

Essex. There are multiple factors that influence an individual's academic achievement and professional satisfaction. In an academic setting, both an individual's mindset and personal motivation towards education have been identified in research as important variables that may determine attainment and enjoyment. Both students and teachers alike can benefit from evaluating and monitoring their mindset and motivation throughout their educational journeys. Lutz hopes to introduce the reader to a basic understanding of mindsets and motivation and how they may influence both academic achievement and professional satisfaction in the classroom. The chapter draws upon important theories in and research from neuroscience and psychology on mindsets and motivation, and concludes with practical applications that readers may choose to examine further to help support a growth mindset and positive motivation in both themselves and their students.

In Chapter 7, Laurie Faith, Bettina Hohnen, Victoria Bagnall and Imogen Moore-Shelley offer an account of how an approach centred around executive functioning skills can develop self-regulation, metacognition and motivation in learners. The chapter provides an overview of the development of executive functioning skills in primary and secondary school-aged children and outlines an approach for building executive functioning skills that is currently being used in primary and secondary schools in the United Kingdom and Canada. The concept of executive functioning and its role in education are also explored in the chapter by Annie Brookman-Byrne and Iroise Dumontheil (Chapter 10).

The fourth section addresses the topic of well-being, with two chapters on the themes of sleep and gratitude, respectively. In Chapter 8, sleep expert Frances Le Cornu Knight explains the vital role of sleep in creating optimal conditions for learning and healthy development throughout adolescence. Le Cornu Knight synthesises the current research exploring the status of sleep and reasons for apparent sleep deprivation in the adolescent population today before considering the value of sleep for academic achievement and well-being. In light of this research, Le Cornu Knight presents a challenge to educators to seriously consider the potential value of introducing a later school start to enable adolescents to regularly get more sleep during weeknights. The chapter closes with recommendations for schools and teachers on promoting the vital role of sleep to pupils and advocating strategies that they can adopt to improve sleep hygiene.

Chapter 9 explores the impact that gratitude can have on the social lives of students, in terms of both their feeling of subjective social well-being and their social cohesion at school. Sarah A. Buckingham and Joseph O. L. Buckingham begin by outlining what we understand by 'gratitude' before summarising existing research showing the connection between expressions of gratitude and pro-social behaviour. They go on to explore the development of gratitude and the extent to which individual differences in the ability to express gratitude may be explained by environmental and personality factors. A review of the connection between gratitude and subjective well-being leads to the conclusion that a great deal of life satisfaction is connected to the amount of gratitude experienced. Furthermore, recent neuroscientific research supports the claim that feelings of gratitude are linked with the activation of brain areas associated with thinking about other people, judging subjective value, emotion, motivation and reward. The chapter concludes with a challenge to all educators to nurture the development of gratitude in pupils and makes some practical suggestions as to how schools can engage with particular interventions and programs to support this.

The final section, 'Subject-Specific Research', contains two chapters offering studies that apply research in educational neuroscience and psychology to three specific subjects: mathematics, science and music. In Chapter 10, Annie Brookman-Byrne and Iroise Dumontheil provide an overview of the neural changes that happen throughout adolescence. The authors proceed to consider how our new understanding of adolescent brain development can be used to enhance teaching and learning. They argue that any experience of social rejection is heightened during adolescence, and, therefore, ensuring that students feel socially included in the classroom is an important way to reduce anxiety and promote better learning. Brookman-Byrne and Dumontheil consider the role of inhibitory control in the acquisition of counterintutitive concepts that are typically found in science and mathematics. The chapter ends with a series of suggestions of ways that teachers might encourage adolescents to employ more widespread use of inhibitory control mechanisms in order to strengthen this executive function, which is still developing throughout adolescence.

In Chapter 11, Daniel Müllensiefen and Peter Harrison explore how music can influence adolescents' cognitive and socio-emotional development and how music, as a model of brain plasticity, could form an effective teaching intervention. The chapter reviews the existing literature investigating musical transfer effects and questions the extent to which we can infer causation from participation in music to changes in cognitive or socio-emotional abilities from the existing research. The authors argue that it is not always possible to infer causal effects because of the nature and design of many studies. In an attempt to close this gap in the empirical literature, Müllensiefen and Harrison report results from a new study that allows us to address causal questions with a longitudinal study design. The study aims to track the development of musical abilities together with cognitive and socio-emotional skills across adolescence. Preliminary results suggest that musical learning can be effective in changing growth mindset attitudes. However, Müllensiefen and Harrison argue that our current knowledge of brain plasticity and the physical changes that occur in the brain as a direct result of musical learning can be used to support mindset teaching interventions. The authors conclude with a suggested framework for developing such a musical mindset intervention.

Controversies and applications

1

Educational neuroscience and educational neuroscientism

Jonathan Beale

The greatest problem facing educational neuroscience and psychology is crossing the bridge between theory and practice: how to move from scientific theories and evidence to their practical application in education. Crossing this bridge too hastily leaves educational neuroscience and psychology open to the accusation of 'scientism': excessive belief in the power or value of science. Scientism would be manifested in attitudes such as the dogmatic assumption that scientific methods or findings can be immediately or straightforwardly applied in education.

How can neuroscience and psychology be applied in education without risking scientism? Scientism is an elusive concept, so this chapter offers an account of what scientism is (the first three sections). It is argued that education should be included among the areas that are the most difficult to reduce to explanations in scientific terms (the third section). The account of scientism is used to outline three examples of ways in which neuroscience and psychology could be applied in education that would be open to accusations of scientism (the fourth section). Three indicators of scientism when scientific theories or evidence are applied in education are described. Alongside each indicator, suggestions are offered on what we should watch out for to avoid being scientistic when applying theories or evidence from neuroscience and psychology in education (the final section) – or, to avoid what we might call 'educational neuroscientism'.

What is scientism?

'Scientism' is an elusive concept that has appeared increasingly in recent years, especially in philosophical debates. It tends to be levelled as a criticism against views that make controversial claims about the nature, value or power of science. The term is usually treated as pejorative, and those levelling it as a criticism often take it to be fairly obvious what 'scientism' is and what is wrong with being 'scientistic'. But the variety of views against which scientism is levelled suggest that it is neither clear what scientism is nor what is wrong with being scientistic. Scientism possesses many features and takes many forms. Many definitions have been offered, some pejorative and some neutral. A growing number of those accused of scientism are happy to bear the term with pride, as a neutral or even an honorific term. Those donning it as an honorific term reply to their critics by arguing that scientism is a reasonable philosophical position.[1]

'Scientism' was coined in roughly the mid-19th century. Its original meaning is neutral: 'the methods, mental attitude, doctrines, or modes of expression ... characteristic of scientists'.[2] This use, which is now rare, was its only meaning until the early 20th century, when it gained a pejorative use, which we could crudely define as 'excessive belief in the power of science' (Haack, 2013 [2009], 2–3) or excessive 'science enthusiasm' (Boudry and Pigliucci, 2017, 2). This is its common use nowadays. Such definitions raise a more specific question: *what is it* to have excessive belief in the power of science or excessive science enthusiasm? This is where scientism becomes more difficult to define.

Most forms of scientism make or imply controversial claims about the nature, value or power of science. Sometimes the views look patently untenable, but sometimes they do not look controversial. For example, in the *Oxford Dictionary of Philosophy*, Simon Blackburn defines scientism as follows:

> Pejorative term for the belief that the methods of natural science, or the categories and things recognized in natural science, form the only proper elements in any philosophical or other inquiry
>
> *[Blackburn, 1994, 344]*

This just looks like another way of expressing philosophical naturalism: the view that the natural world is all that exists and that it should be studied using the methods best suited to the study of the natural world – that is, those of the natural sciences. According to naturalism, or at least the form sometimes called 'methodological naturalism', we can find complete explanations for all phenomena without appeal to anything beyond the natural world. Since naturalism (in its many forms) is the orthodox position in contemporary philosophy, scientism, based on Blackburn's definition, does not seem to be controversial.

The most common targets for allegations of scientism are controversial claims about science's expansion. Consequently, the most common way of defining scientism is as a thesis about science's limits or lack of limits. For example, Mikael Stenmark argues that scientism is synonymous with 'scientific expansionism': the view that the boundaries of science (that is, typically the natural sciences) could and should be expanded in such a way that something that has not previously been understood as science can now become a part of science

[Stenmark, 2003, 783]

We cannot, however, treat scientism synonymously with scientific expansionism because scientism takes expansionist and *non-expansionist* forms. The latter includes views where the natural sciences are unwarrantedly assigned a higher value over non-scientific areas of inquiry and culture but no attempt is made to expand the limits of natural science. For example, Tom Sorell, author of the seminal monograph on scientism, *Scientism: Philosophy and the Infatuation with Science* (1991), defines scientism as follows:

Scientism is a matter of putting too high a value on science in comparison with other branches of learning or culture

[Sorell, 1991, x]

This could be manifested in ways that do not involve any expansion of science. What is essential to scientism, based on Sorell's definition, is an evaluative judgement of the value of science over non-scientific areas of inquiry and culture – for example, to hold that the arts or humanities are of little or no value compared to the sciences.

A look at scientism's history helps to identify non-expansionist forms and the important role of scientific expansionism in the concept's origins. 'Science', in the context of scientism, almost always concerns the natural sciences. 'Science' acquired its narrower modern use during the mid-19th century, when it became synonymous with natural science. This is its dominant sense today. 'Scientism' was coined not long afterwards (the *Oxford English Dictionary* cites its earliest occurrence as 1877). In the early 20th century, 'scientism' gained a pejorative connotation, largely following reactions against scientific expansionism – that is, against attempts to expand the bounds of the natural sciences by applying their methods to other disciplines. Some perceived this as excessively ambitious and worried that certain disciplines would become regarded as obsolete in comparison with science. Some allegations of scientism were directed at practitioners of non-scientific disciplines, particularly those working in the non-natural sciences, for imitating the teaching or vocabulary of the natural sciences in their fields.

In his seminal tripartite set of papers on scientism, 'Scientism and the Study of Society' (*Economica*, 1942–1944), F. A. von Hayek describes such imitation as definitive of scientism: 'we shall', he wrote, 'wherever we are concerned … with that slavish imitation of the method and language of Science, speak of "scientism" or the "scientistic" prejudice' (von Hayek, 1942, 269). This is one of the first explicit pejorative definitions of scientism.

In the first of his papers on scientism, Hayek offers an illuminating summary of its origins. Hayek argues that scientism, understood as the 'slavish imitation' of science, emerged during the first half of the 19th century. During this time, the increasing success of the natural sciences 'began to exercise an extraordinary fascination on those working in other fields'. This led to those working in other disciplines – particularly the non-natural sciences – to 'imitate ... the teaching and vocabulary' of the natural sciences. Disciplines outside the natural sciences 'became increasingly concerned to vindicate their equal status by showing that their methods were the same as those of their brilliantly successful sisters' – that is, the natural sciences. This ran the risk of those disciplines imitating methods from the natural sciences 'rather than ... adapting their [own] methods more and more to their own particular problems' (von Hayek, 1942, 268).

If Hayek's historical account is roughly correct, it is plausible that the focus laid on the natural sciences in the concept of scientism and the term's negative connotation have been brought about largely as a result of the success of the natural sciences. Their success has led to a widespread belief that the methods of the natural sciences can be extrapolated; it has led some practitioners of other disciplines to imitate their methods; and it has led some to think that the natural sciences are more valuable than other fields.

Scientism, based on Hayek's account, denotes imitation for science as a result of deference. This need not involve attempts to expand science. If such imitation is a form of scientism, the concept cannot be treated synonymously with 'scientific expansionism', *pace* Stenmark. While the most common type of scientism may well be what Stenmark calls scientific expansionism, it is not the only form scientism takes and it cannot be used as a means of defining it.

The limits of science

Scientism cannot be defined without considering the following question: *what are the limits of science?* To address this question, consider the most extreme view: science has *no* limits. The editors of a recent volume on scientism, *Science Unlimited: The Challenges of Scientism*, call this view 'science unlimited' (Boudry and Pigliucci, 2017, 2). This view is rare. Even the logical positivist Rudolf Carnap, who claimed that '*Science ... has no limits*', immediately qualified that statement by writing that 'this does not mean that there is nothing outside of science and that it is all-inclusive' and the 'total range of life has still many other dimensions outside of science' (Carnap, 1967 [1928], 290). Yet, some philosophers have tried to offer examples of endorsements of 'science unlimited'. Stenmark describes the strongest form of scientism as follows:

> In its most ambitious form, scientism states that science has no boundaries: eventually science will answer all human problems. All the tasks human beings face will eventually be solved by science
>
> *[Stenmark, 2003, 783]*

Stenmark quotes the following as an example. Jawaharlal Nehru, the first prime minister of independent India, wrote:

> It is science alone that can solve the problems of hunger and poverty, of insanitation and illiteracy, of superstition and deadening custom and tradition, of vast resources running to waste, of a rich country inhabited by starving people. … At every turn we seek its aid. … The future belongs to science and to those who make friends with science
>
> *[Nehru, 1960, 564]*

Stenmark quotes this to illustrate that some politicians are 'champions' of scientism (Stenmark, 2001, 15). Sorell quotes this to illustrate how widespread scientism is. 'Views like Nehru's', Sorell writes, 'were once quite widely held' and 'were perhaps typical of the scientism of the politicians of the 1950s and 1960s' (Sorell, 1991, 2). But we should be careful to not take this quote too seriously. It is taken from a speech Nehru gave at a national science conference and seems like a hyperbolical passage, typical of the kind someone in his position might be expected to give at such an event.

It is difficult to find anyone who endorses what Stenmark describes as the 'most ambitious form' of scientism. Perhaps the closest we can get is those who endorse the view that science can encompass all of those domains often claimed to be especially problematic to bring within the domain of natural science: religion and the supernatural, philosophy, intentionality and morality. The final of those is commonly held to be that which most eludes science's reach. In the essays in the aforementioned volume on scientism (Boudry and Pigliucci, 2017), several contributors argue that science has few limits, but no matter how far we expand its boundaries, science cannot provide an objective basis for morality. The view that science can do so seems to be what is meant by 'science unlimited' in that volume. Examples cited in that collection of those who hold that science can provide an objective basis for morality are Sam Harris (*ibid.*, 22, 44, 123, 189) and Michael Shermer (*ibid.*, 97–101, 106, 189). Harris is the most commonly cited target. Harris's *The Moral Landscape* (Harris, 2010) puts forward the view that science can determine values (Pigliucci, 2017, 189). According to Harris, we can derive 'should' and 'ought' from certain facts about the world (Kalef, 2017, 97).

Perhaps education should be added to those domains that are especially problematic for science to encompass. It is difficult to see how teaching and learning could ever be entirely reduced to or based upon what has come to be known as the 'science of learning'. Education is a vastly complex field and a humanistic enterprise, involving a variety of methods and approaches for teaching many disparate disciplines to a range of people. Teaching and learning involve human interpretation across a broad spectrum of contexts. Education involves judgements about learning on the basis of a wide set of criteria, the input of many areas of inquiry and managing human behaviour across age groups where psychological, emotional, intellectual and physical development is rapid and significant.

While it would be controversial to argue that all human experiences cannot be explained on *some level* in neuroscientific and psychological terms, this does not entail that other ways of understanding human experience are reducible to the conceptual sphere of the natural sciences, or the sciences more broadly construed, such as neuroscience and psychology, or the collection of sciences involved in the interdisciplinary programme known as the 'science of learning' (which draws upon evidence from the natural, cognitive and psychological sciences). It also does not entail that other ways of understanding human experience are not extremely useful and important. If we were to try to reduce explanations and frameworks for understanding human beings to the domains of neuroscience and psychology, and in the process do away with the kinds of descriptions offered by some other disciplines, we would risk losing an important way of understanding others, the world and ourselves.

Consider, for example, an instance of what is sometimes called the 'cognitive value' of literature. A great writer can teach us much about human experiences through the ways in which he or she expresses particular experiences through writing, even – and perhaps especially – in fictional contexts. Great writers can teach us about experiences in highly accessible and relatable ways. Literature offers a richer means of expressing human experience than learning about experiences through the conceptual repertoire of neuroscience and psychology. Great literature sometimes even offers richer ways of understanding human experiences than the ways of understanding we gain by having those experiences ourselves. For example, Shakespeare can express the vicissitudes life throws our way better than most of us are able to describe, conceptualize or understand. In other words, great writers enable us to *think* about our own experiences in new and richer ways.

Teaching requires knowledge both of the subject taught and of how to teach it. The latter is a form of 'ability knowledge': knowledge of how to do something. While we can pass on certain kinds of knowledge to others through instructions and explanations – for example, knowledge of facts ('propositional knowledge') – we often cannot teach ability knowledge in this way. One could, for example, acquire a highly detailed knowledge of musical notation but not be able to sight-read.

Dylan Wiliam recently employed this epistemological distinction to support an argument concerning the limitations of research in education. An expert teacher's ability knowledge cannot, he argues, be explained to another person such that the knowledge is then possessed by both parties. To use his example, while you could explain to someone how to solve quadratic equations such that they could solve them themselves, you could not explain to someone how to ride a bike such that they could ride a bike themselves. Regardless of the level of quality and detail of the instructions and explanations, a person cannot ride a bike until he or she has learned how to do it for himself or herself. Similarly, Wiliam argues, 'teacher expertise cannot be put into words': while we can offer guidance, 'there is no set of instructions that will be guaranteed to work' (Wiliam, 2019).

Connecting this point to the role of research in education, Wiliam argues that while it is important for teachers to know about research in order to 'make smarter decisions about where to invest their time', there are many areas of teaching where there is either no research evidence or research evidence is not applicable within a specific context of teaching and learning. Wiliam argues that education therefore can be 'research *informed*' but not 'research *based*' because '[c]lassrooms are just too complicated for research ever to tell teachers what to do' (Wiliam, 2019).

Certain areas of education can be research based, such as particular teaching strategies. For example, Barak Rosenshine's influential 'Principles of Instruction' are research-based teaching strategies.[3] But education as a whole is too complex to be an entirely research-based field. Education has epistemic, moral and civic aims. Its aims include developing virtuous character skills and dispositions, inspiring and motivating students to learn and helping students to flourish. Many factors contribute to the learning process, such as the atmosphere in the classroom and the levels of curiosity, enthusiasm and motivation among the students.

This brings us to what is perhaps the main objection we should raise against Rosenshine's 'Principles…'. One of the three sources of evidence for his principles is the teaching strategies of 'master teachers': teachers whose classrooms made the highest gains in standardised achievement tests (Rosenshine, 2012, 12). But surely the honorific title 'master teacher' ought to cover a broader set of pedagogical accomplishments, particularly student engagement, yet very little is said in Rosenshine's 'Principles…' about engagement.

We can use scientific research to provide support to and develop the effectiveness of teaching and learning methods, but if we had to *base* the effectiveness of teaching and learning on research, much of what takes place in the classroom would lack research support. In some cases this would be because there is not *yet* the relevant research, but in others it would be because research in certain areas would not be able to tell us much. This is because education is a complex, humanistic enterprise which involves many aspects, some of which are not reducible to exhaustive explanation in scientific terms.

Wiliam's argument concerning the role of research in education can be applied more specifically to the role of neuroscience and psychology in education, drawing attention to some of their limitations. Education cannot be *based* on scientific research, but it can be *informed* by it. A research-based practice is undertaken on the basis of the research supporting it. For example, medicine is prescribed on the basis of empirical evidence showing that it can prevent or be used as treatment for a disease. By contrast, a research-informed practice is informed by research but need not make recourse to research to justify its employment. For example, many teaching methods have been successfully employed for a long time without research showing why they are effective. But the lack of research evidence supporting their effectiveness does not imply that we should give them up in favour of methods the effectiveness of which is supported by research evidence. or think of them as less pedagogically valuable.

Awareness of these limitations puts us in a better position to apply neuroscience in education without the risk of scientism. Failure to acknowledge them puts educational neuroscience at risk of becoming educational neuroscientism.

Three options for defining scientism

Given the many uses to which scientism is put, there seem to be three options for how we should approach a definition of scientism.

Eliminativism

We could eliminate the term altogether. Russell Blackford argues that we should adopt this approach. Scientism, Blackford argues, should be 'shelved' (Blackford, 2017, 27). But this seems excessive; we can surely salvage the term, but not univocally.

Relativism

We could be relativistic about how scientism should be defined. Don Ross takes this approach:

> There is no fact of the matter about what scientism is, only facts about what different sets of people take scientism to be; and … there is much disagreement across these sets
>
> *[Ross, 2017, 225]*

However, acknowledging the caveats that, first, there is wide disagreement over definitions and applications of 'scientism' and, second, there are many criteria for identifying scientism and its manifold uses could lead us to a position other than relativism.

Cluster concept

The relations between forms of scientism could be understood as those which unite the concept but are not to be understood in terms of necessary and sufficient conditions or a finite set of shared criteria. Scientism is perhaps best understood as a cluster concept (see Beale, 2019, 85). Scientism might be a good example of what Wittgenstein called a 'family resemblance' concept, where the relations between the instances of what we can legitimately call 'scientism' are loose and varied, such as the relations between the members of what we call a 'family' (e.g. blood relatives, step relatives, in-laws, godparents and so on) (see Wittgenstein, 2009 [1953], section 67). This is the position Ian James Kidd and I have suggested:

> Scientism is perhaps a good example of a family resemblance concept – a plurality of related things differing in significant ways
>
> *[Beale and Kidd, 2017, 1–2]*

Even if scientism is a cluster concept, we can offer a crude definition of its pejorative use. Defining scientism as 'excessive belief in the power of science' is misleading because a view that seems scientistic because it *overvalues* science need not involve a claim about science's *power*. Sorell's definition as 'overvaluing science' is also misleading because a view that betrays excessive belief in the *power* of science need not involve any claim about science's *value*. We should therefore make the pejorative definition of scientism disjunctive: *excessive belief in the power or value of science* (see Beale, 2019, 85). This covers the definitions offered by those who have made the most influential contributions to the debate concerning scientism, such as Stenmark, Sorell and Susan Haack, and perhaps all views against which scientism is levelled as an accusation – albeit crudely. To cover all forms of scientism, pejorative and neutral, it is perhaps best understood as a family resemblance concept.

On this definition of the pejorative use, some specification needs to be made on *how much* value or power is assigned to science over non-science. Sorell's work on scientism is useful here. Scientism, according to Sorell, is 'the belief that science ... is *much the most* valuable part of human learning':

> What is crucial to scientism is not the identification of something as scientific or unscientific but the thought that the scientific is much more valuable than the non scientific, or the thought that the non-scientific is of negligible value
>
> *[Sorell, 1991, 9]*

We could say that scientism is ultimately a matter of believing that natural science is *much* more powerful or valuable than non-science, where 'powerful' generally denotes *explanatory power*. This is consistent with the earlier point that to be scientistic a view needs to be controversial.

Sorell's definition draws attention to an important feature of scientism. To count as scientistic, in the pejorative sense, a view about the application of science to non-scientific areas of inquiry or culture needs to be *controversial*. An interdisciplinary approach between neuroscience and education cannot be scientistic simply because it holds that certain findings from neuroscience can be used to improve approaches towards education. This would not betray excessive belief in the power or value of science. To be scientistic, the claim needs to be much more ambitious.

Examples of what would count as scientism in educational neuroscience

With scientism defined, here are three examples of views concerning the application of neuroscientific theories or evidence in education against which accusations of scientism would be warranted.

Neuroscientific methods and findings can be immediately or straightforwardly applied in educational contexts

Claims about the application of neuroscientific methods or findings to education need to be justified, because their application is not straightforward, for at least two reasons. First, education is not a branch of science. Second, education is a vastly complex field and a humanistic enterprise. So clear links need to be provided between scientific evidence and its application to education.

It is not possible to provide a good education without recourse to educational neuroscience

An example of this would be holding that education that is not informed by neuroscience is inadequate. The uncontroversial view that neuroscience can *improve* education does not entail that without attention to neuroscience, education is in some way deficient. The latter would follow from the former if educational neuroscience were shown to improve education to a highly significant degree. The latter would also follow from the former if attention to educational neuroscience could result in educators following much more effective teaching and learning practices, and the effectiveness of those practices were well supported by evidence from educational neuroscience. In such cases, education would be deficient as a consequence of insufficient attention to educational neuroscience.

To illustrate, consider the following. Evidence suggests that effective feedback improves learning and student progress to a highly significant extent. So it would be uncontroversial to argue that education without effective feedback is inadequate. Until a similar claim could be made about educational neuroscience, one could not convincingly argue that education without attention to educational neuroscience is inadequate.

The claim that education that is not informed by educational neuroscience is inadequate may one day have greater force. It could do so if the field continues to make significant advances. Regardless of where educational neuroscience goes in the future, to hold that it has the potential to *improve* education is uncontroversial.

One cannot be a proficient teacher without an understanding of educational neuroscience

A similar point applies here: while knowledge of educational neuroscience may *improve* a teacher's proficiency, it does not follow that a teacher is not proficient unless he or she possesses such knowledge. For that claim to be justified, it would need to be shown that knowledge of educational neuroscience improves a teacher's proficiency to a *highly significant* degree.

The following analogy illustrates what constitutes a healthy approach towards crossing the methodological bridge between taking findings from neuroscience and psychology and applying them in education. One can be an outstanding musician with little or no formal education in music theory. But it is *extremely likely* that music theory will improve even the best of musicians; and the *best musical education* includes music theory as a component. Moreover, the *most equipped* musicians will be well educated in music theory. To apply this analogy to educational neuroscience and psychology, while knowledge of educational neuroscience and psychology is not *necessary* to be an outstanding teacher, it undoubtedly has the potential to be useful, and the *most equipped* teachers possess the knowledge yielded by these fields.

Indicators of scientism in educational neuroscience

Based on the preceding account, three indicators of scientism that are most relevant to our concerns in educational neuroscience and psychology are outlined below. Connected with each of these, suggestions are offered for how we can reduce the risk of scientism when applying theories or evidence from neuroscience or psychology in education.

Dogmatically assuming that scientific methods or findings can be applied in non-scientific domains or overemphasising the extent to which they can be applied

We should (1) not *assume* that neuroscientific methods or findings can *always* be applied in education and (2) be careful with claims about how far they can be applied. For any neuroscientific evidence or study, a case needs to be made for its application in education. This relates to the first example of scientism outlined earlier: the view that neuroscientific methods or findings can be immediately or straightforwardly applied in education. This is the most important methodological hazard facing educational neuroscience as it concerns the central problem it faces: how to move from scientific theories and evidence to their application in education.

Using scientific or quasi-scientific language to try to make work look more impressive, without the evidential support for such uses of language

We should have good reason to use the language or conceptual repertoire of neuroscience in educational research and its dissemination. Examples are concepts such as 'neuroplasticity', 'synaptic plasticity' or references to parts of the brain such as areas of the limbic system (e.g. the amygdala, the hypothalamus, or the hippocampus). It is important to use these with good reason because in our scientific age, such concepts and language can be misappropriated to make work sound more technical, impressive, rigorous or evidence-based.[4]

Usually, the employment of such concepts and language is done with good reason; the peer-review process of academic journals, for example, should ensure this. But, with such concepts increasingly entering the parlance of contemporary education, they are increasingly employed more widely and liberally: in education publications for a general audience; at conferences aimed at educators in wide sectors of education, or educators in general; in professional development training sessions; and so on. In order to be discerning consumers and disseminators of research, we should be aware of the ways that such concepts and terms can be misappropriated to give a misleading impression of technicality, rigour, or extensive evidential support.

The same caveat goes for psychological concepts, but these can be used more liberally than neuroscientific concepts because psychology is a science operating on a less fundamental level than neuroscience, so the concepts are less specific – that is to say, they are concerned with the human mind and human behaviour rather than the structure or function of the brain and nervous system. So, psychological concepts such as 'emotional contagion', 'motivational contagion', 'mentalization' and so on can be used with greater freedom, but the caveat still applies, albeit with less force. Such concepts have entered the vernacular of contemporary education, particularly Carol Dweck's influential concept of 'growth mindset' (see Dweck, 2007 [2006]), which now occupies a staple place in many teacher training and professional development programmes. We need to be careful about how we use and interpret these concepts and other psychological concepts commonly employed in education.

The following three principles help to avoid the risk of scientism when applying theories, evidence or concepts from neuroscience or psychology in education. Such concepts should be used

1. on the basis of good evidence,
2. within a sound neuroscientific and/or psychological methodology (rather than, for instance, being used casually or carelessly in an article for a general audience),
3. (with 1 and 2 met) in order to justify the practical implementation of research in education, by illustrating ways that such concepts are relevant to educational practices.

Holding that to explain something scientifically is to explain it away

To explain something in neuroscientific terms is not to explain it *away*. Just because all areas of human thought and behaviour can be causally explained in neuroscientific terms *on some level*, this does not show that other ways of understanding human behaviour can be *reduced* to an explanation in neuroscientific terms. Neuroscientific explanations of areas especially relevant to teaching and learning, such as how the brain processes information, or the neurological underpinnings of emotional regulation, should not be interpreted as *reducing* teaching and learning to exhaustive explanation in neuroscientific terms. Teaching and learning require much more than the evidence, theories, concepts and language offered by neuroscience and psychology. We saw earlier two obstacles standing in the way of attempts to apply explanatory scientific reductionism to teaching and learning: the complexity of teaching and learning and, drawing on the work of Wiliam, the kind of knowledge required in the practice of teaching.

Concluding remarks

This chapter has offered an account of scientism and some practical guidance on how to avoid scientism in educational neuroscience and psychology. It has been argued that scientism, in the pejorative sense, is best understood as excessive belief in the power or value of science. As a position, scientism is best understood as a cluster concept, such as one where its various forms are related by what Wittgenstein called 'family resemblance'. Scientism takes expansionist and non-expansionist forms (*pace* Stenmark). For a view to count as scientistic, it must be controversial.

Based on the account of scientism offered, three examples of scientism in education were outlined related to views on the application of theories and evidence from neuroscience and psychology in education: (1) assuming that *neuroscientific methods and findings can be immediately or straightforwardly applied in educational contexts*, (2) holding that *it is not possible to provide a good education without recourse to educational neuroscience* and (3) holding that *one cannot be a proficient teacher without an understanding of educational neuroscience*.

Three indicators of scientism in educational neuroscience and psychology and some ways of avoiding them were also outlined. The first indicator is *dogmatically assuming that scientific methods or findings can be applied in non-scientific domains, or overemphasising the extent to which they can be applied*. To avoid this, we should, first, not *assume* that neuroscientific methods or findings can always be applied in educational contexts and, second, be careful in how far we claim they can be applied.

The second indicator is *using scientific or quasi-scientific language to try to make work look more impressive, without the evidential support for such uses of language*. To avoid this, we should have good reason to use the language or conceptual repertoire of neuroscience in educational research and its dissemination. The same caveat applies to psychological concepts, but these can be used more liberally than neuroscientific concepts because psychology is a science operating on a less fundamental level than neuroscience, so the concepts are less specific. Three principles were put forward for using concepts from neuroscience and psychology in education in such a way that avoids risking scientism: (1) they are used on the basis of good evidence, (2) they are used within a sound neuroscientific and/or psychological methodology and (3), with (1) and (2) met, they are used in order to justify the practical implementation of research into education by illustrating ways in which such concepts are relevant to educational practice.

The third indicator is *holding that to explain something scientifically is to explain it away*. To avoid this, neuroscientific explanations of areas specifically relevant to teaching and learning, such as how the brain processes information or stores memories, or the neurological underpinnings of emotional regulation, should not be interpreted as *reducing* teaching and learning to a domain that could be exhaustively understood in neuroscientific terms.

It is important that we are aware of the limitations of educational neuroscience and psychology. Awareness of these limitations enables us to avoid hazards when applying neuroscience and psychology in education; have realistic expectations of what might come from their application; and make sensible decisions about education on the basis of the evidence emerging from them. Educational innovations are sometimes interpreted in a panacean manner. Placing excessive promise in such innovations can lead to poorly judged decisions about educational strategies and policies and to the consolidation of a misplaced divide between educational 'traditionalists' and 'innovators'. Science and technology are the domains that make the greatest and most rapid advances; while they deserve high praise and promise, they are also the domains where excessive praise and promise are most often placed. Excessive praise and promise in science can lead to scientism. Through awareness of what scientism is, the problems with it and the ways it can become manifest when we apply theories or evidence from educational neuroscience in education, educational neuroscience is better placed to avoid educational neuroscientism.[5]

Notes

1 See, for example, Fodor, 1998, 189; Ladyman *et al.*, 2007, 61; Shermer, 2002, 35; Rosenberg, 2011; Rosenberg 2017, 203. For an overview of these views, see Beale, 2019, 75.

2 *Webster's Third New International Dictionary of the English Language*. The *Oxford English Dictionary*'s primary definition is 'the habit or mode of expression of a man of science'.

3 First published in 2010 by the International Academy of Education; republished in 2012 as 'Principles of Instruction: Research-based Strategies That All Teachers Should Know', in *American Educator* (Rosenshine, 2012).

4 Uses of such language to achieve such ends is one of the 'signs of scientism' outlined by Haack in her seminal article on scientism, 'Six Signs of Scientism' (Haack, 2013 [2009]).

5 Many thanks to Amy Fancourt, Iro Konstantinou and Jonnie Noakes for comments. The account of scientism offered in this chapter draws on my article, 'Scientism and Scientific Imperialism' (Beale, 2019); I am grateful to the editors of the *International Journal of Philosophical Studies* for permission to draw on the material in that article.

References

Beale, J. (2019). Scientism and scientific imperialism. *International Journal of Philosophical Studies*, *27(1)*, 73–201.

Beale, J., and Kidd, I. J. (Eds.). (2017). *Wittgenstein and Scientism*. London: Routledge.

Blackford, R. (2017). The sciences and humanities in a unity of knowledge. In Boudry, M., and Pigliucci, M. (Eds.), *Science Unlimited: The Challenges of Scientism*. Chicago: University of Chicago Press.

Carnap, R. (1967 [1928]). *The Logical Structure of the World* [*Der Logische Aufbau der Welt*] (trans. Rolf A. George). Berkeley: University of California Press.

Dweck, C. (2007 [2006]). *Mindset: The New Psychology of Success* (updated edition). London: Penguin Random House.

Fodor, J. (1998). *In Critical Condition: Polemical Essays on Cognitive Science and the Philosophy of Mind*. Cambridge, MA: MIT Press.

Haack, S. (2013 [2009]). Six signs of scientism. In *Putting Philosophy to Work: Inquiry and Its Place in Culture* (2nd ed.). New York: Prometheus Books.

Harris, S. (2010). *The Moral Landscape: How Science Can Determine Human Values*. New York: Free Press.

Kalef, J. (2017). Scientism and the is/ought gap. In Pigliucci and Boudry, 2017.

Ladyman, J., and Ross, D., with David Spurrett and John Collier. (2007). *Every Thing Must Go: Metaphysics Naturalized*. Oxford, UK: Oxford University Press.

Nehru, J. (1960). *Proceedings of the National Institute of Science of India: Biological Sciences* (Vol. 26, p. 27). Bengalura, Karnataka, India: The Institute.

Pigliucci, M. (2017). Scientism and pseudoscience: in defense of demarcation projects. In Boudry, M., and Pigliucci, M. (Eds.), *Science Unlimited: The Challenges of Scientism*. Chicago: University of Chicago Press.

Rosenberg, A. (2011). *The Atheist's Guide to Reality: Enjoying Life without Illusions*. New York: W.W. Norton.

Rosenberg, A. (2017). Strong scientism and its research agenda. In Boudry, M., and Pigliucci, M. (Eds.), *Science Unlimited: The Challenges of Scientism*. Chicago: University of Chicago Press.

Rosenshine, B. (2012). Principles of instruction: research-based strategies that all teachers should know. *American Educator*, Spring, 12–19 and 39.

Ross, D. (2017). Economics and allegations of scientism. In Boudry, M., and Pigliucci, M. (Eds.), *Science Unlimited: The Challenges of Scientism*. Chicago: University of Chicago Press.

Shermer, M. (2002). The shamans of scientism. *Scientific American*, *287(3)*, September. Available at www.michaelshermer.com/2002/06/shamans-of-scientism/.

Sorell, T. (1991). *Scientism: Philosophy and the Infatuation with Science*. London: Routledge.

Stenmark, M. (2001). *Scientism: Science, Ethics and Religion*. Aldershot, UK: Ashgate.

Stenmark, M. (2003). Scientism. In J. W. V. Huyssteen *et al.* (Eds.), *Encyclopedia of Science and Religion*. New York: Macmillan.

von Hayek, F. A. (1942). Scientism and the study of society (part I). *Economica, 9* (35), 267–91.

Wiliam, D. (2019). Dylan Wiliam: teaching not a research-based profession. *Times Educational Supplement*, 30 May 2019. Available at www.tes.com/news/dylan-wiliam-teaching-not-research-based-profession.

Wittgenstein, L. (2009 [1953]). *Philosophical Investigations* [*Philosophische Untersuchungen*] (trans. G. E. M. Anscombe, P. M. S. Hacker and Joachim Schulte). West Sussex, UK: Wiley-Blackwell.

2

How BrainCanDo has been applied at Queen Anne's School

Gill Little

BrainCanDo is working!

As deputy head for teaching and learning at Queen Anne's School, I am privileged to be working in such a forward-thinking and inspired school in which the use of research in educational neuroscience and psychology underpins both our culture and teaching and learning environment. This work is led and coordinated by our BrainCanDo research team.

Keeping abreast of such research and embedding it holistically enable us to provide an excellent environment for effective and innovative learning. Our aim is to engage all stakeholders (including teachers, students, parents, governors and the public) to provide an awareness of what we do and how it helps students to improve their cognitive attainment, foster a love of learning and enable a healthy, productive approach to personal development.

In this chapter, I will share with you some of the methods that we use, their outcomes and how they are monitored. The methods of engagement used will be considered separately for staff, students and other stakeholders, including parents, governors and the public.

Staff training and engagement

Developments in neuroscientific and psychological research in recent years have given us a greater understanding of the human brain, particularly the changes that occur during adolescence. We believe that by educating teachers about how an adolescent's brain is developing and psychology is changing, they can become better informed about how learning happens. Also, knowing how emotional regulation and social motivation change throughout adolescence can help teachers to employ the most effective strategies to improve the quality of teaching and learning. In order to support teachers to make use of this research, we use a variety of staff development strategies which are described herein.

The BrainCanDo 'Teacher Handbook'

When staff first join Queen Anne's School, they are all issued a 'Teacher Handbook' written by our BrainCanDo research team. The handbook is divided into chapters that explore several themes relating to educational neuroscience and psychology and provides practical strategies to help teachers to bring their understanding of educational neuroscience and psychology into the classroom. At the end of each chapter, practical examples drawn from best practice are given that help to clarify ways in which our understanding of the brain and the ways that adolescents learn can be effectively applied to our teaching and learning practices.

For example, the chapter in the handbook on the 'social brain' illustrates how humans, being naturally gregarious, have developed a robust network of areas of the brain specifically devoted to keeping track of other people and interpreting their actions, motives, thoughts and other mental states, especially when these other states differ from their own. This is known as a 'mentalising network' (Meyer and Lieberman, 2012). Intuitively, it would appear that this mentalising network should be suppressed when we are working on an analytical task, as a silent working environment would be more conductive for engagement. However, use of the mentalising network in fact is known to engage students; therefore, we should not always battle against this and require complete silence in the classroom. Instead, we should make use of the mentalising network in the classroom, for example, through peer tutoring when learning an analytical task, to enhance learning in the classroom (Lieberman, 2012).

Practical classroom applications suggested in the 'Teacher Handbook' that incorporate the benefits of the mentalising network include

- Designing classroom tasks that require socialising, as teaching any content socially will engage the 'social brain'.
- Employing peer marking as a means of improving students' understanding of assessment. As students gain a better understanding of the marking scheme, they will be better placed to get into the mind of the examiner and more effectively reflect on what they did during a test and how they could improve their performance.

Dissemination of effective teaching strategies

A range of opportunities is used to regularly reinforce and update staff on the benefits of using research from educational neuroscience and psychology to inform their teaching and learning practices. At the beginning of each academic year, we have a BrainCanDo INSET (originally an acronym for 'IN-SErvice Training day') session in which staff are encouraged to engage in group exercises with a variety of research articles and consider ways in which the ideas could be implemented in their approaches to teaching and learning.

For example, we recently shared the principles proposed by Henry Fletcher-Wood in his book, *Responsive Teaching* (Fletcher-Wood, 2018). The principles are based on an understanding of how students learn from cognitive science. The principles can help teachers to develop teaching strategies that can enhance students' metacognition and motivation in order to improve learning. Three of the principles shared are related to 'cognitive load theory' and the need to

- select the level of intrinsic load, as this is the level of challenge required for learning new concepts;
- remove extraneous load, as this occupies working memory but does not add to the formation of long-term memory; and
- add germane cognitive load, as this contributes to the storage of information in long-term memory.

In addition, throughout the year, the BrainCanDo team disseminate research articles to provoke, inspire and motivate staff to reflect on their teaching practices and incorporate research-based strategies. Such articles come from a variety of sources, including the Education Endowment Foundation (EEF) and the Chartered College of Teaching, as well as a range of books on pedagogy and neuroscience which staff can access via the school library to further develop their knowledge and understanding. Some of the disseminated articles are written by members of the BrainCanDo research team and other members of the teaching staff at Queen Anne's.

Involve staff in research in educational neuroscience and psychology

Since the founding of BrainCanDo, there has been an increase in the number of teachers at Queen Anne's who seek to engage with evidence-informed teaching practice. For example, several members of staff have written articles for educational journals. Articles written for the Chartered College of Teaching journal *Impact* include

- 'Jigsaw reading – how can a puzzle engage the social brain?' (McNeil, 2018). This article discusses how making reading into a more active exercise engages the social brain and so can help learning. For 'jigsaw learning', a piece of text is subdivided between small groups of students. Each student in the group becomes an 'expert' on the group's section. The groups of students are rearranged so that each 'expert' delivers his or her information to the new group, meaning that information is shared involving receptive and productive skills. This format helps students to become more socially engaged and take on the role of both student and teacher as they interact with one another (Lom, 2012). This was one of the articles used in the group exercises among staff at a recent BrainCanDo INSET.

■ 'Developing effective learning through emotional engagement in the teaching of ethics' (Beale, 2018). This article discusses how the use of thought experiments to introduce normative theories can engender emotional responses in such a way as to aid students' learning. This is underpinned by the understanding that emotional engagement is associated with positive outcomes for student success, including academic achievement (Bulger et al., 2008). Beale's article shows how he uses this approach in his teaching of ethical dilemmas such as the 'trolley problem'.

> A runaway tram is on course to collide with five people on the tracks ahead. You, a bystander, are near a lever, which you could pull to divert the tram onto different tracks, on which there's one person. If you pull the lever, one dies; if you do nothing, five die. Should you pull the lever?
>
> Imagine the same scenario but, instead of pulling a lever, you face the predicament of whether to push a very large man off a bridge into the path of the tram. This will prevent the tram killing the five but the man will die at your hand. Should you push him?
>
> *[Beale, 2018, 56]*

In the lesson employing this thought experiment, the class were divided into small groups with variant cases of the problem, giving them very short times to respond and debate their reasoning. Having to commit to decisions about each dilemma encourages students to be more emotionally invested in the problems and, subsequently, more attentive to the lesson content.

■ 'Applying the expert learning culture at Queen Anne's School' (Little, 2018). This article discusses the value of metacognition for learning and illustrates how the principles of metacognition are applied through the school's tutorial system, for self-reflection with respect to academic attainment and attitude towards learning (further details are discussed in the section 'Metacognition as the key to change').

In addition, staff are invited to join a 'learning study group' that is modelled on the learning study model used by G. Whitman and I. Kelleher in their book, *Neuroteach* (Whitman and Kelleher, 2016). The group is entirely voluntary and meets once a term. The purpose is for each group member to select an area of educational research to form the basis of a piece of action research in which he or she engages over the course of the year, feeding back the findings to the group for discussion and development. Having proposed an area of research in the first term, staff devise pedagogical strategies reflecting that research, trial, monitor and refine them, reflect and tweak them and try again. At the end of the academic year, the group disseminate their findings to all teaching staff. In this way, staff are actively engaging with research and applying it to their teaching practices, often in novel ways, and sharing their findings with the Queen Anne's teaching community both for dissemination and feedback. The research projects have been wide ranging and include studies about feedback methods and their effectiveness, collaborative learning, the use of pastoral tracking to develop character virtues, the use of multiple-choice testing and other spaced learning retrieval strategies.

For example, in light of the recent changes to General Certificate of Secondary Education exams (GCSEs) and A levels which require students to learn a significant volume of work on the basis of which they are assessed at the end of two-year courses, an area of research conducted by a member of a recent Learning Study Group was the use of retrieval strategies. The research was based on understanding the difference between working memory and long-term memory. For effective learning, we must find ways of storing information in our long-term memory so that it is available to be used in the working memory when needed. The work of Robert Bjork et al. (2010) distinguishes between *storage strength* and *retrieval strength*; Bjork et al note that it is storage strength that determines how well something has been learnt. They also note that successfully retrieving information will increase the storage strength. They argue that teachers need to be testing students at frequent, regular intervals to be sure that they have learnt. Using this notion, a member of the Learning Study Group experimented with the 'forgetting curve' proposed by Hermann Ebbinghaus (1880), which is based on the concept of spaced repetition, where material is learned and then reviewed after increasingly large time gaps. When the teacher applied this theory with a geography class, she found that it facilitated the students' learning; she demonstrated this via the improvement in marks that the students achieved through the staged repetition of a test. A number of teachers have been inspired by these findings and have adopted the strategy.

Application of BrainCanDo in the classroom

The preceding examples illustrate some of the ways in which research from or connected with BrainCanDo has been employed in teaching. At Queen Anne's, there is a rich variety of approaches and strategies for teaching and learning to enable excellence in the classroom which are founded on our understanding of neuroscience and psychology. Our expectation is that all departments have approaches to learning informed by BrainCanDo embedded in their departmental strategic development plan, schemes of work and lesson planning. In addition, our BrainCanDo research team request feedback from staff on approaches to teaching and learning that they find effective. Next is a summary of some of the feedback, including some quotes from teachers.

Our teachers understand that *student engagement* is important to effective teaching and learning and that emotion is inextricably linked to learning, particularly in adolescents. If a student is bored or anxious, then his or her brain will not be in an optimal state to learn new information. Conversely, humour and laughter activate the dopamine reward networks in the brain, and this is linked to improved long-term retention of knowledge and to greater engagement and motivation.

> Humour is important – there is a lot of laughter in my lessons.
> [The teacher provides an] open, friendly approach which allows them to feel at ease in a non-threatening atmosphere.

Cognitive engagement measures the investment that students place in their own learning and their capacity to recognise the relevance of their school-work to everyday life. Research has shown that student engagement is associated with more positive current and future outcomes such as academic achievement (Bulger et al., 2008). Our teachers were asked how they encourage their students to take ownership of their learning.

> By not giving up and trying to work out their solutions to their creative problems.
> By giving time in lessons for students to reflect on feedback and improve or correct their work.

The topic of *emotional contagion* has been considered extensively at Queen Anne's through our collaborative research with the University of Reading. Our teachers understand the need to cultivate a positive emotional environment within the classroom and their own pivotal role in doing that.

> If I am upbeat and positive, the mood in the classroom follows and vice versa.

The importance of keeping lessons as *interactive* as possible was recognised as a key factor in good teaching and learning. Teachers at Queen Anne's understand that the adolescent brain, in girls in particular, is geared towards social interaction, and therefore, they value interaction as a way to maximise student learning.

> Less talking at them from me, more questioning to try to provoke responses – e.g. by asking thought-provoking questions and things that engage them emotionally.

Another major focus through the BrainCanDo programme has been on *mindset*. As a school, we have looked at various ways through which we can foster a positive growth mindset in our students, with teachers engaging in activities to nurture resilience and perseverance.

> I offer opportunities to re-work a piece of work to show how progress can be made.
> I am also realistic with students, so for topics which are challenging for their age/ability, I say they will find it hard but with practice [it] will become easier.

BrainCanDo has also looked at how *autonomy* is linked to the development of internal or 'intrinsic' motivation in learners. In their *Self-Determinism Theory*, R.M. Ryan and E.L. Deci (2018) define 'intrinsic motivation' as 'the doing of an activity for its inherent satisfaction rather than for some separable consequence'. Intrinsically motivated students, as opposed to those who are extrinsically motivated, value learning and are more motivated to want to try new things, which can lead to better academic outcomes. Research suggests that 'providing choices to students of all age levels often increase[s] their intrinsic motivation' and improves academic performance (Marzano, 2010, 14, 101). Teachers at Queen Anne's understand the importance of creating opportunities for choice.

> In term 1, students in LS4 [a teaching room in the Sixth Form Centre] can choose their final outcome. ... There are usually four options ranging from very easy to extremely difficult. They choose which one they think would suit their ability.

The curiosity provoked by an element of mystery also raises levels of intrinsic motivation. Our teachers recognise this power of the *unknown*.

> Students never know exactly what they will be doing in any one lesson.

Student engagement

In addition to the students at Queen Anne's experiencing a teaching and learning environment that is underpinned by their teachers' understanding of best practice informed through neuroscience and psychology, we also provide teaching to students on how the brain works in terms of its relation to their wellbeing and learning. We do this in a number of ways, including: the BrainCanDo research team leading assemblies and workshops, inviting expert guest speakers to give talks and workshops on areas of neuroscience and psychology (some of which are outlined later) and using our BrainCanDo student prefects to help promote the BrainCanDo philosophy, both within Queen Anne's and at the schools with which we have links locally and through our foundation. We also have a tutorial system and well-being programme which are run throughout the school in which a number of the ideas discussed in assemblies and workshops are reinforced.

Following are some examples of areas of neuroscience and psychology in which we have actively engaged the students.

Growth mindset

We apply the principles of the 'growth mindset' throughout the school's culture. Growth mindset holds that it is a person's mindset, not his or her innate abilities or talents, that ultimately determines that person's success (Dweck, 2006). Our BrainCanDo team deliver workshops to the students about growth mindset and its impact on learning, education and personal development. In the workshops, students are able to explore their own current type of mindset and how it impacts their approach to learning. They also explore mental exercises and different approaches to learning that could be used to change fixed mindsets to growth mindsets, with the aim of helping them to become more resilient learners.

Metacognition as the key to change

In addition to the opportunities for metacognition in the classroom, the principles of metacognition are applied throughout school life (Little, 2018). We have embedded opportunities through the school's tutorial system, which involves one-on-one discussions between each student and his or her tutor. This system recognises that for motivational reasons, self-assessment is most effective when done more privately, occurring between one teacher and one student (Pintrich and Schrunk, 2002). Data from the school's tracking system are used to monitor academic progress at these one-on-one discussions and are used by the pupils to set specific, measurable, attainable, realistic and time-sensitive (SMART) targets. We also use an 'Attitude to Learning' audit as part of the one-on-one discussions in which we encourage students to reflect on aspects of their attitudes towards learning and set themselves targets for improvement. Aspects include participation in class, willingness to seek help, willingness to work collaboratively and receiving and reflecting on feedback.

Learning initiatives

We have actively involved the students in a wide range of learning initiatives associated with neuroscience and psychology, including the following examples.

The brain and how it works

This is a workshop that is held with lower school students to explore the human brain and how powerful it is. Information on how the brain influences who we are, how neural connections within the brain change throughout our lives and how concentration, focus and procrastination are influenced by our unique brain connections are delivered through fun activities, videos and group discussions.

Exam stress and revision strategies

Workshops led by our BrainCanDo team are delivered to explore different revision strategies and how to handle exam stress. Students are able to work together to discuss strategies and also to try out mental tools that can combat negative stress.

Mental well-being

Our school's well-being programme, which is taught throughout the school, includes sessions on mental well-being and how this impacts students' daily lives. It also considers a variety of mental tools and strategies that can be used to influence positive well-being.

Sleep health

Students are taught about the importance of sleep and its impact on the brain. For example, sleep experts Dr Nicola Barclay from the University of Oxford's Sleep and Circadian Neuroscience Institute and Dr Frances Le Cornu Knight from the University of Bristol have delivered lectures open to all our students and parents about sleep and the teenage brain. The lectures have included explanations of the shifting biological rhythms in adolescence, the impact that this has on the sleep and wake cycle and what teenagers can do to practise good sleep hygiene.[1]

The importance of music and exercise

At Queen Anne's we offer a wide and varied co-curricular programme in which there is ample opportunity to engage in a variety of music and sporting activities, as these can play an important role in stimulating the brain. We teach students the importance of such activities in many ways, including through our well-being programme but also through workshops. For example, in 2018, we held a student conference that focused on music, exercise and memory techniques (see Box 2.1).

Box 2.1 Student conference on music, exercise and memory techniques

Music and the brain

An interactive musical session was led by Paul Smith, author of the VOCES8 Method and founding member of VOCES8. The students were led through a fascinating workshop that intertwined various musical instruments, sounds and vocal noises to create engaging rhythms and melodies. This was linked to the field of education, as potential techniques were discussed that our students could use and apply to a number of different subjects. Both listening to music and playing a musical instrument (including singing) have been found to have a positive impact on revision and overall academic attainment.

Exercise and the brain

The focus of this session was how exercise can help improve mental performance. The students were informed about how exercise can provide a good break from long revision sessions and releases a number of different hormones that impact the brain. The students learned how serotonin is released and can help regulate sleep cycles and boost mood, how dopamine can positively influence attention span, how norepinephrine can impact motivation and mental stimulation and how exercise reduces levels of the stress hormone cortisol. With this information, the students were led by Zumba and fitness instructor Anna Monita Burgess in a fun cardiovascular exercise session of Zumba.

Memory techniques

This was a fascinating and exciting session run by UK Memory Champion James Paterson on the practical application of memory techniques to enable advanced recall. Students were in awe of his abilities to recall the first 314 numbers of pi (and in reverse order!) and recollect the order of an entire deck of playing cards, for which the students were in charge of shuffling the deck and left him only five minutes of looking at the cards to memorise them! In an impressive display of memory, he then showed the students that they, too, could learn techniques to help in advanced recall.

Student involvement in neuroscience research

Along with other schools in the United Grey Coat and Westminster Foundation, our students have been involved in a four-year research programme run by researchers from Goldsmiths, University of London, to see whether participating in the musical life of the school has a significant impact on academic success. The underlying theory is that participation in musical activities leads not only to enhanced memory but also to improved attention, motor coordination and speech processing. Although this is ongoing action research, the positive findings to date mean that we encourage our students to become involved in the various musical activities on offer. MVSIC = +

Our students are also part of an 'Emotional Contagion' project led by the University of Reading. This research investigates the dynamics of student social interaction and emotional connections and how they have an impact on the motivation to learn and how this can be managed in the classroom, for example, in terms of grouping and seating arrangements. The research involves a series of surveys and the scanning of students' brains using a functional magnetic resonance imaging (fMRI) scanner. Findings from this project are fed back to students and staff in the school through regular presentations from the research team in assemblies and staff meetings.

Applications of research in educational neuroscience and psychology

In addition to directly participating in research in educational neuroscience and psychology, the school is constantly looking for opportunities to apply research within the wider school environment; for example, a gratitude project and a - later day start time project have been undertaken. Research, for example, by Roland Zahn et al. (2009) suggests that practising gratitude has many positive impacts, including improved attention, enthusiasm, sleep and energy. Being thankful has also been linked to decreases in anxiety and depression. In November 2018, a school assembly was used to launch a workshop called 'Nice November'. The benefits of gratitude were explained to the students. They were told that when people are asked to summon feelings of gratitude, they find greater activation in areas of the brain associated with the production of 'feel good' chemicals such as endorphin, oxytocin, serotonin and dopamine. Moreover, evidence suggests that when we practise thankfulness, the brain releases these chemicals which make us feel good. After the assembly, students were issued a 'gratitude journal' that they were expected to write in at the end of each day about things for which they were grateful. In addition, they were issued 'gratitude notelets' that they could complete to express their gratitude for something or someone. These were done anonymously and displayed in school on a 'tree of thanks' (Figure 2.1). There were many wonderful thoughts, including

- I just want to say thank you for: 'all of the lovely smiles I received today'.
- I just want to say thank you for: 'my mum calling me this morning just to ask how I was'.
- I just want to say thank you for: 'amazing friends'.
- I just want to say thank you for: 'you smiling and saying hello'.

Additionally, over the past two years, Lower Sixth Form students have been involved in pilot studies of later start times. An increasing volume of research suggests that early school start times have a negative impact on student health and academic outcomes (Banks and Dinges, 2007; Boergers et al., 2014). In particular, female students are more likely to become obese, use legal and illegal drugs and have lower academic performance when chronically deprived of sleep, and since adolescents tend to wake up naturally later than adults, early start times increase the likelihood of chronic sleep deprivation. We therefore experimented with a later start time with our Sixth Form students for a week in the summer of 2018 when we moved the daily timetable back for two hours to try to be more aligned with the students' circadian rhythms. The findings showed that students gained, on average, an extra hour of sleep per night, giving them around eight hours of sleep per night, closer to the recommended length of night-time sleep. Students also reported that they were able to wake naturally rather than be woken by an

Figure 2.1 The 'tree of gratitude' at Queen Anne's School (November 2018).

alarm clock. Teachers found that there was an improvement in the students' attention and ability to control their impulses by taking time to consider the impact of what they might say or do. Given the positive findings, the research was repeated in the summer term of 2019 for an extended period of four weeks to gather further evidence that could lead to a decision to change the timing of the school day for the Sixth Form. Some of this research is discussed in Chapter 7.

Engagement of parents, governors and the public

We are keen to promote our ongoing involvement in research on educational neuroscience and psychology, and the developments of our school's BrainCanDo programme, to parents, governors and the public. To this end, we offer opportunities to attend lectures and workshops to share in our engagement and learning.

Lectures and workshops

We hold BrainCanDo conferences which are attended by staff, governors and the public. Themes have included 'Education for the 21st Century' (2015), 'Music in Learning' (2016) and 'Pathways from Neuroscience to the Classroom' (2018); see Box 2.2 on the final of these.

Box 2.2 'Pathways from Neuroscience to the Classroom' conference

The keynote speech was given by Professor Michael Thomas from the Centre for Educational Neuroscience in London, in which he questioned the value of psychology and neuroscience to educators and debunked some of the neuromyths that have found their way into education. In addition, Dr Dean Burnett, neuroscientist, comedian and *Guardian* columnist, gave an entertaining presentation about emotional contagion in teenagers.

The conference also included lively panel discussions; one was led by Queen Anne's head teacher, Julia Harrington, who focused on some of the opportunities and challenges inherent in trying to meaningfully bring psychology and neuroscience research into educational practice. Another was led by Professor Patricia Riddell and Dean Burnett, who discussed the impact that emotional contagion has on teenagers both within and outside the classroom and what educators can do to effectively work with this process.

We also used the conference as an opportunity to share some of the ongoing research updates from each of our BrainCanDo university collaborators. These included projects investigating the role of self-affirmation in cognitive performance, the impact of music on mindset and academic achievement and the power of emotional contagion in motivation and learning.

Additionally, we hold a number of lectures and workshops each year; themes have included

- 'What do we remember, when we remember music' (Professor Adam Ockleford, secretary for the Society for Education, Music and Psychology Research (SEMPRE), and Daniel Mullensiefen, a music psychologist and member of the Music, Mind and Brain research group at Goldsmiths, University of London).
- 'The psychology of effective revision' (Mr Ben Stephenson, director of the Sixth Form, Queen Anne's).
- 'Wobbles, warbles and fish – the neural basis of dyslexia' (John Stein, emeritus professor of neuroscience, Department of Physiology, Anatomy and Genetics and fellow of Magdalen College, Oxford).

Communicating with parents and prospective parents

We ensure that we keep our parents and prospective parents fully informed of any developments in our BrainCanDo programme. For example, we introduce the concept of BrainCanDo and the use of neuroscience and psychology to inform our teaching and learning to prospective parents at open mornings. For our current parents, we give regular updates in our 'Weekly Bulletin', and we encourage parents to attend our lecture and workshop series.

Outcome

Value added

The school consistently adds value to students' academic performance; in particular, at the GCSE level. The amount of added value varies between students and from year to year; however, over the past six years, in which we have embedded BrainCanDo in the school's culture, the value-added scores are significantly above the expectations forecast from baseline scores (the scores are generated from the Centre for Evaluation and Monitoring tests operated by Cambridge Assessment and Cambridge University Press). We consider that part of this success is attributable to our application of neuroscience and psychology within the school's culture and to our approaches to teaching and learning.

In particular, our evidence shows that there is very significant added value for students who participate in music and/or sport, especially among those who perform at a very high level. Our BrainCanDo research team have interviewed some of these students. Following is an insight into the mindsets of two of the students who achieved very high value-added scores.

At the GCSE level, Student A achieved an average value-added score of 1.8 grades above expectations from baseline scores. To achieve this, she said that she used a range of strategies to maximise her performance. For example, her attitude towards learning was very positive. When asked whether she felt confident going into her exams, she said:

> I tried my hardest and to me that was enough. Sometimes nerves can work to your advantage. I told myself before each exam – 'you only know what you know', especially at that late stage. There was nothing further I could do and worrying about it definitely would not have helped in any way.

She also felt very well mentally prepared. She said:

> I put a lot of effort into managing my time and making an efficient time-table. Learning from the previous ways that I approached exams (mocks, etc.) helped me to learn about how many hours I can work per day, how often to have breaks, and what time of day I work best. I also found that my experiences in competing in high level sporting competitions really benefitted my mental resilience when it came to exams. Competing has forced me to find ways to control negative thoughts and nerves really well. These experiences enabled me to focus on the things I can control, and to remain positive.

Her advice is: 'Stay active and get enough sleep'.

At A level, Student B achieved an average value-added score of 2.3 grades above expectations from baseline scores. She believes that she used her growth mindset to her advantage. She said:

> I work hard consistently and work to the best of my abilities in every lesson and on every piece of prep. I think I'm also a good student just in terms of attitude. I'm a very happy person and I think that definitely helps!

She also said:

> I would be disappointed if I didn't do my very best in the exams. I made sure to embody this mindset when I wasn't in the mood for revising to kind of spur me on.

Her advice is: 'Work hard and keep smiling'.

There is significant positive feedback from students on the impact Brain-CanDo has had on their experience of school life. Following is a quote from a former student who achieved three A* grades at A level and went on to study anthropology at the University of Durham:

The BrainCanDo lecture that highlighted the importance of understanding how the brain works was beneficial to me. It taught me ways to help in exam season, mainly the importance of managing stress levels through methods such as creating lists and healthy sleep routines. I also really enjoyed the experiment in Maths when we did two tests (one playing classical music and one without) and the whole class performed better with music playing! I found this really fascinating and now I study listening to music without lyrics.

Conclusion

The preceding is an illustration of the extent to which Queen Anne's has embedded research in educational neuroscience and psychology within the school's culture. We are delighted with the outcomes that have had a very positive impact on the staff and student body as well as the school's culture. We will continue to actively engage in research so that we provide the best opportunities for our staff and students for 21st-century teaching and learning.

Note

1 For an overview of some of Frances Le Cornu Knight's research on sleep and practical advice for education based on this research, see Chapter 8 in this volume.

References

Banks, S., and Dinges, D. F. (2007). Behavioural and physiological consequences of sleep restriction. *Journal of Clinical Sleep Medicine, 3*(5), 519–28.

Beale, J. (2018). Developing effective learning through emotional engagement in the teaching of ethics. *Impact: Journal of the Chartered College of Teaching* (3), 56–7.

Bjork, R., Storm, B., and Storm, J. (2010). Optimizing retrieval as a learning event: when and why expanding retrieval practice enhances long-term retention. *Memory and Cognition, 38*(2), 244–53.

Boergers, J., Gable, C. J., and Owens, J. A. (2014). Later school start time is associated with improved sleep and daytime functioning in adolescents. *Journal of Developmental and Behavioural Pediatrics, 35*(1), 11–17. doi:10.1097/DBP.0000000000000018.

Bulger, M., Mayer, R., and Almeroth, K. (2008). Measuring learning engagement in computer-equipped college classrooms. *Journal of Educational Multimedia and Hypermedia, 17*(2), 129–43.

Dweck, C. (2006). *Mindset: How You Can Fufil Your Potential*. New York: Ballantine Books.

Ebbinghaus, H. (1880). Urmanuskript 'Ueber das Gedächtniß'. Passau: Passavia Universitätsverlag.

Fletcher-Wood, H. (2018). *Responsive Teaching*. London: Routledge.

Lieberman, M. (2012). Education and the social brain. *Trends in Neuroscience and Education*, *1*, 3–9. Available at www.scn.ucla.edu/pdf/Lieberman(2012)TINE. pdf (accessed 24 August 2019).

Little, G. (2018). Applying the expert learning culture at Queen Anne's School. *Impact: Journal of the Chartered College of Teaching* (3). Available at https://impact. chartered.college/article/little_expert-culture-school/(accessed 24 August 2019).

Lom, B. (2012). Classroom activities: simple strategies to incorporate student-centred activities with undergraduate science lectures. Journal of Undergraduate Neuroscience Education *11*(1): A64–71. Available at www.ncbi.nlm.nih.gov/pmc/articles/ PMC3592730 (accessed 31 October 2017).

Marzano, R. (2010). The highly engaged classroom. Marzano Research Laboratory, Centennial, CO. Available at www.marzanoresources.com/resources/ tips/hec_tips_archive#tip24 (accessed 24 August 2019).

McNeil, L. (2018). Jigsaw reading – how can a puzzle engage the social brain? *Impact: Journal of the Chartered College of Teaching* (3). Available at: https:// impact.chartered.college/article/mcneil_jigsaw-reading-puzzle-brain/ (accessed 24 August 2019).

Meyer, M., and Lieberman, M. D. (2012). Social working memory: neurocognitive networks and directions for future research. *Frontiers in Psychology*, *3*, 571.

Pintrich, P. R., and Schrunk, D. H. (2002). *Motivation in Education: Theory, Research, and Applications*. Upper Saddle River, NJ: Merrill Prentice-Hall.

Ryan, R. M., and Deci, E. L. (2018). *Self-Determination Theory: Basic Psychological Needs in Motivation, Development, and Wellness*. New York: Guilford Press.

Whitman, G., and Kelleher, I. (2016). *Neuoroteach: Brain Science and Future of Education*. Lanham, MD: Rowman and Littlefield.

Zahn, R., Moll, J., Paiva, M., et al. (2009). The neural basis of human social values. *Cerebral Cortex*, *19*(2), 276–83.

Becoming a successful learner

3

Developing character education in schools: An evidence-based approach

Iro Konstantinou and Jonnie Noakes

Introduction

The UK educational system, it is fair to say, is primarily centred around examinations. There are assessments and exams from a very young age, all the way to the last year of schooling. Alongside Standard Attainment Tests (SATs) and General Certificate of Secondary Education (GCSE) exams, those who wish to move on to higher education take A-level exams. The latest results by the Organisation for Economic Co-operation and Development (OECD) Programme for International Student Assessment (PISA) report in 2015 show that the averages in mathematics, science and reading have remained largely unchanged since 2006 and that there are still attainment gaps across the socio-economic divide. There are also increasing concerns with regards to the mental well-being of pupils. Pupils report high levels of anxiety and an increase in the level of emotional and mental disorders (NHS, 2017), while only an unsatisfactory 28% of pupils reported a high satisfaction with life (OECD, 2017).

Therefore, it can be argued that there is an urgent need for schools to reconsider what they place emphasis on and adopt an approach that looks beyond the testing of cognitive skills to also equip pupils with the abilities required to become engaged citizens who can thrive in a diverse society. It is not only the alarming statistics on well-being but also more practical shortcomings that call for an increased demand in the development of such skills within education. Currently, schools do not have enough provisions in place to prepare pupils for the workplace and the new era of diverse forms of employment and plethora of working patterns. According to a report by the British Chamber of Commerce, 88% of employers felt that school leavers were unprepared for the workplace and lacked the attributes and attitudes required for the workplace. Moreover, the publication *New Vision for Education* by the World Economic Forum (2015, 2) argues that

> [t]o thrive in today's innovation-driven economy, workers need a different mix of skills than in the past. In addition to foundational skills like literacy and numeracy, they need competencies like collaboration, creativity and problem-solving, and character qualities like persistence, curiosity and initiative.

Or, as UNESCO (2015, 5) suggests:

> The world is changing – education must also change. Societies everywhere are undergoing deep transformation, and this calls for new forms of education to foster the competencies that societies and economies need, today and tomorrow. This means moving beyond literacy and numeracy, to focus on learning environments and on new approaches to learning for greater justice, social equity and global solidarity.

Taking into consideration the above-mentioned areas – academic achievement, well-being and competencies needed for an increasingly diverse world and workplace – this chapter argues that there is one overarching element that could provide the foundations for better-equipped pupils. If character education is embedded within a school's curriculum, co-curriculum and wider culture, there is an argument to be made about the wider impact it may have. Here we provide a number of ways identified through our work at the Tony Little Centre for Innovation and Research at Eton College to foster some of the character skills and traits that may equip students for a changing world.

A report by Birdwell et al. (2015) and the Character Awards by the Department for Education have shown some key findings in how schools need to approach character education for any meaningful impact to be observed. They suggest the following:

1. A whole school ethos;
2. Student-led recording evidence of personal development, accompanying school-led approaches to measure character;
3. Use of reward or award systems schemes;
4. Structured reflection periods;
5. Personal tutors or coaches;
6. Older students working with younger students;
7. Opportunities to take part in voluntary programmes and social action in school and in the local community;
8. Consideration of moral issues in a cross-curricular manner;
9. Involvement of parents, guardians and families; and
10. Classes in public speaking and philosophy and ethics.

At Eton, we are currently in the process of creating our own taxonomy of character in order to create a common language of what character traits and dispositions we value in the curruiculum and co-curriculum across the school. We are looking at what we currently say we value as a community, and through a process of collecting empirical data from staff and students, we are trying to understand how these character traits and values can be embedded across the curriculum and co-curriculum. Even though we have not completed this process, we have outlined what we currently do and how certain processes which we already employ support character development.

In this chapter, we outline evidenced-informed practices that can promote a number of character skills and values and give examples of some of the research we have conducted or are conducting in those areas. First, we outline some of the debates on the definitions of character traits, or non-cognitive skills as they are more widely known, and offer an account of the empirical basis of why character education matters.

Distinctions between cognitive and non-cognitive skills

Cognitive skills invite little dispute as to how they can be defined, although there is a wider debate as to how they can be developed. According to the *American Psychological Association Dictionary of Psychology*, cognitive ability are the skills involved in performing the tasks associated with perception, learning, memory, understanding, awareness, reasoning, judgment, intuition, and language.

Non-cognitive skills, by contrast, are less universally defined. A multitude of frameworks has been adopted when it comes to defining non-cognitive skills and how they might be fostered (Lucas, 2019). They are referred to using terms such as 'character traits', 'soft skills' and 'social and emotional skills', which encompass a broad range of competencies, such as self-regulation and empathy. Some others use the term '21st-century skills', which is more closely aligned with problem solving and critical thinking. Borghans et al. (2008, 974) define non-cognitive skills as personality traits or patterns of thought, feelings, and behaviour. Additionally, as West et al. (2015, 2) point out, 'non-cognitive, therefore, has become a catchall term for traits or skills not captured by assessments of cognitive ability and knowledge'.

Bill Lucas (2019), a professor of learning and diretor at the Centre for Real World Learning at the University of Winchester, suggests that not only do we need to place value on these traits and skills, but we also need to reach a consensus as to what is likely to be different in the coming years, as only then we will be able to educate children in a well-rounded way. He suggests some of the following:

1. The increasing complexity of problems such as climate change, global migration and growing resistance to lifesaving drugs;
2. The increasing interconnectedness and global nature of our relationships;
3. The potential of automation via artificial intelligence and its impact, often contested, on life and work;
4. Increased self-employment; and
5. An ageing society (Lucas, 2019, 9).

Lucas proposes that

> in direct response to each of these elements it can be argued that the kinds of capabilities, competencies or dispositions that we need are likely to include:
>
> 1. Complex problem-solving that is frequently multi- and inter-disciplinary by nature and always ethically driven.
> 2. Critical thinking and high-level project- and time-management.
> 3. Digital literacy, design and computational thinking.
> 4. Intercultural collaborative problem-solving and emotional and social intelligence.
> 5. Creativity, adaptability, meta-cognition.
> 6. Creativity, communication, adaptability.
> 7. Learning to learn
>
> *[Lucas, 2019, 10]*

Moreover, Hokanson and Karlson (2013) point to the need for non-cognitive skills to be addressed explicitly and be valued equally as cognitive skills. As schools are preparing students for a borderless world, the authors argue that knowledge and facts have become much more accessible, and consequently, they are not unique to any one person, learner or worker. Therefore, what could distinguish those who aim to enter the workforce in the future from others are character strengths such as creativity and grit.

Undeniably, popular interest in measuring and developing students' non-cognitive skills has become prominent in educational discussions (see e.g. Tough, 2012). Governments across the world have started to emphasise the role of character, behaviour and skills in schools. For example, Tough (ibid.) focuses on the Knowledge is Power Program (KIPP) in schools in the United States, which has put character education into practice in 162 American schools, focusing on the character 'strengths' of zest, grit, optimism, self-control, gratitude, social intelligence and curiosity.

Closer to home, the UK government has stressed the importance of character education in its various manifestations in schools. In 2015, the then Secretary of State for the Department of Education, Nicky Morgan, launched the 'Character Award', a monetary prize for the schools that best promoted character. The list of what the Department of Education considered most important included the following:

- perseverance, resilience and grit;
- confidence and optimism;
- motivation, drive and ambition;
- neighbourliness and community spirit;
- tolerance and respect;
- honesty, integrity and dignity; and
- conscientiousness, curiosity and focus (White et al., 2017).

Nicky Morgan's successor, Justine Greening, placed priorities elsewhere, and the initiatives introduced by Morgan were discontinued. However, the Secretary of State for the Department of Education for 2018–2019, Damian Hinds, believed that not enough disadvantaged children get the opportunity to develop character and resilience through the curriculum and co-curriculum. He shared his vision on character within education and outlined five foundations on which character education should be based. These are

- sport (which might include competitive sport and activities such as running, martial arts and swimming, as well as activities such as rock climbing and hiking);
- creativity (filmmaking, music composition, creative writing);
- performing (dance, theatre, drama, debating, public speaking);
- volunteering and membership (litter picking, fundraising, Duke of Edinburgh Cadets); and
- the world of work (practical work experience or mentoring by professionals) (DfE, 2019).

Hinds' vision sought to bring various organisations and the state and public education sector together, as he believed that the lack of resources in a particular school should not deter pupils from seeking opportunities to participate in those activities. Instead, he believed that there should be better communication across the different organisations and schools to ensure that all children can develop character and resilience.

The current Secretary of State, Gavin Williamson, has taken a slightly different approach, and he talks about behaviour and the fact that schools will be supported by the government to promote good behaviour. This was followed by the announcement that school head teachers could promote good behaviour through rewards and sanctions, such as detention and expulsions.

Moreover, the new proposed Ofsted Inspection Framework which was launched in May 2019, placed a renewed emphasis on behaviours and attitudes. Schools are now assessed on these areas, and the assessment covers two distinct facets: (1) the behaviour and discipline in schools and (2) the 'pupils' wider personal development and their opportunities to grow as active, healthy and engaged citizens' (Ofsted, 2019, 11). This is described as the provider prepares learners for life in modern Britain by

- equipping them to be responsible, respectful, active citizens who contribute positively to society;
- developing their understanding of fundamental British values;
- developing their understanding and appreciation of diversity; and
- celebrating what we have in common and promoting respect for the different protected characteristics as defined in law (Ofsted, 2019).

Such policies require character dispositions or skills such as those mentioned earlier to be embedded within schools; however, research on non-cognitive skills remains in its infancy. The preceding brief overview of the different frameworks that define non-cognitive skills illustrates how little agreement there is on which skills are important, how they can be taught and embedded in the various aspects of the school and how they can be reliably measured, seeing as school contexts vary tremendously. A quick summary of traditional and non-traditional methods of measuring such skills is extremely wide ranging and includes approaches such as self-assessments, biodata, interviews, letters of recommendation, analysing writing samples, situational judgement tests, implicit association tests and conditional reasoning tests (Lipnevich et al., 2013).

Why does teaching character matter?

There is good evidence to suggest that embedding character education in schools can have a positive link to both academic achievement and mental well-being. For example, the University of Chicago's Consortium on Chicago School Research focuses on a distinct range of non-cognitive skills which they have found to be those that are most strongly associated with academic performance. These are academic behaviours, academic perseverance, academic mindsets, learning strategies and social skills such as study skills, attendance, work habits, time management, help-seeking behaviors, metacognitive strategies and social and academic problem-solving skills (Farrington et al., 2012). In the United Kingdom, one of the biggest reviews of the literature conducted by University College London found eight characteristics that are malleable and have been found to have a positive impact on children's academic achievement and overall well-being (Gutman and Schoon, 2013). These were: self-perception, motivation, perseverance, self-control, metacognitive strategies, social competencies, resilience and coping and creativity.

Another example includes a study by Boyer and Sedlacek (1988) that found that an understanding of diversity, racism and involvement in community service was a strong predictor of persistence and was related to academic achievement. This can resonate with the Jubilee Centre Framework, which suggests that civic virtues contribute to good character. Similarly, Reuber (2007) found that a 'high degree of self-regulation increases success in school as well as income, occupational prestige and happiness significantly'. He concludes that the costs for parental and school investment in promoting such non-cognitive skills are minimal compared to their long-lasting effects. Farrugia et al. (2016) found that academic mindsets had a strong link to academic performance and retention in higher education students.[1] Another study that supports similar findings is by Müllensiefen et al. (2015), and these authors found that 'musical abilities and active engagement with music have been shown to be positively associated with many cognitive abilities as well as social skills and academic performance in secondary school students'.[2]

Research that is more specifically focused on mental well-being is the body of literature that draws from positive psychology and the wider work of Seligman, which looks at character strengths expressed through thoughts, feelings and behaviours (Seligman and Csikszentmihalyi, 2000). These behaviours are classified in the 'Values in Action' classification, which describes twenty-four character strengths organised under six broad virtues: wisdom and knowledge, courage, humanity, justice, temperance and transcendence. These character strengths are described as valuable for one's academic achievement and well-being. They 'can be seen as the components of a good character, and are described as the inner determinants of a good life, complemented by other external determinants (such as family, education, and health)' (Wagner and Ruch, 2015).

Mental and physical well-being have attracted renewed attention in adolescence as the numbers of pupils with mental health issues have soared in recent years (The Children's Society, 2018). However, the fulfilment of well-being is not a straightforward path. This tension appears in the various theories and the many models aiming to bridge happiness with the concept of self-actualisation. For example, Ryff's model (cited in Olsson et al., 2012, 1080) develops the theory of personal well-being, which 'defines well-being with respect to six domains of human growth: autonomy, personal growth, self-acceptance, life purpose, mastery and positive relatedness'. Positive education centres around education for both traditional skills and happiness; it has been designed to form the basis of a 'new prosperity' that values accomplishment, achievement and wellbeing (Seligman et al., 2009).

At this stage, we should mention the work of the University of Birmingham's Jubilee Centre for Character and Virtues, which is currently conducting the most comprehensive work to date on character education in UK schools. Their framework draws on Aristotelian accounts of *eudaimonia*, or human flourishing. Their suggestion is that to flourish is not only to be happy but also to fulfil one's potential. The role of character education in schools is to teach how to acquire, develop and strengthen virtues that sustain a well-rounded life and a thriving society. Character education should aim to teach students how to become confident, compassionate and effective contributors to society, successful learners and responsible citizens. The Jubilee Centre's definition of character encompasses a set of virtues which produce specific moral emotions (such as empathy and sympathy), inform motivation and guide conduct (Jubilee Centre, 2017). The ultimate goal of the development of character is the development of practical wisdom: the ability to choose the best option out of several, even during difficult situations. These decisions are made, for instance, when students show respect for others but also for themselves, are neighbourly and take actions that are morally justifiable. For practical wisdom to be achieved, the Jubilee Centre outlines and demarcates between four categories of virtue that play supporting roles to one another and are each required for a well-rounded life. Their framework is given in Figure 3.1 (Jubilee Centre, 2017).

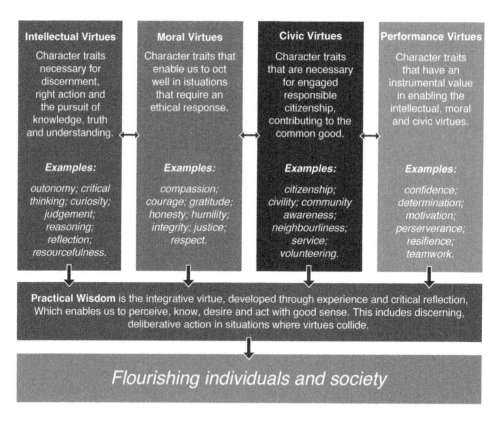

Figure 3.1 A framework for character education in schools (Jubilee Centre, 2017).

Motivation and self-regulation

The importance of self-knowledge and self-understanding lies at the core of some of the most influential philosophies propounded in both the Eastern and Western traditions. In both traditions, there is a common belief that self-knowledge can lead to wisdom. Socrates, for example, taught that the unexamined life is not worth living, and at the core of his philosophy lay the Delphic maxim, 'Know thyself'. The ability to attain self-knowledge through introspection is one of the foundations of modern psychology. More recently, the academic Yuval Noah Harari, author of *Sapiens* (2011) and *Homo Deus* (2017), suggested that what schools currently teach will be almost completely irrelevant in a few years. The rise of 'fake news', artificial intelligence and the almost constant surveillance by social media and online platforms require that schools prepare students with different skills. According to Harari, the skills needed are those which promote the ability of humans to reinvent themselves, namely mental balance and emotional intelligence.

If you are able to develop such skills, Harai argues, you will be able to 'know thyself' (γνῶθι σεαυτόν) and have a better grasp of yourself than Google or Facebook or any other algorithms will ever have. In this sense, liberal education, an education paradigm largely adopted in the United Kingdom, can redefine itself beyond the limiting and limited terms of what is perceived as the ability to pass knowledge from teachers to students. A new approach to education could be promoted that focuses on the importance of self-knowledge with an emphasis on understanding oneself and self-reflection. According to Haberberger (2018), this can be achieved by focusing on developing the following nine categories of skill:

1. critical thinking and broad analytical skills,
2. learning how to learn,
3. independent thinking,
4. empathy,
5. self-control,
6. self-assurance as a leadership ability,
7. mature social-emotional judgement,
8. egalitarian liberal values, and
9. participation in and enjoyment of cultural experience.

There is evidence to suggest that promoting such skills can lead to academic attainment. For example, Daniela (2015) found that the competence of self-regulated learning enhanced the relationship between motivation and performance. Similarly, Barry J. Zimmerman (1989) argues that the ability to set own goals, or self-instruction, can lead to better academic performance. As another example, a study by Wintre et al. (2011) found that being able to manage one's time and set goals leads to greater success in higher education.

In 2018, we conducted a study at Eton in which we identified the character skills that are important to the Eton community. Motivation and perseverance came in the top 5 of the 39 options we gave staff and students. Interestingly, we found that motivation is supported at the school through emphasizing the role of effort in success, providing the right level of challenge, offering teacher support and using formative assessment (Research Schools International (RSI), 2019). For example, by emphasising effort, students are taught that their successes are not a result of innate intelligence or chance but are a function of the effort they put into achieving their goals. Motivation, as the boys commented, can also be developed on the sports field when being coached. When it comes to providing challenge, we know that if skills exceed the level of challenge, students can feel disengaged and bored in a learning activity; likewise, when a student's skills are an inadequate match for the level of challenge at hand, the combination can trigger anxiety, which can also result in disengagement (Watts and Alsop, 2000). In order for a student to be effectively motivated, the challenge and skill level must be matched (Csikszentmihalyi, 1991). Therefore, providing students with the right level of challenge is crucial in order to motivate them. This is something that has been prioritised at Eton, as a lot of the training given within teaching and learning looked at differentiation in the classroom. Through our data collection, we also found that boys believed they were challenged to achieve their best work by pointing them towards further resources they could explore or by giving them extension activities.

Another way this can be achieved is by ensuring that students know about their strengths and weaknesses and are given time to reflect on them. This agrees with the earlier argument which suggests that knowing oneself is crucial in a changing world. This can be achieved through strategies such as teaching students metacognitive skills such as reflection and planning, giving them the tools to overcome difficulties by being able to break down difficult pieces of work into smaller chunks or allowing them to choose the medium of the work they produce. All these strategies can be instrumental ways to promote motivation and also promote self-regulated learning. At Eton, we found that this is something that is being promoted. The school prides itself on promoting individuality and giving students the opportunity to flourish based on their unique strengths, while teachers and adults in boarding houses provide the necessary support for students to explore areas of interest outside the classroom.

Social connectedness and community cohesion and empathy

A comprehensive book on the teenage brain by Sarah-Jayne Blakemore, *Inventing Ourselves: The Secret Life of a Teenage Brain* (2018), has shown the importance of peer relationships during adolescence.[3] Through neuroscientific findings, she gives examples of antibullying campaigns that would have achieved greater success if they had been run by students rather than teachers. She discusses how teenagers are more likely to take risks and engage in risky behaviour if they are with their peers, even though they are perfectly capable of making rational and safe choices when by themselves. On the basis of findings such as these, it is not difficult to see how important social groups and connections are to adolescents, as one of their primary concerns is to 'fit in' with their peers – to belong and be part of a social group. A large number of studies have shown how important it is for humans to have a sense of belonging and social connectedness, as this can lead to greater well-being throughout one's life (Baumeister and Leary, 1995; Demir and Weitekamp, 2007; Holder and Coleman, 2009). Similarly, Jose et al. (2012) found that youths who reported higher levels of social connectedness at one point in time subsequently reported higher well-being, such as greater life satisfaction, confidence and aspirations, at a later point in time.

In 2016–2017, we conducted a study on happiness among boys at Eton (RSI, 2017). Students across the school identified four elements they believed contributed to their happiness. These were

1. social support, from friends and community;
2. a sense of autonomy – that is, the freedom to make decisions about one's life;
3. gratitude, for the diversity of opportunities at Eton; and
4. competence – that is, the ability to do what one wants in order to achieve.

Undeniably, the community of the school is a focal point in determining which character traits are promoted and how character is perceived among students and staff. 'Buying into' the character of the school and being able to engage with the ethos fostered in the school are some of the most important determinants in the academic engagement and well-being of students.

However, broadening the boys' experiences of community engagement may also be a powerful way to develop their character. To this extent, we have conducted a study looking at the development of character traits in year 12 boys (aged 16–17 years) who undertake community engagement as part of Eton's outreach initiatives. We specifically focused on respect, openness to experience, teamwork, gratitude and empathy.[4] Here we outline some examples of how community engagement – or other forms of volunteering that schools promote – can be a platform to develop character.

We believe that the boarding environment of the school encourages respect, as students and adults live together in one big community. Therefore, not showing respect would be frowned upon as it would go against the ethos of the school. This was also something we found in our project with RSI (2019), where pupils noted that the school promotes respect. In the context of our project, we wanted to see whether respect for others, and the local community more broadly, increased through the boys' participation in community engagement. For the boys, respect often meant being open and kind, being understanding of the various skill levels of those they were teaching, being patient when others or themselves were tired and working around what the others needed. Respect was also again closely linked to empathy; a pattern we identified with most of these character traits was that the boys saw them as interlinked.

One of the boys described his experience teaching younger pupils music and how this encouraged respect.

> The first song we sang was 'Any dream will do', a classic choir song. For all of them [this] was probably the first time they were split into harmonies etc. and having to split into teams and respecting their skill levels and under-standing what they could all do.

Another main theme that the boys repeated was the fact that being in Eton often meant that they were mainly socialising with people who came from similar backgrounds to them. Therefore, engaging in activities in the wider community could be beneficial to build character. A boy gave the example of working at a stable where people with physical disabilities would go to try horseback riding. He saw this as an opportunity to develop empathy and be more concerned for people who were not in his social circle. As he describes it,

> seeing how difficult it is even to keep a straight posture. I see how difficult it is ... helping others to get accustomed to riding a horse. ... It is more difficult to feel empathetic if you never met someone with cerebral palsy and it is nice to get to know ... helps to get to know them and they become your friends, so you feel more empathetic rather [than] if it is towards someone you don't know.

Following this study, we aim to implement community engagement, and volunteering, following some of these principles:

1. The idea of service would be championed at all levels of the school and woven into the school's communications strategy, consistently articulated senior management and others. Time for volunteering would be considered when planning out the school week.
2. Volunteering would be emphasised as an educational experience. Placements would be planned with the aim of nurturing key virtues, such as respect, patience, empathy, gratitude and openness.
3. We would maintain a healthy relationship with the individuals and organisations that allow our boys to volunteer with them. Community engagement is a two-way process, and the boys learn at least as much as they give. The guidance, training and supervision provided by placement hosts constitute a significant part of the boys' education.
4. We would create opportunities for boys to volunteer in different ways throughout their time at school, with a clearly articulated pathway for service work from F block (year 9) to B block (year 13) (Arbuthnott, 2019).

Growth and academic mindsets

Carol Dweck (2012) defines 'mindsets' – or 'implicit theories' – as psychologists have defined them – as people's lay beliefs about the nature of human attributes, such as intelligence or personality. Some people hold a fixed mindset (or an entity theory) and believe that human attributes are simply fixed traits. For example, they might believe that each person has a fixed amount of intelligence which he or she cannot change or that each person has a certain personality or moral character which he or she cannot do much to alter. By contrast, other people hold a growth mindset (or an incremental theory). For example, they may believe that all people, no matter who they are, can become substantially more intelligent, say, through their effort and education or that all people can take steps to develop their personality or moral character over time.[5]

Through our interest in growth mindset, we decided to research the concept among students in year 12. Baseline data were collected from 187 students, who were divided into an experimental group ($n = 93$) and a control group ($n = 94$). Teachers at Eton delivered a course that focused on growth mindset and brain plasticity. The course was delivered to the experimental group once a week over three weeks. The control group only took the course after the data were collected, but in the meantime, the group continued their studies as usual. Findings revealed what we had hypothesised and what agrees with similar interventions: students in the experimental group developed a growth mindset and positive self-efficacy beliefs. They gave responses which suggested that learning that the brain has the ability to change can improve self-efficacy and belief in one's abilities.

Even more interestingly, it was found that the pupils who participated in the growth mindset course developed more positive pro-social attitudes. We compared students' pro-social attitudes and social support from before and after the course to measure how the growth mindset course impacted their attitudes and beliefs about social relationships. To be sure that the measured effect was in fact due to the course, we compared the scores of the experimental group of students, who took the course, to the scores of the control group of students, who did not yet take the course. The growth mindset course led to a statistically significant increase in students' prosocial scores. While there was a slight difference in pro-social scores between the experimental and control groups before the course began, the pro-social scores for the experimental group increased after taking the course, whereas the pro-social scores for the control group did not show any change. What underlying shifts in thinking might contribute to students adopting more pro-social attitudes after taking the growth mindset course? To explore this, we examined our qualitative data. As expected, analysis of these data from students in the control group did not uncover notable changes. Analysis of these data from students in the experimental group indicated that after taking the growth mindset course, many students became more aware of how pro-social attitudes and behaviours benefit learning. Specifically, we noticed that many students become more conscious of how kindness and helpfulness support learning after taking the growth mindset course. In practical terms, this meant that those students felt that they received better social support and were able to value social support and character values more highly. They were more likely to link kindness with academic success, show support to others and see how social support can be important to their own academic success (RSI, 2016).

Resilience, grit and perseverance

Angela Duckworth et al. (2007) agree that there is a long list of positive characteristics that are important to one's success. Among those listed are 'creativity, vigour, emotional intelligence, charisma, self-confidence, emotional stability, and physical attractiveness' (*ibid.*, 1087). They state that some of these might be crucial for one area but not so for another. However, they suggest that one character trait in particular is crucial if an individual is to achieve success, in whichever pursuit they are engaged in: grit. Grit is defined as 'perseverance and passion for long-term goals' (*ibid.*). Grit entails working strenuously toward challenges, maintaining effort and interest over extended periods of time despite failure, adversity and plateaus in progress. The 'gritty' individual approaches achievement as a marathon; his or her advantage is stamina. Whereas disappointment or boredom signals to others that it is time to change trajectory and cut losses, the gritty individual stays the course (*ibid.*, 1087–88).

Similarly to grit, 'resilience' refers to a person's ability to bounce back after adversity, hardship or failure: 'abandoning the imprint of the past' (Cyrulnik, 2009, 5). Moreover, Southwick and Charney (2018) note that resilience is a 'prized characteristic' among employers, a fact emphasised by the World Economic Forum (2015), which listed 'grit, persistence and adaptability' as key character attributes that will increasingly be in demand (as cited in Weston, 2019, 12). According to Bernard (2004), resilience is associated with students who have higher levels of social skills and have problem-solving skills, a sense of autonomy and self-efficacy and a sense of purpose, hope and optimism.

One of the most comprehensive frameworks that is implemented primarily in the United States but also in the United Kingdom is the Penn Resilience Programme (PRP). As described by the Positive Psychology Centre at the University of Pennsylvania:

Central to PRP is Ellis' Adversity-Consequences-Beliefs (ABC) model, the notion that our beliefs about events impact our emotions and behaviour. Through this model, individuals learn to detect inaccurate thoughts, and to challenge negative beliefs by considering alternative interpretations. PRP also teachers a variety of strategies that can be used for solving problems and coping with difficult situations and emotions. Individuals learn techniques for assertiveness, negotiation, decision-making, social problem-solving, and relaxation.

Karen Reivich (2008) has suggested seven learnable skills that teachers can promote in the classroom to help students develop their resilience:

1. emotional awareness,
2. impulse control,
3. realistic optimism,
4. flexible thinking,
5. empathy,
6. self-efficacy and
7. risk-taking.

Jackson and Watkin (2014) also suggest an inventory of skills that can boost resilience accompanied by some practical tips on how these can be fostered in young people (Table 3.1).

In the academic year 2019–2020, we commissioned BrainCanDo to trial a resilience programme among year 9 studentss across eleven state and independent schools. The programme is based on the Virtues in Action Character Strengths and will train teachers to run sessions on self-regulation, coping with failure, gratitude, learned optimism, empathy and problem solving. We aim to measure the levels of resilience in students and their attitudes towards dealing with problems. We hope that the findings will allow us to implement a similar programme in more schools in the future and extend the sessions so that they expand over more than one term. This project forms part of our attempt to embed evidenced-informed practices related to character education firmly within the curriculum and co-curriculum.

Table 3.1 Inventory of skills.

ABC	Learning to recognise the impact of your 'in the moment' thoughts and beliefs on behavioural and emotional consequences of adversity
Thinking traps	Recognising the errors in thinking we are often unaware of; for example, jumping to conclusions
Detecting icebergs	Building an awareness of the deep-seated beliefs we have of how the world works and how this can impact our emotions and behaviour
Calming and focusing	Finding ways to step back from adversity, create breathing space and think more resiliently
Challenging beliefs	A process by which the breadth and thus accuracy of our understanding of events can be enhanced, leading to more effective and sustained problem-solving behaviours
Putting it in perspective	Learning to stop the spiralling of catastrophic thinking and turn it into realistic thinking
Real-time resilience	Putting it all into practice in the moment, which is reliant on mastering the other skills and offers a 'fast skill' that does not rely on having the time to think through a resilience reaction in depth

Source: Jackson and Watkin (2014, 15).

Conclusion

The importance of placing character at the heart of education is well evidenced, in terms of its positive impact on both attainment and well-being. The increased focus on character skills in employability also makes a strong argument for why schools and education providers should be considering character as an integral part of their mission. Even though we did not provide an exhaustive description of all the character traits or dispositions which could be deemed important, we have mapped our journey in exploring a number of them at Eton College as well as through our commissioned work with BrainCanDo. We have outlined a number of strategies that can promote motivation and self-regulation, social connectedness and empathy, growth mindset and resilience. Despite only being at the early stages of our research, both empirically and conceptually, we believe in the value of placing these questions at the centre of our research, especially at a time when we know so much about the workings of the teenage brain and what strategies can prove beneficial to students.

Notes

1 Academic mindsets are four beliefs which influence our behaviours as learners and affect our motivation, strategies and perseverance. These are (1) I belong in this learning community, (2) I can change my abilities through effort (a growth mindset), (3) I can succeed, and (4) this work has value and purpose for me (Mindsetworks, 2019).
2 See Chapter 11 for a more in-depth analysis of this study.
3 See Chapter 5 for a summary of adolescent brain development and an analysis of the neuroscientific underpinnings of the increased importance of peer relations during this period.
4 For the full report, see Konstantinou and Harrison (2019), Community engagement: mapping its impact on character development in C block boys, www.etoncollege.com/userfiles/files/ECCE%20report%20.pdf.
5 See Chapter 6 for a comprehensive discussion on the literature of mindsets.

References

American Psychological Association. (2020). *APA Dictionary of Psychology*. Available at https://dictionary.apa.org/cognitive-ability 931.3.2020.
Arbuthnott, T. (2019). ALEX Eton leadership programme with the Oxford character project. *Eton Journal for Innovation and Reserch in Education*, 2. Available at www.etoncollege.com/userfiles/files/CharacterEducationJournalNov2019.pdf (accessed 31 March 2020).

Baumeister, R., and Leary, M. (1995). The need to belong: desire for interpersonal attachments as a fundamental human motivation. *Psychological Bulletin*, *117*, 497–529. doi:10.1037/0033-2909.117.3.497.

Bernard, B. (2004). *Resiliency: What We Have Learned*. San Fransiso: WestEd.

Birdwell, J., Scott, R., and Reynolds, L. (2015). *Character Nation: A Demos Report with the Jubilee Centre for Character and Virtues*. London: Demos.

Blakemore, S. J. (2018). *Inventing Ourselves: The Secret Life of the Teenage Brain*. London: Public Affairs.

Borghans, L., Duckworth, A., Heckman, J., and Ter Weel, B. (2008). The economics and psychology of personality traits. *Journal of Human Resources, 43*(4), 972–1059.

Boyer, S. P., and Sedlacek, W. E. (1988). Noncognitive predictors of academic success for international students: a longitudinal study. *Journal of College Student Development, 29*(3), 218–23.

Csikszentmihalyi, M. (1991). *Flow: The Psychology of Optimal Experience*. New York: Harper Perennial.

Cyrulnik, B. (2009). *Resilience: How Your Inner Strenght Can Set You Free from the Past*. London: Penguin.

Daniela, P. (2015). The relationship between self-regulation, motivation and performance at secondary school students. *Procedia – Social and Behavioural Sciences, 191*, 549–2553.

Demir, M., and Weitekamp, L. A. (2007). I am so happy 'cause today I found my friend: friendship and personality as predictors of happiness. *Journal of Happiness Studies, 8*(2), 181–211.

Department for Education (DfE). (2019). Education secretary sets out vision for character and resiience. London: DfE. Available at www.gov.uk/government/news/education-secretary-sets-out-vision-for-character-and-resilience (accessed 3 December 2019).

Duckworth, A. L., Peterson, C., Matthews, M. D., and Kelly, D. R. (2007). Grit: perseverance and passion for long-term goals. *Journal of Personality and Social Psychology, 92*, 1087–1101.

Dweck, C. S. (2012). Mindsets and human nature: promoting change in the Middle East, the schoolyard, the racial divide, and willpower. *American Psychologist, 67*(8), 614–22.

Farrington, C. A., Roderick, M., Allensworth, E., et al.(2012). Teaching adolescents to become learners: the role of noncognitive factors in shaping school performance: a critical literature review, University of Chicago Consortium on Chicago School Research. Available at www.greatschoolspartnership.org/wp-content/uploads/2016/11/Teaching-Adolescents-to-Become-Learners.pdf (accessed 3 December 2019).

Farruggia, S. P., Han, C., Watson, L., et al. (2016). Noncognitive factors and college student success. *Journal of College Student Retention: Research, Theory and Practice, 20*(3), 308–27. doi:10.1177/1521025116666539.

Gutman, L. M., and Schoon, I. (2013). The impact of non-cognitive skills on outcomes for young people: a literature review. Education Endowmen Foundation, London.Available at https://pdfs.semanticscholar.org/f4a5/2db3001 fb6fb22eef5dc20267b5b807fd8ff.pdf (accessed 3 December 2019).

Haberberger, C. (2018). A return to understanding: making liberal education valuable again. *Educational Philosophy and Theory*, *50*(11), 1052–59.

Harari, Y. N. (2011). *Sapiens*. London: Harvill Secker.

Harari, Y. N. (2017). *Homo Deus*. New York: Harper Perennial.

Hokanson, B., and Karlson, R. M. (2013). Borderlands: developing character strengths for a knowmadic world. *On the Horizon*, *21*(2), 107–13. doi:10.1108/10748121311323003.

Holder, M. D., and Coleman, B. (2009). The contribution of social relationships to children's happiness. *Journal of Happiness Studies*, *10*(3), 329–49.

Jackson, R., and Watkin, C. (2014). The resilience inventory: seven essential skills for overcoming life's obstacles and determining happiness. *Selection and Development Review*, *20*(6), 13–17.

Jose, P. E., Ryan, N., and Pryor, J. (2012). Does social connectedness promote a greater sense of well-being in adolescence over time? *Journal of Research on Adolescence*, *22*, 235–51. doi:10.1111/j.1532-7795.2012.00783.

Jubilee Centre. (2017). *A Framework for Character Education in Schools*. Brimingham, UK: University of Brimingham. Available at https://uobschool.org.uk/wp-content/uploads/2017/08/Framework-for-Character-Education-2017-Jubilee-Centre.pdf.

Lipnevich, A. A., MacCann, C., and Roberts, R. D. (2013). Assessing non-cognitive contsructs in education: a review of traidtional and innovative approaches. *Oxford Handbooks Online*. Available at www.salzburgglobal.org/fileadmin/user_upload/Documents/2010-2019/2016/Session_566/Lipnevich_et_al_2013_Assessing_NonCognitive_Constructs_in_Education_OUP_Book.pdf.

Lucas, B. (2019). Why we need to stop talking about 21st century skills. *Eton Journal for Research and Innovation in Education*, 2. Available at www.etoncollege.com/userfiles/files/TLC_brochure_2019_FAW(2).pdf.

Müllensiefen, D., Harrison, P., Caprini, F., and Fancourt, A. (2015). Investigating the importance of self-theories of intelligence and musicality for students' academic and musical achievement. *Frontiers in Psychology*. Vol 6, doi:10.3389/fpsyg.2015.01702.

National Health Service (NHS) (2017). 1.4 millions people referred to NHS mental health therapy in the past year. Available at https://www.england.nhs.uk/2017/12/1-4-million-people-referred-to-nhs-mental-health-therapy-in-the-past-year/(accesed 31 March 2020).

Office for Standards in Education, Children's Services and Skills (Ofsted). (2019). The education inspection framework. Ofsted, London.Available at https://assets.publishing.service.gov.uk/government/uploads/system/uploads/attachment_data/file/801429/Education_inspection_framework.pdf (accessed 3 December 2019).

Olsson, C. A., McGee, R., Nada-Raja, S., and Williams, S. M. (2012). A 32-year longitudinal study of child and adolescent pathways to well-being in adulthood. *Journal of Happiness Studies* 14, 1069–83.

Organisation for Economic Co-operation and Development (OECD) (2017). *PISA 2015 Results (Volume III): Students' Well-Being*, PISA, OECD Publishing, Paris. Available at http://dx.doi.org/10.1787/9789264273856-en.

Positive Psychology Centre. (2019). *Resilience in Children*. Philadelphia: University of Pennsylvania Press. Available at https://ppc.sas.upenn.edu/research/resilience-children.

Reuber, M. (2007). Noncognitive skills and success in life: the importance of motivation and self-regulation. Discission Paper No. 07/14. Univeristy of Konstanz. Available at https://pdfs.semanticscholar.org/daf8/0e2296329e5cdb39939d6b1d3f827812b3d2.pdf (accessed 9 April 2019).

Reivich, K. (2008). *The Seven Ingredients of Resilience*. Available at https://www.cnbc.com/id/25464528 (accessed 31 March 2020).

Research Schools International (RSI). (2016). *Eton partners with researchers to support students' mindsets and social relationships*. Eton College, Windsor, UK. Available at www.etoncollege.com/userfiles/files/RSI%20Eton%20Research%20Report%2015-16.pdf. (accessed 31 March 2020)..

Research Schools International (RSI). (2017). *RSI research on happiness at Eton College*. Eton College, Windsor, UK. Available at www.etoncollege.com/userfiles/files/RSI%20Eton%20Report%20on%20Wellbeing%20final.pdf. (accessed 31 March 2020).

Research Schools International (2019). *Character Education Research at Eton College*. Windsor: Eton College. Available at https://www.etoncollege.com/userfiles/files/Character%20Education%20at%20Eton%20final.pdf. (accessed 31 March 2020).

Seligman, M. E., Ernst, R. M., Gillham, J., et al. (2009). Positive education: positive psychology and classroom interventions. *Oxford Review of Education, 35*(3), 293–311.

Seligman, M. E. P., and Csikszentmihalyi, M. (2000). Positive psychology: an introduction. *American Psychologist, 55*, 5–14.

Southwick, S. and Charney, D. (2018). *Resilience: The Science of Mastering Life's Greatest Challenges*. Cambridge, UK: Cambridge University Press.

The Children's Society. (2018). *The Good Chidlhood Report*. Children's Society, London. Available at www.childrenssociety.org.uk/what-we-do/resources-and-publications/the-good-childhood-report-2018 (accessed 3 December 2019).

Tough, P. (2012). *How Children Succeed: Grit, Curiosity, and the Hidden Power of Character*. New York: Houghton Mifflin Harcourt.

UNESCO. (2015). *Rethinking Education: Towards a Global Common Good?* Paris: UNESCO.

Wagner, L., and Ruch, W. (2015). Good character at school: positive classroom behavior mediates the link between character strengths and school achievement. *Frontiers in Psychology, 6*. doi:10.3389/fpsyg.2015.00610.

Watts, M., and Alsop, S. (2000). The affective dimensions of learning science. *International Journal of Science Education, 22*(12), 1219–20.

West, M., Kraft, M., Finn, A., et al. (2015). Promise and paradox: measuring students' non cognitive skills and the impact of schooling. *Educational Evaluation and Policy Analysis, 38*(1), 148–70.

Weston, K. (2019). Cultivating resilience in children and young people. *Eton Journal for Innvation and Research in Education.* Eton College, Windsor, UK. Available at www.etoncollege.com/userfiles/files/CharacterEducationJournal Nov2019.pdf.

White, C., Gibb, J., Lea, J., and Street, C. (2017). *Develoing Character Skills in Schools.* Government Social Research Service, London. Available at https:// assets.publishing.service.gov.uk/government/uploads/system/uploads/attach ment_data/file/634712/Developing_Character_skills-Case_study_report.pdf.

Wintre, M. G., Dilouya, B., Pancer, S. M., et al. (2011). Academic achievement in first-year university: who maintains their high school average? *Higher Education, 62,* 467–81.

World Economic Forum. (2015). New vision for education. WEF, Cologny, Switzerland. Available at www3.weforum.org/docs/WEFUSA_NewVisionfor Education_Report2015.pdf (accessed 3 December 2019).

Zimmerman, B. J. (1989). Models of self-regulated learning an academic achievement. In B. J. Zimmerman and D. Schunk (Eds.), *Self-Regulated Learning and Academic Achievement: Theory, Research, and Practice.* New York: Springer-Verlag.

4

The impact of working memory and learning difficulties in the classroom

Amy Fancourt and Joni Holmes

Introduction

Working memory (WM) is the mental workspace that allows us to manipulate and store information temporarily. It has a vital role to play in learning new skills and has been linked to academic progress in a variety of different subjects, including mathematics, English and science. WM capacity increases steadily over age; however, some children do not develop WM at the same rate as others. Failure to follow the typical developmental trajectory for WM skills can result in poor WM and a number of concomitant difficulties in the classroom. For example, a child with poor WM may find it difficult to follow instructions, copy information down from the board or follow typical group interactions. This can result in task failure and distractible and disruptive behaviour.

There are two main approaches to supporting children with poor WM. First, we can attempt to train WM in order to improve capacity. However, research has shown that although there may be some success in training WM, this does not then necessarily translate to improved academic progress or educational attainment for these children. Second, we can modify our classroom teaching practices so that we become more attuned and responsive to the needs of children with WM limitations. Research has consistently demonstrated that if teaching practices are modified in such ways, a child with limited WM can be adequately supported and enabled to achieve good academic progress.

How is memory organised?

The multi-store model of memory proposed by Atkinson and Shiffrin (1968) suggests that there are two main memory stores: short-term memory and long-term memory. These two parts of memory work very differently and store information in very different ways. Our short-term memory can hold around seven distinct pieces of information for a very brief time, and without constant repetition of this information, it is forgotten. Generally, we hold information in short-term memory acoustically by verbally repeating it to ourselves either silently or out loud. Long-term memory has an infinite capacity, and once learned, information will remain in this memory store for a lifetime. The way in which we store information in long-term memory is by assigning meaning to it. For example, we are able to recall our knowledge of important factual information a long time after learning it, and we are able to remember significant events in our lives. These are types of long-term memories that mean something to us.

When we first encounter new information, we have to pay attention to this information for it to even enter the memory system. Once this information has entered short-term memory, we then need to assign some meaning to it in order for it to be transferred and stored in long-term memory. The meaning we give to the information will then help us to retrieve this knowledge when we next need it. We can only really say that learning has happened once information has been transferred to long-term memory and can be successfully retrieved and used.

Since the introduction of the multi-store model of memory in 1968, there has been a lot of further work investigating how short-term memory and long-term memory work; it is now widely recognised that the picture is a little more complex than first understood. For example, we now know that there are different types of long-term memories and that these different types operate independently and are stored in different areas of the brain (Cohen and Squire, 1980; Tulving, 1972). This means that it is possible for a person to have difficulty remembering what they ate for lunch yesterday and yet still be able to ride a bike or play the piano. Similarly, we now understand that short-term memory is more than just a verbal store and that it has many more active parts to it. The WM model was introduced by Alan Baddeley and Graham Hitch in 1974 as a way of explaining the more active parts of short-term memory (Baddeley and Hitch, 1974).

What is working memory and what does it do?

The term 'working memory' (WM) describes our ability to mentally store and manipulate information over brief periods of time (Baddeley, 2017). Throughout the day, we are bombarded with input that we need to make sense of and respond to. It is our WM that enables us to organise and effectively respond to this input. WM enables us to store information in our mind for short periods of time and then actively use this information in some way. Our WM is a mental workspace that is important for a number of different daily tasks. For example, the ability to read, carry out simple mental arithmetic, learn how to use new technology or gadgets and follow a series of instructions or directions all rely heavily on our WM ability. For children at all stages of development, WM plays an important role in learning new skills. It enables children to meet classroom demands and maintain focused behaviour in environments that are complex and filled with distractions.

WM is not a part of the brain but a faculty of the mind. It is a theoretical concept that is used to explain how active memory works. One of the most widely accepted models of WM is that of Baddeley and Hitch (1974; Baddeley, 2000). According to this model, WM has multiple systems. There are two storage components, the phonological loop and the visuo-spatial sketchpad. The visuo-spatial sketchpad is responsible for processing visual and spatial information (e.g. a route on a map) and for enabling us to remember this information for a brief period of time. The phonological loop does the same, but for verbal and auditory information. These two components work together, and our attention is directed to processing information in the phonological loop and the visuo-spatial sketchpad by the central executive. The central executive is part of WM that controls focused attention and helps us to avoid distraction. The fourth component of the WM model is the episodic buffer. This integrates information from the different components of WM with material held in long-term memory.

Interestingly, WM capacity is not the same thing as intelligence. There are clear distinctions between a child's intelligence quotient (IQ) and his or her WM ability, and each factor plays a role in a child's overall academic achievement (Gathercole et al., 2006). Having said this, it is often found that children with a low-range IQ also have poor WM (Elliott et al., 2010).

How much information can working memory hold on to?

The amount of information we can hold and manipulate in our WM is known as our 'WM capacity', and this changes with age. In general, the younger you are, the smaller is your WM capacity. WM capacity increases steadily with age until a child reaches around 15 years of age, at which point it becomes similar to that of adults (Alloway et al., 2006). For some children, WM capacity does not develop at the same rate as other children of the same age. This means that they have a smaller capacity for remembering information compared to other children their age.

Who has poor working memory?

Impairments in WM are a feature of many different developmental disorders and diagnoses of special educational needs. For example, poor WM has been reported in children with speech, language and reading difficulties, including those with specific language impairment (SLI) and dyslexia (Archibald and Gathercole, 2007). It is also common in children with attention problems linked to learning difficulties (Holmes et al., 2014; Simone et al., 2018) and in children with specific mathematical difficulties such as dyscalculia (Holmes and Adams, 2006; Mammarella et al., 2018). Children with behavioural difficulties such as attention deficit/hyperactivity disorder (ADHD) typically perform poorly on tests of both verbal and visuo-spatial (nonverbal) working memory (Holmes et al., 2014). Interestingly, one study reported that the only cognitive difference between children with poor WM for their age but no other diagnoses and children with ADHD was that those with poor WM were slower to respond on several tasks relative to the group with ADHD (Holmes et al., 2014). The ADHD group were rated by teachers as being more impulsive and oppositional than the low WM group, but both groups were rated as being equally highly inattentive (Holmes et al., 2014). It has been suggested that WM problems may be the cause of the inattentive and distractible behaviour seen in children with ADHD. In order to successfully complete any task, WM is needed to support the maintenance of task goals as well as the different elements of the ongoing mental activity needed to achieve the goal. Poor WM function could result in a shift of attention away from the task in which a child is currently engaged. This could result in the loss of information needed for successful task completion, as well as in forgetting the task instructions. Consequently, the child experiences task failure or gives up on the activity (Holmes et al., 2014).

WM deficits are a risk factor for poor educational progress and outcomes in children who have not received a formal special educational needs and disabilities (SEND) diagnosis (Gathercole and Alloway, 2008). Poor performance on a WM test may be a useful prospective marker for children who are likely to make slow progress at school but have not been formally diagnosed with any other learning difficulty (Elliott et al., 2010). One study measured the extent to which WM deficits are present in children with reading and mathematical difficulties in a large sample of children aged between 5 and 15 years (Gathercole et al., 2016). All children included in the study were reported to have difficulties with attention, learning and memory, and the findings revealed that performance on reading and mathematics assessments was significantly correlated with verbal and visuo-spatial WM abilities. Thus, it seems that academic underachievement in literacy and mathematics is linked to underlying deficits in WM. Interestingly, despite the poor performance in reading and mathematics, these children had age-appropriate vocabulary scores and low to average nonverbal reasoning abilities. The authors note that the co-occurrence of learning difficulties alongside WM deficits may mean that we could use WM screening as a tool to prospectively identify children at risk of poor academic attainment.

Although WM alone cannot explain the wide range of different learning difficulties in all their complexity, understanding the nature of WM difficulties in these children can be valuable for appropriately targeting educational support

(Gathercole et al., 2016). It is clear that poor WM creates barriers to effective engagement and mental activity that are pivotal within the classroom. Given the connection with educational outcomes, early recognition of WM difficulties and the provision of effective educational support and targeted interventions are of great importance in improving outcomes for many children (Holmes et al., 2010). Classrooms and teaching methods that have been designed to purposefully compensate for WM difficulties or avoid WM-related failures should be a key feature of targeted support interventions put in place for struggling learners (Gathercole et al., 2016).

Assessing working memory

There are a few different standardised assessments that can be used to assess a child's WM abilities. The 'Working Memory Rating Scale' was developed by Tracey Alloway and Susan Gathercole (Alloway et al., 2009) and was designed to be used by teachers for early identification of children with WM difficulties. This measure was developed from another test called the 'Automated Working Memory Assessment' which has been tested and standardised on very large samples of data; this means that age-normed scores are available. The presence of age-normed scores enables us to measure an individual child's WM capacity and compare it to the typical WM capacity score for children of the same age. Children are typically identified as having poor WM if their scores on this measure fall at least one standard deviation below the mean score. If a child is identified as having poor WM by this standard, he or she is potentially at risk of poor educational progress (Holmes et al., 2010).

These memory assessment measures are used by educational psychologists and learning support professionals who are trained to administer the tests and interpret the results. If you suspect that any student you teach does have poor WM, then please consult the learning support department in your school so that a complete WM assessment can be made.

What difficulties do children with poor working memory face?

Academic problems

WM skills are strongly linked to a child's ability to learn in a range of academic domains, including reading, mathematics and science (Gathercole and Pickering, 2000; Holmes and Adams, 2006; Jarvis and Gathercole, 2003; Peng and Fuchs, 2016; Peng et al., 2016; Swanson and Saez, 2003; Wang and Gathercole, 2013). Performance on WM assessments predicts a child's further academic performance and attainment at 7, 11 and 14 years of age (Gathercole et al., 2004; Jarvis and Gathercole, 2003).

WM supports many complex activities in which children engage in school. It plays an important role in the development of counting and the remembering of number bonds. Children with WM difficulties often resort to using primitive finger-counting strategies that have relatively low WM demands (Geary et al., 2004). The knock-on effect is that the child does not establish a robust network of arithmetic facts in long-term memory that are vital to the use of effective solution strategies for maths problems in adulthood (Hamann and Ashcraft, 1985; Kaye, 1986). Poor WM impairs learning number facts (Geary, 2004), efficiently trans-coding numbers (Camos, 2008), computational skills (Wilson and Swanson, 2001) and solving mathematical problems that are couched in everyday language (Swanson and Sachse-Lee, 2001).

When learning to read and comprehend a passage of written text, a child has to perform a number of psychological activities simultaneously: the child has to map between sounds, letters and words; he or she also has to hold sentences in memory; and he or she has to retrieve and integrate information about the meaning of each word and previous sentences from long-term memory. The phonological store in WM supports the maintenance of sounds and sound sequences for correct word identification (Prebler et al., 2013). WM also supports the active processing of incoming information and enables it to be merged with previous knowledge for reading comprehension. It also supports the retrieval of semantic knowledge of familiar words from long-term memory (Booth et al., 2010; Carretti et al., 2009; Sesma et al., 2009).

There are many reasons why a child may struggle to cope with the demands of a typical classroom situation. A classroom is often noisy with background sounds which can make it difficult to concentrate on what the teacher is saying or the task at hand. The complexity of social interactions creates a further obstacle to be navigated as a child is working in the classroom. Poor WM ability can further add to these challenges, making it very difficult for a child to cope with a typical classroom setting. When we consider what exactly WM does, it is easy to see why a deficit in WM should have such significant consequences for a child's educational progress.

What is the typical profile of a child with poor working memory?

One of the reasons why children with poor WM find it so difficult to meet the demands of a typical classroom setting is because many classroom activities exceed their WM capacities – in other words, there is just too much information to process and remember. As a consequence, children with poor WM often display the following signs of struggling:

- *Poor academic progress for their age.* For example, 80% of children with poor WM score poorly in reading and mathematics relative to their peers (Jaroslawska et al., 2016).

■ *Difficulties following multistep instructions* (Engle et al., 1991; see also Elliott et al., 2010). For example, if a typical 7-year-old has a WM capacity of around ten items, he or she may just about be able to remember and follow a set of instructions such as the following from the teacher:

> Come into the classroom, hang your coats up, take off your outdoor trainers and put on your plimsolls. Put your book bags in your tray, and then take out your reading books, reader cards and come and sit on the carpet.

If we break this sentence down, there are eight different instructions to remember and follow. For a typical 7-year-old with an average WM capacity of around ten, this is manageable. But if a child has a poor WM and has a WM capacity of six, this set of instructions becomes impossible to remember and follow. When the WM is unable to keep up with the demands that such complex instructions carry, the child will forget what he or she is doing, and this can result in inattentive or poor behaviour.

■ *Struggling to keep pace in demanding and complex activities such as writing or copying from a board.* For example, you may find that children with poor WM miss out letters, skip whole words or blend parts of different words from different sentences together. If a child with poor WM was asked to copy the title of a piece of work from the board, such as 'My Holiday', and the date '17th June' they could actually end up writing 'My Holune' (Holmes et al., 2010). Often such children will not recognise their errors and will not self-correct their work, so this can result in failure (Gathercole and Alloway, 2008).

■ *Planning and organising information* (Alloway et al., 2009). A child with poor WM may find it very challenging to plan his or her time effectively or to plan ahead. This may make it difficult to keep up with the demands of homework or project work requiring this level of organisation. The child may also struggle to keep an ordered file of notes or an organised exercise book.

■ *Difficulties keeping focus in practical situations* (Kane et al., 2004). A child with poor WM may find it difficult to follow, or to write, a sequenced set of instructions needed to carry out a practical experiment or follow a recipe when cooking.

■ *Difficulties with problem solving* (Swanson et al., 2008). Any problem that requires moving through a series of steps in order to work out a solution will be challenging for a child with poor WM.

■ *Keeping track of progress in complex tasks* (Gathercole et al., 2006). Children with poor WM may experience mind wandering, and this can make it difficult to concentrate for extended periods of time on the completion of a task that has been set.

- *Distractible and inattentive behaviour* (Alloway et al., 2009).

  - A child with poor WM may find it difficult to sit and concentrate on the task he or she has been given to do. This may be reflected in poor behaviour.
  - A child with poor WM may demonstrate typical social interactions but can also show some difficulties managing complex and demanding social situations. Children with poor WM are often reserved in group discussions in the classroom but are much more adept at managing less formal social interactions with peers outside the classroom (Gathercole et al., 2008).
  - A child with WM difficulties may not participate fully during group-based class activities and may appear very withdrawn. However, at break and lunch times, the child may be highly sociable.

- *Difficulties with emotional control and regulation.* According to teacher reports, around 50% of children identified as having poor WM are perceived as having concomitant difficulties with emotional control and regulation. Alloway et al. (2009) reported that 38% of their sample of children with poor WM also had severe difficulties with emotional control that reached clinical significance. Furthermore, 45% of 5- to 6-year-olds and 48% of 9- to 10-year-olds with poor WM showed significant problem behaviours associated with poor emotional control. This may reflect the increased likelihood of co-morbidity in children with WM difficulties such that the presence of poor WM increases the risk of also being diagnosed with a SEND such as ADHD. Alternatively, the behavioural difficulties may be a direct result of the challenges associated with the limited processing abilities of a child with poor WM.

How can we best support children with working memory difficulties?

There are two main ways in which we can seek to overcome the challenges faced by children with poor WM. The first approach is to try to improve a child's individual WM capacity directly through training. The idea here is that if a child's WM capacity can be increased, then this should lead to better academic performance. An alternative approach is to modify the learning environment so that the demands placed on WM are reduced. This second approach involves considering situations that could lead to memory overload and developing a range of different techniques and strategies to support a child so that he or she does not reach this point of overload.

The impact of WM training programmes is currently limited, and the chances of improvements on specific WM tasks transferring to improvements in underlying WM more broadly are low. Moreover, the benefits of WM training do not appear to generalise to improvements in everyday functioning (Dunning et al., 2013). In a recent meta-analysis of eighty-seven publications relating to WM training, improvements on WM measures were found. However, improvements on these WM measures were not reflected in improvements in other abilities underpinned by WM, such as language comprehension, reading or mathematical abilities (Melby-Lervag et al., 2016). Thus, the transfer from WM training to improvement in actual educational outcomes is limited. Given the evidence suggesting that WM training is not linked to improvements in academic or educational outcomes for children, it is important to find another way to support learning in the classroom for these children.

The second approach is very much rooted in the notion that teachers should be made aware of the warning signs of WM difficulties and taught how best to adapt their teaching methods to reduce the cognitive load placed on children's memories. Teachers can also work with the children themselves to encourage them to use strategies to compensate for their WM limitations (Holmes et al., 2010).

What can teachers do in the classroom to support children with working memory difficulties?

In this section, we will look at some examples of how classroom teaching can be adapted to best support children with WM limitations. Although these strategies are designed to improve access to learning for children with poor WM, by including these strategies, classroom teaching for all learners can be improved. Every child has a WM capacity; this may vary, and some children have a larger capacity than others. Ultimately, however, every child will reach WM capacity at some point. Therefore, it is important for teachers to be mindful of the limited processing capacity of children when planning lessons and designing classroom activities. We want all learners to be engaged in classroom activities, but, ultimately, if these activities exceed processing capacity, then learning is impeded. This idea is known as 'cognitive load theory'. Cognitive load theory recognises that all people, adults and children, have a WM capacity, that learning for everyone is hampered and that task failure occurs when this WM capacity is overloaded (De Jong, 2010). Therefore, we want to design a curriculum and plan lessons with classroom activities that are within the WM capacities of the children in our classrooms.

Susan Gathercole and colleagues have identified seven key principles designed to decrease task failures, improve confidence and increase rates of learning in children with WM difficulties (see Elliott et al., 2010). First, teachers can be aware of the symptoms of underlying WM difficulties in children. It is absolutely pivotal that teachers are taught about the concept of WM and what happens when a child experiences WM difficulties. Once aware of the challenges faced by many children in their classrooms, teachers can begin to work on adapting their classroom practice to reduce the memory load they are placing on children. Central to this is the need for teachers to monitor how children with poor WM are coping with mentally challenging activities and to actively look for warning signs of cognitive overload. Teachers should also take the time to regularly evaluate learning activities to identify those that will be problematic for children with limited WM capacities. For example, a long written text or activities that include large amounts of unfamiliar material will place additional demands on WM and thereby prove problematic for children with limited WM capacities. Once this situation is evaluated, teachers are in a position to restructure activities so that they weigh less heavily on WM. This can be achieved by reducing the amount of information that a child must hold in memory at any one time and increasing the familiarity and meaningfulness of the material with which children are engaged. Teachers should regularly repeat task-specific instructions and pair children with poor WM with those who do not struggle to remember information so that the child experiences fewer WM-related task failures. Finally, teachers should do everything within their power to encourage children to help themselves by developing compensatory strategies to overcome their WM limitations.

Here are some suggestions as to how classroom practice can be modified to accommodate the range of different WM capacities reflected in learners:

1. *Break tasks and instructions down into smaller steps.* Wherever possible, simplify instructions so that children only have one or two pieces of information to remember. Alternatively, write instructions down on the board so that if children forget what has been said, they can go back to the instructions and check again.
2. *Present information more than once.* If a concept is important and forms the foundation for later learning, revisit the concept on more than one occasion, as this will help to connect with knowledge stored in long-term memory.
3. *Create a comfortable environment where forgetting is not punished but understood.* In this way, when a child forgets, he or she is able to ask what to do rather than falling into negative or disruptive classroom behaviour.

These suggestions may sound simple and obvious, yet the research shows that they can have a huge impact on the success (or failure) of children's learning outcomes (Elliott et al., 2010). One study showed that when teachers modified their practice to accommodate the needs of children with limited WM, this had a significant impact on the progress the children made in literacy and mathematics. Teachers commented that by implementing the above-mentioned strategies in a focused way, they were able to reinterpret children's classroom behaviour and recognised that many task failures were due to forgetting rather than children having a lack of attention, effort or motivation. Elliott et al. (2010) devised an intervention that could be implemented within the existing curriculum with the aim of improving children's WM capacity and their subsequent academic performance by creating a more optimal classroom environment and learning experience. The biggest factor in this intervention was supporting teachers to ensure that the cognitive load and demands placed on the WM of children did not exceed their abilities.

Elliott et al. (2010) worked with a total of 3,189 children from twenty-five local education authority primary, infant and junior schools in County Durham, North-East England. The schools were selected to reflect the national demographic profile of children receiving free school meals (an indicator of socio-economic status) and performance on national assessments in reading, writing and mathematics. Children completed assessments before and after the intervention and were tested individually in a quiet area of the school. The assessments included a measure of visual and verbal WM ability, a reading comprehension task, a mathematical reasoning task, a measure of receptive vocabulary and a test of general ability (or IQ). The intervention period lasted for eight months and began in each school as soon as the pre-intervention assessment was complete. Prior to the intervention, the classroom teachers, teaching assistants, special educational needs coordinators (SENCOs) and senior management teams in each of the schools were given a series of twilight training sessions, and throughout the intervention period, the schools were supported by a full-time research assistant.

During the training sessions, staff in the schools were given the booklet 'Understanding Working Memory: A Classroom Guide', produced by Susan Gathercole and Tracey Alloway (2007). During the training, participants were taught about WM and the extent to which this system underpins many different classroom activities. Teaching staff were given guidance about how to modify and reduce WM loads in the classroom by using following eight principles:

1. Recognise failures in WM.
2. Monitor the child for warning signs of poor WM.
3. Evaluate the WM demands of activities.
4. Reduce WM loads, if necessary.
5. Be aware that increasing the processing demands can increase WM load.
6. Frequently repeat important information.
7. Encourage the use of memory aids.
8. Help the child to develop the use of memory-supporting strategies.

The staff who attended the training session were given feedback sheets to complete in which the eight principles were listed. Participants were asked to indicate on their feedback sheets how frequently they had applied the eight principles and give examples of how these principles had been applied. Numeracy and literacy lessons were observed to check that teachers were successfully applying the intervention strategy.

At the end of the intervention, it was found that although children's WM abilities remained unchanged, there were significant gains in the academic performance of the students of the teachers who successfully integrated the aforementioned eight principles into their classroom practice. Observations revealed that the most effective teachers were already attuned to the needs of their students with WM problems and were using appropriate strategies spontaneously. Elliott et al. (2010) note that one of the biggest reasons why there is such a connection between sensitive teaching and academic gains in younger children is that if a child is constantly left to struggle with cognitive overload while responding to teachers who are not at all sympathetic or understanding, it is very likely that the child will become disheartened, lose focus and disengage altogether from the education system. Naturally, this level of disengagement will result in poor academic performance. If teachers truly understand the role that WM plays in so many aspects of classroom teaching and learning and recognise when a child has a limited WM, they can become empowered to transform the way they teach so that it becomes more sensitive and attuned to the needs of their students.

Can children be taught to compensate for their own working memory difficulties, and does this lead to improved educational attainment?

It is possible to enhance WM by training children to use various strategies to support their memory. For example, children can be encouraged to repeatedly rehearse aloud information they need to remember. They may also be encouraged to use memory aids or mnemonic strategies such as creating a story or generating visual images of the information they are trying to learn (Holmes et al., 2010). It has been found that individual differences in strategy use are related to WM abilities in adults and that developmental increases in WM capacity are mediated by the onset of strategy use (Gathercole, 1999). Strategy use is not spontaneous in young children, but they will attempt to use strategies when instructed to do so, and therefore, it may be that training children to use memory strategies for themselves may boost WM functioning (St Clair-Thompson and Holmes, 2008).

St Clair-Thompson and Holmes (2008) found that giving children memory strategy training resulted in significant improvements in WM in those children. In this study, 6- to 7-year-olds and 7- to 8-year-olds were given a computerised adventure game called 'Memory Booster' (Leedale et al., 2004). This game taught and encouraged the use of rehearsal, visual imagery, story generation and grouping. Children were given two thirty-minute-long training sessions per week for six to eight weeks, and the younger children showed improvement in their ability to follow a set of instructions. Interestingly, the benefits of memory training were limited to the younger children; the 7- to 8-year-olds showed no improvements following this period of training. In a further follow-up study, St Clair-Thompson (St Clair-Thompson and Holmes, 2008) recruited 254 children 5 to 8 years of age and divided them such that half participated in the Memory Booster training and half did not. The author reported that the children who had completed the Memory

Booster training showed improvements in mental arithmetic and their ability to follow instructions but did not show any gains in standardised assessments on reading or mathematics. Taken together, these findings seem to indicate that memory strategy training may confer some benefits for classroom-related activities that are problematic for children with poor WM. However, the extent to which these transfer to gains in educational attainment is limited.

Summary

WM is central to many aspects of daily functioning, from remembering what we need to pick up from the shops to mental arithmetic. Multiple complex demands are placed on WM in the classroom, and these can lead to cognitive overload. Children with limited WM might be identified in the classroom by indicators such as poor written work where letters or words are missing, apparently inattentive or distractible behaviour, inaccuracy when copying details from the board and trouble following multistep instructions. Once recognised, it is within the power of the teacher to modify his or her teaching practices to best meet the needs of children with limited WM capacities. Research has shown that becoming more attuned to the needs of students and seeking to devise learning activities that reduce the demands placed on WM resources can lead to significant gains in literacy and numeracy. Ways in which classroom practice can be modified to support children with WM difficulties are to break complex tasks down into smaller steps, simplify instructions wherever possible, revisit the most important foundational concepts on a regular basis and create a comfortable environment in which a child is permitted to forget. Just increasing awareness and making a few simple modifications to teaching practice can have a large impact on the behaviour and progress of children with WM difficulties.

Another way in which we can effectively support children with WM difficulties is by working directly with each child to help him or her find memory strategies to effectively compensate for his or her memory limitations. Such strategies may include encouraging the use of visual imagery, story generation or rehearsal to help the child learn information that needs to be remembered. One study showed that by employing such techniques, children with WM limitations showed marked improvements in their everyday memory abilities and were better able to follow task instructions and remain on task (St Clair-Thompson and Holmes, 2008).

It is clear that WM is of central importance to teaching and learning across many areas of the curriculum. WM difficulties are present in a number of developmental disorders and SEND diagnoses and have been tangibly linked to poor educational progress and outcomes. We are in a position to be able to recognise WM difficulties when they occur and to put in place appropriate and targeted interventions to better support learning in students with poor WM. It is our responsibility as teachers to do whatever we can to adapt and modify our teaching practice so that it is student centred and meets the needs of every learner.

References

Alloway, T. P., Gathercole, S. E., Kirkwood, H., and Elliott, J. (2009). The working memory rating scale: a classroom-based behavioral assessment of working memory. *Learning and Individual Differences, 19*(2), 242–45.

Alloway, T. P., Gathercole, S. E., and Pickering, S. J. (2006). Verbal and visuospatial short-term and working memory in children: are they separable? *Child Development, 77*(6), 1698–1716.

Archibald, L. M., and Gathercole, S. E. (2007). Nonword repetition in specific language impairment: more than a phonological short-term memory deficit. *Psychonomic Bulletin Review, 14*(5), 919–24.

Atkinson, R.C. & Shiffrin, R.M. (1968). Human memory: a proposed system and its control processes. In K.W. Spence & J.T. Spence (Eds.), *The psychology of learning and motivation: Advances in research and theory. (Vol. 2).* New York: Academic Press. Pp. 89–195.

Baddeley, A. (2017). *Exploring Working Memory: Selected Works of Alan Baddeley.* London: Routledge.

Baddeley, A. D. (2000). The episodic buffer: a new component of working memory? *Trends in Cognitive Sciences, 4*(11), 417–23.

Baddeley, A. D., and Hitch, G. (1974). Working memory. In G. H. Bower (Ed.), *The Psychology of Learning and Motivation: Advances in Research and Theory* (Vol. 8, pp. 47–89). New York: Academic Press.

Booth, J. N., Boyle, J., and Kelly, S. (2010). Do tasks make a difference? Accounting for heterogeneity of performance of children with reading difficulties on tasks of executive function: findings from a meta-analysis. *British Journal of Developmental Psychology, 28*(1), 133–76.

Camos, V. (2008). Low working memory capacity impedes both efficiency and learning of number transcoding in children. *Journal of Experimental Child Psychology, 99*(1), 37–57.

Carretti, B., Borella, E., Cornold, C., and De Beni, R. (2009). Role of working memory in explaining the performance of individuals with specific reading comprehension difficulties: a meta-analysis. *Learning and Individual Differences, 19*(2), 246–51.

Cohen, N. J., and Squire, L. R. (1980). Preserved learning and retention of pattern analyzing skill in amnesia: dissociation of knowing how and knowing that. *Science, 210,* 207–9.

De Jong, T. (2010). Cognitive load theory, educational research, and instructional design: some food for thought. *Instructional Science, 38*(2), 105–34.

Dunning, D. L., Holmes, J., and Gathercole, S. E. (2013). Does working memory training improve the classroom performance of children with poor working memory? A randomised controlled trial. *Developmental Science, 16,* 915–25.

Elliott, J. G., Susan, G., Alloway, T. P., and Holmes, J. (2010). An evaluation of a classroom-based intervention to help overcome working memory difficulties and improve long-term academic achievement. *Journal of Cognitive Education and Psychology*, *9*, 227–50.

Engle, R. W., Carullo, J. J., and Collins, K. W. (1991). Individual differences in working memory for comprehension and following directions. *Journal of Education Research*, *84*(5), 253–62.

Gathercole, S. E. (1999). Cognitive approaches to the development of short-term memory. *Trends in Cognitive Sciences*, *3*(11), 410–19.

Gathercole, S. E., and Alloway, T. P. (2007). *Understanding Working Memory: A Classroom Guide*. London: Harcourt Assessment.

Gathercole, S., and Alloway, T. P. (2008). *Working Memory: A Practical Guide for Teachers*. Thousand Oaks, CA: SAGE Publications.

Gathercole, S., Woolgar, F., Kievit, R. A., et al.. (2016). How common are deficits in children with difficulties in reading and mathematics? *Journal of Applied Research in Memory and Cognition*, *5*(4), 384–94.

Gathercole, S. E., Alloway, T. P., Willis, C., and Adams, A. M. (2006). Working memory in children with reading disabilities. *Journal of Experimental Child Psychology*, *93*(3), 265–81.

Gathercole, S. E., and Pickering, S. J. (2000). Working memory deficits in children with low achievements in the national curriculum at 7 years of age. *British Journal of Educational Psychology*, *70*, 177–94.

Gathercole, S. E., Pickering, S. J., Ambridge, B., and Wearing, H. (2004). The structure of working memory from 4 to 15 years of age. *Devlopmental Psychology*, *40*(2), 177–90.

Gathercole, S. E., Durling, E., Evans, M., Jeffcock, S., & Stone, S. (2008). Working memory abilities and children's performance in laboratory analogues of classroom activities. *Applied Cognitive Psychology*, *22*, *1019–1037*.

Geary, D.C. (2004). Mathematics and learning disabilities. *Journal of Learning Disabilities*, *37(1)*, *4-15*.

Geary, D. C., Hoard, M. K., Byrd-Craven, J., and De Soto, C. (2004). Strategy choices in simple and complex addition: contributions of working memory and counting knowledge for children with mathematical disability. *Journal of Experimental Child Psychology*, *88*, 121–51.

Hamann, M. S., and Ashcraft, M. H. (1985). Simple and complex mental addition across development. *Journal of Experimental Child Psychology*, *40*, 49–72. doi:10.1016/00220965(85)90065-7.

Holmes, J., and Adams, J. W. (2006) . Working memory and children's mathematical skills: implications for mathematical development and mathematics curricula. *Educational Psychology*, *26. pp. 339-366*.

Holmes, J., Gathercole, S., and Dunning, D. (2010). Poor working memory: impact and interventions. In J. Holmes (Ed.), *Advances in Child Development and Behaviour* (Vol. 39, pp. 1–43). Burlington, VT: Academic Press. 2010.

Holmes, J., Hilton, K. A., Place, M., et al.. (2014). Children with low working memory and children with ADHD: same or different? *Frontiers in Human Neuroscience*, *8*, 1–13.

Jaroslawska, A. J., Gathercole, S. E., Logie, M. R., and Holmes, J. (2016). Following instructions in a virtual school: does working memory play a role? *Memory & Cognition*, *44*(4), 580–89.

Jarvis, H. L., and Gathercole, S. E. (2003). Verbal and non-verbal working memory and achievements on national curriculum tests at 11 and 14 years of age. *Educational and Child Psychology*, *20*, 123–40.

Kane, M. J., Hambrick, D. Z., Tuholski, S. W., Wilhelm, O., Payne, T. W., & Engle, R. W. (2004). The generality of working memory capacity: a latent variable approach to verbal and visuospatial memory span and reasoning. *Journal of Experimental Psychology: General*, *133*, 189–217.

Kaye, D. B. (1986). The development of mathematical cognition. *Cognitive Development*, *1*, 157–70.

Leedale, R., Singleton, C., and Thomas, K. (2004). *Memory booster (computer program and manual)*. Lucid Research, Beverley, UK.

Mammarella, I. C., Caviola, S., Giofrè, D., and Szűcs, D. (2018). The underlying structure of visuospatial working memory in children with mathematical learning disability. *British Journal of Developmental Psychology*, *36*(2), 220–35.

Melby-Lervag, M., Redick, T. S., and Hulme, C. (2016). Working memory training does not improve performance on measures of intelligence or other measures of 'far transfer'. *Perspectives in Psychological Science*, *11*(4), 512–34.

Peng, P., and Fuchs, D. (2016). A meta-analysis of working memory deficits in children with learning difficulties: is there a difference between verbal domain and numerical domain? *Journal of Learning Disabilities*, *49*(1), 3–20.

Peng, P., Namkung, J., Barnes, M., and Sun, C. (2016). A meta-analysis of mathematics and working memory: moderating effects of working memory domain, type of mathematics skill, and sample characteristics. *Journal of Educational Psychology*, *108*(4), 455–73.

Prebler, A. L., Krajewski, K., and Hasselhorn, M. (2013). Working memory capacity in preschool children contributes to the acquisition of school relevant precursor skills. *Learning and Individual Differences*, *23*, 138–44.

Sesma, H. W., Mahone, E. M., Levine, T., et al.. (2009). The contribution of executive skills to reading comprehension. *Child Neuropsychology*, *15*, 232–46.

Simone, A. N., Marks, D. J., Bédard, A. C., and Halperin, J. M. (2018). Low working memory rather than ADHD symptoms predicts poor academic achievement in school-aged children. *Journal of Abnormal Child Psychology*, *46* (2), 277–90.

St Clair-Thompson, H. L., and Holmes, J. (2008). Improving short-term and working memory: methods of memory training. In N. B. Johansen (Ed.), *New Research in Short-Term Memory* (pp. 125–54). New York: Novascience.

Swanson, H. L., Jerman, O., and Zheng, X. (2008). Growth in working memory and mathematical problem solving in children at risk and not at risk for serious math difficulties. *Journal of Educational Psychology*, *100*, 343–79. doi:10.1037/0022-0663.100.2.343.

Swanson, H. L., and Sachse-Lee, C. (2001). Mathematical problem solving and working memory in children with learning disabilities: both executive and phonological processes are important. *Journal of Experimental Child Psychology*, *79*, 294–321.

Swanson, H. L., and Saez, L. (2003). Memory difficulties in children and adults with learning disabilities. In H. L. Swanson, S. Graham, and K. R. Harris (Eds.), *Handbook of Learning Disabilities* (pp. 182–98). New York: Guildford Press.

Tulving, E. (1972). Episodic and semantic memory. In E. Tulving and W. Donaldson (Eds.), *Organization of Memory* (pp. 381–403). New York: Academic Press.

Wang, S., and Gathercole, S. E. (2013). Working memory deficits in children with reading difficulties: memory span and dual task coordination. *Journal of Experimental Child Psychology*, *115*(1), 188–97.

Wilson, K. M., and Swanson, H. L. (2001). Are mathematical disabilities due to a domain-general or a domain-specific working memory deficit? *Journal of Learning Disabilities*, *34*, 237–48.

Motivation

5

Motivational contagion in education

Laura Burgess, Patricia Riddell and
Kou Murayama[1]

What is social contagion?

Think back to what it was like to step through the school gates on the morning of your first day at secondary school. You were most likely nervous, and not so much about the fact that you were going to start learning new things, but most likely because of the sea of new faces with whom you would suddenly be interacting. A few hours later, you may have forgotten all about those social pressures because you were already forming fast friendships with several new peers.

From that moment on, the people you interacted with at school started to influence you, and social networks started to form. Through adolescence especially, friends often share experiences, both positive and negative. Being in touch with each other's emotions and sharing these moments contribute to the influence that occurs. For example, Sarah might receive a poor grade on an assignment, and Megan, knowing that this will upset her friend, feels her negative emotion. As a consequence, both Sarah and Megan might support each other in work towards the next assignment and help each other to improve. Therefore, social dynamics are important to consider in the context of the school environment – and beyond. Further, our relationships with others are not fixed; we naturally change our connections at any time and may have various motivations for doing so. These processes through which friends influence one another are examples of 'social contagion'.

From a social perspective, it is important for us to be members of groups because we are both safer in groups and can accomplish more as a group than we can individually. As humans, we develop social understanding of others' emotions and feelings from birth in order to make and retain membership of the first group to which we belong, which is typically our family. The development of empathy is one example of social contagion (Decety and Jackson, 2004).

It begins with affective arousal in infants, an automatic mimicry process by which infants learn about their own emotional responses partly through mimicking the emotional expressions of their caregivers. Next, we develop empathic concern, an attachment process that has been linked to the need for attachment between parents and their offspring in which we develop an understanding of others' needs and emotions. This is an unconscious process in which emotional responses are transferred from one individual to another through social contagion – I feel what you feel. Finally, this evolves into empathic understanding, where we have a reflective awareness of both our own and others' emotions. In the first two of these stages, our empathy towards others is automatic. As development progresses, we become more consciously aware of the emotions of others and their possible interpretations (Decety and Svetlova, 2012). This allows us to predict how others might feel in different situations ('theory of mind') and therefore helps us to interact appropriately with others, for instance, through acts of kindness and avoidance of situations that we know might be hurtful. These processes underlie how we interact with one another as social beings, and such interactions are ultimately one source of influence that can be spread between connected individuals.

In the context of education, it is clear that emotional contagion of this sort occurs in the classroom. Certain children, no matter their age, have the ability to influence the moods and behaviour of their fellow classmates, without showing an explicit intention of doing so. But it is possible that this is not confined to catching emotions from one another. Imagine a group of friends where one individual has a higher interest in science than the other group members – is it possible that the heightened interest of one group member has the power to spark interest in the rest of the friendship group through motivational contagion? The concept of 'motivational contagion' describes an important psychological process that argues that it is possible.

The term 'contagion' is best defined as the process by which behaviours and/or attitudes are involuntarily passed from one individual to another (or 'caught' by an individual from another; Levy and Nail, 1993). This process has been established as a well-accepted phenomenon in psychology, and it is clearly observed by teachers (Safran and Safran, 1985). However, despite this, little research has been carried out on this phenomenon in the context of education.

In this chapter, this gap in the research is highlighted by discussing current literature that demonstrates the different forms that social contagion can take in educational environments. Further, the framework and mechanisms that provide the foundations for social contagion to occur are explained. The chapter evolves to discuss recent empirical research that begins to address some of the questions that arise from the literature review. Finally, the implications of the findings for teachers are provided, including how further research might address outstanding questions through both neuroimaging and modern social network analysis techniques.

What is motivational contagion?

Specifically, the 'contagion of motivation' refers to the spreading of motivation between socially connected individuals. Students have many opportunities to engage with one another at school, and through these social circumstances, students share their motivational experiences and have the power to influence the motivations of the students with whom they are connected, and vice versa (Urdan and Schoenfelder, 2006).

However, contagion of all kinds can occur in many different forms within a school setting. The research into the development of empathy indicates that influence between individuals is almost impossible to avoid. Therefore, all possible social interactions at school should be considered. This includes contagion from teachers to their pupils and vice versa, the influence of peer groups on other peer groups within and beyond the classroom and the influence of one individual student on other individual students (see Figure 5.1).

Contagion and teachers

From day-to-day observation of a learning environment, it is possible to see that the behaviour of teachers has the power to influence that of the students they teach. Diane Christophel (1990) noted that immediacy behaviours (those which convey involvement and availability of communication) of teachers positively modify the motivation of students to learn. Furthermore, the well-known 'Dr. Fox effect' shows an effect of teacher enthusiasm on students' effectiveness ratings of the teacher, as well as achievement of the students (Ware and Williams, 1975). Groups of students attended lectures that varied in content (number of substantive teaching points covered: high, medium and low content) and the enthusiasm, humour and friendliness of the lecturer (high and low seduction). After the lecture, students rated their

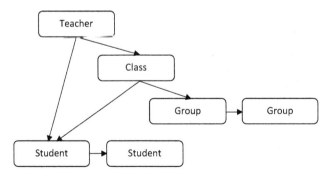

Figure 5.1 Pathways of contagion.

satisfaction with the lecturer and their perceived learning gain and completed a short multiple-choice test as an objective assessment of learning. Satisfaction ratings were high for all levels of content for the high-seduction lectures but varied with level of content for low-seduction levels, with high-content lectures rated as significantly more satisfying than medium- or low-content lectures. In comparison, while level of content affected learning with higher test scores for those who had viewed high- rather than medium-content lectures, there was no significant effect of seduction on learning. Thus, while lecturer enthusiasm affected student ratings, it did not affect learning.

It is not only the obvious behaviours of teachers that have an impact on the learning experience of students, as they are also affected by underlying attitudes and emotions. For instance, teachers' stress levels have been shown to have a direct impact on the students they teach. Eva Oberle and Kimberly Schonert-Reichl (2016) measured student salivary cortisol levels (a hormone closely related to stress) and teacher burnout levels. They found that students whose teachers reported a high level of burnout had higher cortisol levels. Furthermore, Mina Westman and Dalia Etzion (1999) demonstrated that job-induced tension transferred between school principals and teachers, thus elevating the overall stress felt in the school.

Teachers will often note that some classes of students feel better to teach than others. It is possible that these differences in satisfaction with teaching a particular class could be driven by a contagion effect between the teacher's self-perception of his or her attempts to endorse and recognise individual students' performance (confirming behaviour) and the teacher's perception of the engagement of his or her students, as evidenced by their nonverbal behaviour. This was tested in a study in which the relationship between the confirmation behaviours of teachers, teacher satisfaction and teacher perceptions of students' nonverbal classroom behaviours was investigated (Houser and Waldbuesser, 2017). Measures were taken of teachers' perception of their confirmation behaviours, teacher satisfaction with their own teaching and teacher satisfaction with their students' cooperation in class. All three measures significantly predicted teachers' perceptions of their students' nonverbal behaviour in a multiple regression analysis. One interpretation of these findings, based on primitive emotional contagion theory (Hatfield et al., 1993), is that teachers who perceive their behaviour as confirming towards their students are more satisfied with their own teaching and therefore expect to see appropriate nonverbal behaviours in their students. Thus, a virtuous circle might exist in which increased teacher satisfaction results in a contagion effect that drives students' nonverbal confirming behaviours, which further increases teacher satisfaction. Alternatively, teachers' dissatisfaction with their teaching might drive student behaviour that is non-confirming and therefore further decreases teacher satisfaction.

In a similar study, Timothy Mottet and Steven Beebe (2000) demonstrated that there was a significant correlation between the emotional responses of students and teachers over time. Further, long-term teacher enjoyment levels have been shown to have a lasting positive impact on the reported enjoyment of their students (Frenzel et al., 2009). Together this research reinforces the idea of teacher-to-student contagion, emphasizing how much teachers' underlying attitudes and behaviours impact their students.

In addition, contagion effects have also been identified to spread from teachers to students and, through those students, to a further group of peer-taught students (Radel et al., 2010). In this study, the same lesson was delivered to two classes by two teachers with perception of the motivation of the teacher varied between classes. Students in the first class were told that their teacher was being paid to be there and therefore was extrinsically motivated to deliver the class. The other teacher was introduced to the class as a volunteer, intrinsically motivated to lead the session. Those taught by the paid teacher reported lower interest and less engagement when compared to students taught by the volunteer teacher. In a follow-up experiment, further groups of students who were given peer-to-peer teaching by students from each class reported lower interest and engagement when taught by the students in the class with the paid teacher. This demonstrates that contagion between teacher and student is lasting and can have an impact beyond the classroom.

Contagion and peers

Contagion effects have been demonstrated between peers at school as early as pre-adolescence (Hanish et al., 2005). For example, friendship, peer acceptance and group membership have all been shown to predict academic achievement in a sample of 11- to 12-year-old school children (Wentzel and Caldwell, 1997). However, research with secondary school students tends to focus on the challenges faced by adolescents, in terms of peer pressure to engage in risky behaviours, and consequent disengagement at school. Peer pressure is different from social contagion between peers, as 'pressure' implies a more explicit coercion to participate in activities (Dishion and Dodge, 2005). Thus, peer influence can be regarded as a subset of social contagion.

In recent years, much research on social contagion between peers has focused on ways to help educators better understand patterns of behaviour and to design appropriate interventions to influence behavioural reform. In one study, Thomas Berndt and Keunho Keefe (1995) investigated the influence of a friend's behaviours (such as classroom involvement and disruption) and features of the friendship (such as levels of pro-social behaviour, number of arguments and number of incidences of self-esteem support) on school adjustment in a large sample of 12- to 15-year-olds. They found that negative friend behaviours and friendship features had independent impact on adjustment in school, with adolescents being more disruptive when their friends acted disruptively and when friendships consisted of more negative features.

In further research on the negative impact of peer relationships, Geoffrey Cohen and Mitchell Prinstein (2006) used a novel computerized 'chat room' to research 16- to 17-year-old adolescent male conformity to negative health risk behaviours. Participants were encouraged to believe that they were in an online conversation with three best friends whom they had nominated prior to the experiment. In reality, the participant was viewing the responses of actors, whose answers were experimentally manipulated. The researchers found that when peer status was high, as measured by popularity and likeability, conformity to participate in health risk behaviours was increased. Levels of social anxiety held by the students also moderated the level of conformity in that those who were most anxious conformed regardless of peer status. This is an interesting finding, as those who were characterised as being more highly anxious were led more by their desire to please their peers than any conscientious thoughts about avoiding risky behaviours. While this research provides evidence for the negative power of peer influence and supports the suggestion by Judith Harris (2011) that peer influence has a stronger impact on adolescent behaviour than other socialisation sources (such as family members), it leaves open the question of whether peer contagion can also have a positive impact on school behaviours. This reinforces the need for further research to assess both the mechanisms behind peer contagion processes and how to use them to create positive influences in the classroom.

What are the mechanisms for contagion?

Our ability to influence those around us happens naturally as a social mechanism for building and supporting our social connections. This has been demonstrated to be transmitted via several different mechanisms, from those which are innate social processes (e.g. mimicry) to those which are more motivated and goal-directed social behaviours (e.g. self-determination theory and social learning theory).

Mimicry

The term 'mimicry' refers to an instance where a behaviour is copied from others or from an external stimulus. Mimicry is an essential mechanism for our social interactions; we unconsciously mimic others in order to socially bond and express empathy. Mimicry, and the consequent feedback from such mimicry, can be vocal, facial, behavioural and emotional and exists as an automatic and passive response in all forms (Chartrand and Dalton, 2009). There is a strong human tendency to inherently mimic a range of actions, including vocal accents (Adank et al., 2013) and physical mannerisms (Chartrand and Bargh, 1999). Tanya Chartrand et al. (2005) suggest that mimicry requires that we attend and perceive another person's behaviour. From this theoretical perspective, mimicry exists as a motivational mechanism to increase group belonging. Thus, in order to be accepted, people automatically and unconsciously mimic the behaviour of those already positioned highly in the social group while reporting a lack of awareness of their imitative behaviour.

Moreover, emotional mimicry (imitation of emotion) has been tied closely to the theory of primitive emotional contagion described by Elaine Hatfield et al. (1993). In this theory, mimicry and feedback are hypothesised to be mechanisms for contagion. Indeed, in the field of emotion research, the terms 'emotional contagion' and 'emotional mimicry' are often used interchangeably. Both terms describe an automatic and non-conscious process that supports our perception and understanding of the feelings of others.[2] Consequently, it might be argued that emotional mimicry acts as a basic psychological process that drives contagion. Thus, contagion in the classroom might involve emotional mimicry.

Self-determination theory

Self-determination theory (SDT) stipulates that people are naturally motivated to satisfy their need for relatedness (a basic psychological need to feel accepted by others), autonomy and perceived competence (Deci et al., 1991). Relatedness, as a core component of human motivation, is considered a potential driving force behind our will to build relationships (Baumeister and Leary, 1995; Wentzel, 1999). Thus, in the context of secondary school education, social contagion observed among students might be explained by their motivated behaviour to maintain social relationships.

In cases of negative peer influence, adolescents might engage in risky behaviours such as smoking because they are motivated to be affiliated with a particular peer group. Although the term 'peer influence' implies some coercion in this context, from a motivational perspective, this influence might also be mediated by the perceived need to maintain relationships. It is also possible that the need for relatedness could drive positive peer-to-peer contagion.

Social learning theory

Another theory of motivation that can be applied to the social contagion phenomenon is social learning theory (Bandura, 1977, 1986). This proposes that a person's motivation is grounded in the concept of self-efficacy, a personal judgement of the person's capability to achieve a goal or task (Bandura, 1977). Importantly, Bandura (1977, 1986) argues that self-efficacy is formed through the socialisation process, and he identifies several sources of self-efficacy: direct experience, vicarious experience and verbal persuasion. Direct experience of mastering tasks may raise or lower our personal sense of self-efficacy depending on the success of the experience, whereas vicarious experiences influence our sense of self-efficacy through observation of the experiences of others. If we observe the actions of others and see that there is a low rate of failure, or that something 'was easier than it looked', our belief in our own self-efficacy is likely to increase. The final influence on our self-efficacy comes from verbal persuasion, where exposure to suggestions from others can shape our beliefs. Persuasion can be used to encourage people to believe that they possess the capabilities to complete a task, resulting in the person receiving the persuasion putting more effort into the task. Success in the task then reinforces the person's self-efficacy as a result of trying a new approach that alters his or her direct experience.

As an example of these concepts in action, consider the situation we described at the start of the chapter, where a student's interest in science enhances his or her friends' interest in science. Based on social learning theory, if a student is friends with a fellow student who is highly capable and interested in science, his or her enthusiasm may spread through the friendship via his or her verbal encouragement or explanations of science (i.e. verbal persuasion). Alternatively, the recipient of the friendship tie may observe the success and enthusiasm of the friend and as a result begin to enjoy science vicariously (i.e. vicarious experience). It is also possible that the recipient of the tie has more opportunities to enjoy science because the friend is actively engaged in that subject. Consequently, students with high levels of self-efficacy have the potential to create positive contagious effects on their friends in the classroom.

Is motivation similar between friends?

So far, we have presented literature outlining social contagion in the context of schools and shown examples of how contagion manifests and the mechanisms that underlie the process. From this, we suggest that motivation theories can provide interesting and complementary perspectives on the social contagion that occurs in classrooms. A natural next step is to explore the motivation levels of students and investigate whether similarities exist in levels of motivation between friends and within friendship groups.

Motivation has been long established as a leading factor in students' learning and achievement at school, impacting on all forms of academic outcomes (for a meta-analysis, see Robbins et al., 2004). This finding is further supported by research that has demonstrated that motivation is a better predictor of increased academic achievement over time than intelligence scores – a more traditional measure of attainment (Murayama et al., 2013).

It is important to examine what determines the motivational state of students in schools. So far, researchers have investigated the socio-cognitive factors that contribute to the school experience, highlighting learning environment, teacher style and parental beliefs as contributors to student motivation (for a review, see Anderman and Wolters, 2006). However, within this field, little work has been carried out on the influence of school peer groups and networks and school friends on motivation.

Students have many opportunities to spend time with one another at school and build social networks; thus, peer group activity may impact motivation.

Throughout the school day, students have opportunities to make friends during lunch or break times, during group work in the classroom or through involvement in extracurricular activities. Through such social situations, students share their motivational experiences and have the power to influence the motivations of the students to whom they are socially connected. If students do influence each other through social connections, we would expect greater similarity between friends than between students who are not connected socially.

Much of the literature surrounding similarity between friends defines similarities as instances where connected friends have shared influence and therefore become more similar. However, it should also be noted that friendships are often formed on the basis of similarity, since the likelihood of a friendship forming increases when there is similarity in personal characteristics (Kupersmidt et al., 1995). Furthermore, research such as that by Thomas Kindermann (1993, 2007) has shown that friends are selected and friendship networks formed where similarities lie in the motivational orientation of group members. This finding became stronger over time, and despite structural changes to the network (i.e. changes in the members of the friendship groups), the motivational orientation of the group remained relatively stable.

Further research by Michael Nelson and Teresa DeBacker (2008) investigated the association between peers and achievement motivation in a cross-sectional study of 253 students. Self-report measures of classroom climate, achievement-related beliefs, values of a best friend, achievement goals, social goals and self-efficacy were collected. Results suggested that students who felt valued and respected had greater adaptive achievement motivation. Further, adaptive achievement motivation was related to good-quality, close friendships with those who valued education. The converse was also true, in that poor-quality friendships and a disregard for school values were indicative of a maladaptive achievement motivation orientation.

To provide further insight into the relationship between peer groups and academic motivation, we conducted a study to assess the motivational similarity between friendship dyads across friendship networks. We aimed to determine whether levels of academic motivation are similar between connected individuals. We assessed several types of academic motivation, including interest and boredom for school subjects, perceived competence, self-regulation, value for learning, grit and views on intelligence. We predicted that friendship pairs would be significantly correlated on their motivation scores and that there would be a significant relationship between the motivation levels of an individual and his or her social connectedness within the network.

Methods and procedure

Data were collected from 104 Sixth Form students aged 16 to 19 years from a relatively small, mixed-gender school in central London. During a single session, students from two year groups (year 12 and year 13) completed an online motivation survey to assess their academic motivation (i.e. interest, boredom and competence for mathematics and English; self-regulation of learning in mathematics; value for learning; grit; and views on intelligence), followed by a social network survey where students were asked to nominate up to five of their closest friends from their year group.

Data were analysed to provide a measure of the correlation between connected and non-connected friends within the network to test the hypothesis that connected friends would show greater correlation in their motivation than non-connected individuals ('assortativity analysis'; see Newman, 2002). A second analysis determined whether individuals who were highly connected in the network had greater levels of motivation than those who were less well connected ('centrality analysis'; see Newman, 2010).

Results

Data were collected on several different types of academic motivation. Specific subject interest and boredom were measured for mathematics and English lessons, measuring student's engagement with these subjects (Pekrun et al., 2002; Wigfield and Eccles, 2000). Further, students' self-perceptions of their competence in mathematics and English classes were also recorded. The items to assess perceived competence were based on the model of academic self-concept (Marsh, 1990). A scale was also included that measured students' self-regulation in their mathematics classes, self-regulation referring to the students' level of autonomous motivation to participate actively in classes, based on SDT (Ryan and Deci, 2000). Subject general measures of academic motivation included scales that assessed students' sense of value for what they are learning at school (Wigfield and Eccles, 2000), their personal level of grit (i.e. passion and perseverance to achieve long-term goals; Duckworth and Quinn, 2009) and, finally, their views surrounding intelligence and the fluidity of mindset, measured to produce a level of fixed or growth mindset for each student (Dweck, 2000).

Assortativity analysis

A single analysis was conducted including both year groups. A significant finding in this analysis indicates that connected individuals are significantly similar in their scores on the given measure. In the case of a negative r value, the correlation indicates that connected individuals are dissimilar in their scores. Friends were found to be significantly and positively similar in their levels of maths interest, value for learning and perseverance of effort (a sub-measure of grit). This means that connected friendship pairs are correlated and therefore show more similarity than students who are not in friendship pairs. No other measures reached statistical significance. These results are displayed in Table 5.1.

Table 5.1 Summary of meta-analyses of assortativity indices across all year groups for each motivation construct.

Variable	r	Standard error	p	Confidence interval (lower)	Confidence interval (upper)
Mathematics interest	0.181	0.05	0.000[***]	0.084	0.278
Mathematics boredom	0.033	0.06	0.565	−0.079	0.145
Mathematics competence	0.091	0.05	0.093	−0.015	0.196
English interest	−0.081	0.06	0.208	−0.208	0.045
English boredom	−0.074	0.06	0.230	−0.194	0.047
English competence	0.004	0.06	0.946	−0.107	0.115
Learning self-regulation (RAI)	0.162	0.08	0.049	0.001	0.342
Value	0.173	0.06	0.002[**]	0.065	0.281
Grit, consistency of interest	0.104	0.05	0.056	−0.003	0.210
Grit, perseverance of effort	0.155	0.06	0.009[**]	0.039	0.271
Mindset	−0.029	0.07	0.655	−0.157	0.099

[**] $p < 0.01$;
[***] $p < .001$.

Centrality analyses

This analysis is used to determine whether the degree of connectedness within the network predicts levels of motivation. Table 5.2 summarises the results of these analyses for subject-specific variables. Measures of centrality were found to significantly predict levels of math interest, boredom and competence. Thus, individuals who are central to the group have higher levels of interest, lower levels of boredom and higher perception of competence in mathematics than those who are not central. Finally, being central within the network predicted high levels in perseverance of effort (a measure of grit). No other measures were statistically predicted by network centrality.

Discussion of results

This study was designed to investigate similarity in academic motivation between friends at school. The hypothesis that friendship dyads would be similar on our measures of motivation was partially supported, with significant similarity between friends across both year groups identified for mathematics interest, value for learning and perseverance of effort. This suggests that there are aspects of academic

Table 5.2 Results of the regression analyses on all behavioural variables, controlling for year group.

Variable	Degree centrality			Eigenvector centrality		
	Beta	t	p	Beta	t	p
Mathematics interest	−0.37	−2.44	0.017[*]	0.51	3.37	0.001[**]
Mathematics boredom	0.22	1.48	0.142	−0.44	−0.98	0.004[**]
Mathematics competence	−0.07	−1.35	0.181	1.58	3.00	0.004[**]
English interest	−0.03	−0.29	0.771	−0.31	−0.31	0.759
English boredom	0.00	0.04	0.969	0.70	0.70	0.486
English competence	−0.04	−0.64	0.525	1.09	1.79	0.077
Learning self-regulation (RAI)	0.07	0.79	0.435	0.42	0.54	0.590
Value	−0.02	−0.38	0.702	0.88	1.94	0.056
Grit, consistencey of interest	0.00	−0.11	0.911	−0.64	−1.54	0.128
Grit, perseverance of effort	−0.03	−0.20	0.839	0.32	2.16	0.034[*]
Mindset	0.00	−0.04	0.969	−0.27	−0.84	0.402

[*] $p < 0.05$;
[**] $p < 0.01$.

motivation that are shared between friends, providing some support for motivational contagion within the classroom.

Furthermore, our second prediction that those with more influence over the network would score higher on the measures of motivation was partially supported. High centrality was found to predict math interest, boredom and perceived competence, in addition to greater perseverance. This suggests that a person who is very central in his or her network and who therefore has greater opportunity to influence others has greater capacity to spread his or her high levels of perseverance or mathematics interest across the network, as they are more likely to have high motivation themselves.

Our findings support those of Thomas Kindermann (1993) by showing, first, that pairs of friends share similar levels of specific forms of academic motivation and, second, that the position of a student in the network (i.e. students with high eigenvector centrality) can predict the levels of certain motivational variables. Our evidence of similarity between connected individuals supports research by Micheal Nelson and Teresa DeBacker (2008), who found that those with good-quality friendships and high value for education were similar in having adaptive motivation styles (with the negative relationship also being found). Our assortativity analysis suggests that interest, value and perseverance are all similar among friends, while our centrality results support the conclusion that the more central members of a group have higher levels of motivation and therefore more avenues through which to spread their motivation. These findings show partial support for the hypothesis that motivation can be similar between friends, forming a basis for further research that will develop understanding of the complexity of friendship similarity and its positive role in the classroom.

How can this knowledge and research be used?

The literature and research presented in this chapter demonstrate that social contagion can have influence in the classroom. We aim to use this insight to find ways in which to promote positive motivational exchange within classroom environments and to nurture this so that students can persevere in their studies and therefore better achieve their potential.

From a teacher's perspective, being aware of the motivational orientation of the students in a classroom is valuable, especially if the teacher considers students' positions within their social environments. If a student who is central to his or her classroom network has a strong positive motivation, or strong demotivation, towards the taught subject, then a teacher can use this to inform how he or she approaches his or her teaching style to motivate the class as a whole. Having the most central students on board and positively motivated may increase the likelihood that those central students will have positive influence on their fellow classmates, as opposed to using their influence to demotivate those around them. In addition, the motivational orientation of the teacher is also important (Radel et al., 2010). Teachers who are engaging and interested can increase motivation within the class-room by encouraging peer-to-peer learning following their teaching. However, this could be potentially detrimental if the teacher has lower interest and less engagement in his or her teaching and passes this lack of motivation, through his or her students, to those involved in peer-to-peer teaching.

There is an ongoing debate in UK education as to whether ability grouping has any significant benefit to students, with researchers and policy makers often holding opposing views surrounding the costs and benefits of this approach (Francis et al., 2017). The research on social contagion can add to this debate. Frequently, research shows little overall benefit of between-class ability grouping (for a meta-analysis, see Steenbergen-Hu et al., 2016). However, little research investigating the effects of ability grouping includes consideration of social relationships within the classroom. If students select friends who have similar levels of academic per-formance to themselves (Smirnov and Thurner, 2017) and are more likely to select friends who have similar levels of academic motivation to themselves (as identified in the research presented here), then the case for ability grouping may be further supported because students appear to be naturally forming their social networks in this way, meaning that their natural opportunities for friendships are not hindered by the use of ability grouping.

Research on social contagion in friendship also has implications for the use of seating plans within lessons. While seating plans provide more structure to a classroom and greater control for the teacher (Fernandes et al., 2011), they have also been found to restrict natural opportunities for intergroup friendship formation (McKeown et al., 2016). These implications can be considered alongside the advantages and disadvantages of using ability grouping. If students are placed into structured seating within classes where they are also grouped by ability, the opportunity for natural friendship group formation is even more restricted. This may be a positive thing, in that students can naturally seek out friendships with those with whom they have similar characteristics. However, by using social network data to inform decisions about seating plans, teachers may be able to encourage constructive friendship formation, establishing those in which positive improvements can be encouraged for both students.

Summary

Overall, this chapter has outlined the varied forms of social contagion and provided examples of these in educational settings. Defined as the involuntary 'catching' of behaviours and/or attitudes (Levy and Nail, 1993), social contagion occurs within schools between teachers and other teachers, between teachers and students and between students and other students within each of their social networks. As such, it is important for teachers not only to consider their own motivational orientation but also to consider the motivational orientations of the students they teach when thinking about the social implications.

In the research presented here, similarity in motivation between friends within school social networks was investigated. This work provided evidence to suggest that certain forms of academic motivation can be shown to be more similar between friends than between those who are not friends. This included motivation types such as subject-specific interest, value for learning and perseverance of effort. Through understanding which types of motivation are similar between friends and also how motivation is linked to a person's position in his or her network, we develop a clearer picture surrounding the relationship between motivation and social contagion. The results presented, along with the literature described, have implications for teaching practice. The use of ability grouping and seating plans in lessons will change the opportunities for friendships to naturally occur and has implications for the opportunity for positive, and negative, influence to spread between students. Further, as shown by the research on contagion between teachers and students, the motivational orientation of teachers is also important in terms of the impact on class motivation on the whole.

To conclude, social contagion plays an important role in all aspects of school life and provides a different perspective from which to consider the motivation of students. Considering students' social connections can be beneficial in understanding how to best foster and support students in increasing their motivation to learn.

Notes

1 This work was supported by a Jacobs Foundation Advanced Research Fellowship (to K. Murayama), the F. J. McGuigan Early Career Investigator Prize from the American Psychological Foundation (to K. Murayama), the Leverhulme Trust Research Leadership Award (RL-2016-030, to K. Murayama), and the Economic Social Research Council and BrainCanDo Centre for Research (award ref. GS16-086 to L. Burgess).
2 For a review on emotional mimicry, see Hess and Fischer (2014).

References

Adank, P., Stewart, A. J., Connell, L., and Wood, J. (2013). Accent imitation positively affects language attitudes. *Frontiers in Psychology*, *4*, 1–10. doi:10.3389/fpsyg.2013.00280.

Anderman, E. M., and Wolters, C. A. (2006). Goals, values, and affect: influences on student motivation. In P. A. Alexander and P. H. Winne (Eds.), *Handbook of Educational Psychology*. New York: Lawrence Erlbaum Associates.

Bandura, A. (1977). Self-efficacy: toward a unifying theory of behavioral change. *Advances in Behaviour Research and Therapy*, *1*(4), 139–61. doi:10.1016/0146-6402(78)90002-4.

Bandura, A. (1986). *Social Foundations of Thought and Action*. Englewood Cliffs, NJ: Prentice-Hall.

Baumeister, R. F., and Leary, M. R. (1995). The need to belong: desire for interpersonal attachments as a fundamental human emotion. *Psychological Bulletin*, *117*(3), 497–529. doi:10.1037/0033-2909.117.3.497.

Berndt, T. J., and Keefe, K. (1995). Friends' influence of adolescents' adjustment to school. *Child Development*, *66*(5), 1312–29. doi:10.1111/j.1467-8624.1995.tb00937.x.

Chartrand, T. L., and Bargh, J. A. (1999). The chameleon effect: the perception-behavior link and social interaction. *Journal of Personality and Social Psychology*, *76*(6), 893–910. doi:10.1037/0022 3514.76.6.893.

Chartrand, T. L., and Dalton, A. N. (2009). Mimicry: its ubiquity, importance, and functionality. In *Oxford Handbook of Human Action* (pp. 458–83).

Chartrand, T. L., Maddux, W. W., and Lakin, J. L. (2005). Beyond the perception-behavior link: the ubiquitous utility and motivational moderators of nonconscious mimicry. *The New Unconscious*, 334–61.

Christophel, D. M. (1990). The relationships among teacher immediacy behaviors, student motivation, and learning. *Communication Education*, *39*(4), 323–40. doi:10.1080/03634529009378813.

Cohen, G. L., and Prinstein, M. J. (2006). Peer contagion of aggression and health risk behavior among adolescent males: an experimental investigation of effects on public conduct and private attitudes. *Child Development*, 77(4), 967–83. doi:10.1111/j.1467-8624.2006.00913.x.

Decety, J., and Jackson, P. L. (2004). The functional architecture of human empathy. *Behavioral and Cognitive Neuroscience Reviews*, 3(2), 71–100. doi:10.1177/1534582304267187.

Decety, J., and Svetlova, M. (2012). Putting together phylogenetic and ontogenetic perspectives on empathy. *Developmental Cognitive Neuroscience*, 2(1), 1–24. doi:10.1016/j.dcn.2011.05.003.

Deci, E. L., Vallerand, R. J., Pelletier, L. G., and Ryan, R. M. (1991). Motivation and education: the self-determination perspective. *Educational Psychologist*, 26(3–4), 325–46. doi:10.1080/00461520.1991.9653137.

Dishion, T. J., and Dodge, K. A. (2005). Peer contagion in interventions for children and adolescents: moving towards an understanding of the ecology and dynamics of change. *Journal of Abnormal Child Psychology*, 33(3), 395–400. doi:10.1007/s10802-005-3579-z.

Duckworth, A. L., and Quinn, P. D. (2009). Development and validation of the short grit scale (GRIT–S). *Journal of Personality Assessment*, 91(2), 166–74. doi:10.1080/00223890802634290.

Dweck, C. S. (2000). *Self-Theories: Their Role in Motivation, Personality and Development* (1st ed.). New York: Psychology Press.

Fernandes, A. C., Huang, J., and Rinaldo, V. (2011). Does where a student sits really matter? – The impact of seating locations on student classroom learning. *International Journal of Applied Educational Studies*, 10(1), 66–77.

Francis, B., Archer, L., Hodgen, J., et al. (2017). Exploring the relative lack of impact of research on 'ability grouping' in England: a discourse analytic account. *Cambridge Journal of Education*, 47(1), 1–17. doi:10.1080/0305764X.2015.1093095.

Frenzel, A. C., Goetz, T., Lüdtke, O., et al. (2009). Emotional transmission in the classroom: exploring the relationship between teacher and student enjoyment. *Journal of Educational Psychology*, 101(3), 705–16. doi:10.1037/a0014695.

Hanish, L. D., Martin, C. L., Fabes, R. A., et al. (2005). Exposure to externalizing peers in early childhood: homophily and peer contagion processes. *Journal of Abnormal Child Psychology*, 33(3), 267–81. doi:10.1007/s10802-005-3564-6.

Harris, J. (2011). *The Nurture Assumption: Why Children Turn Out the Way They Do* (2nd ed.). New York: Simon & Schuster.

Hatfield, E., Cacioppo, J. T., and Rapson, R. L. (1993). Emotional contagion. *Current Directions in Psychological Science*, 2(3), 96–100. doi:10.1111/1467-8721.ep10770953.

Hess, U., and Fischer, A. (2014). Emotional mimicry: why and when we mimic emotions. *Social and Personality Psychology Compass*, 8(2), 45–57. doi:10.1111/spc3.12083.

Houser, M. L., and Waldbuesser, C. (2017). Emotional contagion in the classroom: the impact of teacher satisfaction and confirmation on perceptions of student nonverbal classroom behavior. *College Teaching*, *65*(1), 1–8. doi:10.1080/87567555.2016.1189390.

Kindermann, T. A. (1993). Natural peer groups as contexts for individual development: the case of children's motivation in school. *Developmental Psychology*, *29*(6), 970–77. doi:10.1037/0012-1649.29.6.970.

Kindermann, T. A. (2007). Effects of naturally existing peer groups on changes in academic engagement in a cohort of sixth graders. *Child Development*, *78*(4), 1186–203. doi:10.1111/j.1467-8624.2007.01060.x.

Kupersmidt, J. B., DeRosier, M. E., and Patterson, C. P. (1995). Similarity as the basis for children's friendships: the roles of sociometric status, aggressive and withdrawn behavior, academic achievement and demographic characteristics. *Journal of Social and Personal Relationships*, *12*(3), 439–52. doi:10.1177/0265407595123007.

Levy, D. A., and Nail, P. R. (1993). Contagion: a theoretical and empirical review and reconceptualization. *Genetic, Social, and General Psychology Monographs*, *119*(2), 233–84.

Marsh, H. W. (1990). The structure of academic self-concept: the Marsh/Shavelson model. *Journal of Educational Psychology*, *82*(4), 623–36. doi:10.1037/0022-0663.82.4.623.

McKeown, S., Stringer, M., and Cairns, E. (2016). Classroom segregation: where do students sit and how is this related to group relations? *British Educational Research Journal*, *42*(1), 40–55. doi:10.1002/berj.3200.

Mottet, T. P., and Beebe, S. A. (2000). Emotional contagion in the classroom: an examination of how teacher and student emotions are related. Annual Meeting of the National Communication Association.

Murayama, K., Pekrun, R., Lichtenfeld, S., and Vom Hofe, R. (2013). Predicting long-term growth in students' mathematics achievement: the unique contributions of motivation and cognitive strategies. *Child Development*, *84*(4), 1475–90. doi:10.1111/cdev.12036.

Nelson, R. M., and Debacker, T. K. (2008). Achievement motivation in adolescents: the role of peer climate and best friends. *Journal of Experimental Education*, *76*(2), 170–89. doi:10.3200/JEXE.76.2.170-190.

Newman, M. E. J. (2002). Mixing patterns in networks. *Physical Review E*, *67*(2), 13. doi:10.1103/PhysRevE.67.026126.

Newman, M. E. J. (2010). *Networks: An Introduction*. Oxford, UK: Oxford University Press.

Oberle, E., and Schonert-Reichl, K. A. (2016). Stress contagion in the classroom? The link between classroom teacher burnout and morning cortisol in elementary school students. *Social Science & Medicine*, *159*, 30–37. doi:10.1016/j.socscimed.2016.04.031.

Pekrun, R., Goetz, T., Titz, W., and Perry, R. P. (2002). Academic emotions in students' self-regulated learning and achievement: a program of qualitative and quantitative research. *Educational Psychologist*, *37*(2), 91–106. doi:10.1207/S15326985EP3702_4.

Radel, R., Sarrazin, P., Legrain, P., and Wild, T. C. (2010). Social contagion of motivation between teacher and student: analyzing underlying processes. *Journal of Educational Psychology, 102*(3), 577–87.

Robbins, S. B., Le, H., Davis, D., et al. (2004). Do psychosocial and study skill factors predict college outcomes? A meta-analysis. *Psychological Bulletin, 130*(2), 261–88. doi:10.1037/0033-2909.130.2.261.

Ryan, R., and Deci, E. (2000). Self-determination theory and the facilitation of intrinsic motivation, social development, and well-being. *American Psychologist, 55*(1), 68–78. doi:10.1037/0003-066X.55.1.68.

Safran, J. S., and Safran, S. P. (1985). Teachers' judgments of problem behaviors. *Exceptional Children, 54*(3), 240–44. doi:10.1177/001440298705400306.

Smirnov, I., and Thurner, S. (2017). Formation of homophily in academic performance: students change their friends rather than performance. *PLoS One, 12* (8), e0189564. doi:10.1371/journal.pone.0183473.

Steenbergen-Hu, S., Makel, M. C., and Olszewski-Kubilius, P. (2016). What one hundred years of research says about the effects of ability grouping and acceleration on K–12 students' academic achievement: findings of two second-order meta-analyses. *Review of Educational Research, 86*(4), 849–99. doi:10.3102/0034654316675417.

Urdan, T., and Schoenfelder, E. (2006). Classroom effects on student motivation: goal structures, social relationships, and competence beliefs. *Journal of School Psychology, 44*(5), 331–49. doi:10.1016/j.jsp.2006.04.003.

Ware, J. E., and Williams, R. G. (1975). The Dr. Fox effect: a study of lecturer effectiveness and ratings of instruction. *Journal of Medical Education, 50*(2), 149–56.

Wentzel, K. R. (1999). Social-motivational processes and interpersonal relationships: implications for understanding motivation at school. *Journal of Educational Psychology, 91*(1), 76–97. doi:10.1037/0022-0663.91.1.76.

Wentzel, K. R., and Caldwell, K. (1997). Friendships, peer acceptance, and group membership: relations to academic achievement in middle school. *Child Development, 68*(6), 1198–209. doi:10.2307/1132301.

Westman, M., and Etzion, D. (1999). The crossover of strain from school principals to teachers and vice versa. *Journal of Occupational Health Psychology, 4*(3), 269–78. doi:10.1037//1076-8998.4.3.269.

Wigfield, A., and Eccles, J. S. (2000). Expectancy-value theory of achievement motivation. *Contemporary Educational Psychology, 25*(1), 68–81. doi:10.1006/ceps.1999.1015.

6

Mindsets and motivation: An introduction to potential influences on academic achievement

Catherine Lutz

Introduction

Why aren't my students achieving higher grades?

Why don't my students seem motivated to learn?

How do I keep my students motivated throughout the year?

Why aren't my students putting in as much effort as they used to?

How can I get my students to believe in themselves?

Is there anything I am doing or could be doing that may be impacting my students' academic attainment and satisfaction?

Questions such as these can creep into educators' minds throughout an academic year. When teachers find themselves beginning to ask these sorts of questions, they can start to feel overwhelmed, deflated, defeated and burnt out. These are by no means rare questions asked by teaching professionals, nor should they be. As educators, we should be looking for ways not only to help our pupils achieve the highest attainment scores possible but also to keep our pupils motivated to learn and positive about the overall learning process.

Mindsets and motivation are two areas of psychology that play a big role in teaching and learning. A 'mindset' is the attitude that an individual possesses, while 'motivation' is the determining factor in how and why we behave in certain ways. When examining mindsets and motivations in a classroom, the psychological underpinnings of both appear to be capable of influencing a student's overall academic performance. However, it is not just the student whose mindset and motivation are important in the pursuit of higher academic attainment; it is the teacher's as well. By assessing the mindsets and motivations of both parties, monitoring their academic and professional needs and cultivating positive attitudes and behaviours, the influential power of mindsets and motivation may be able to be harnessed within the classroom and ultimately improve academic performance and professional satisfaction.

In today's world, where the pursuit of academic attainment trumps all else, it is important to adopt a 'no stone left unturned' approach, allowing different psychological avenues (in this instance, mindsets and motivation) to be explored and applied. By understanding more about the different mindsets that students and teachers have, as well as the influential role that motivation can play, we can hopefully begin to reflect on the questions listed earlier and come up with different approaches that both help our students to succeed and enhance our own professional satisfaction. Therefore, this chapter aims to define mindsets and motivation, explore some of the underlying psychological concepts, from both pupil and teacher perspectives, and conclude by discussing a number of practical applications that may be used by educators to keep themselves and their students motivated and in a positive mindset!

Mindsets

Whether you think you can or whether you think you can't, you're right.
— *Henry Ford (Reader's Digest, 1947)*

This well-known quote from Henry Ford epitomises the power our thoughts can have on our abilities. The implication that what we tell ourselves, in turn, determines what we are capable of doing is both provocative and accurate. It also ties in nicely with the theory behind mindsets. Based on the idea presented and researched extensively by Carol Dweck (2000, 2006, 2007, 2010a, 2010b, 2016), mindsets are, simply put, the attitudes that we possess. Those attitudes influence how we approach situations; how we behave; how we react to news, learn and interact with others; and what we believe ourselves capable of doing. All those examples, plus many more, can be linked back to the type of mindset we individually adopt. Based on Dweck's research, there are two categories of mindset that individuals tend to fall into: growth and fixed. Individuals with a fixed mindset believe that the attributes they were born with (intelligence, athleticism, etc.) are unable to be changed. To them, there is no amount of hard work or effort that will improve their capacity to learn, progress or grow in those areas. They are 'fixed', and there is nothing they can do about it. By contrast, individuals with a growth mindset believe that with hard work and effort, they can improve and 'grow' many aspects and attributes of themselves, such as increased self-esteem and reduced levels of anxiety, aggression and depression (Schleider et al., 2015), as well as intelligence. Individuals with a growth mindset also see challenges as opportunities to improve, utilise feedback to achieve success in the future, and are inspired by the achievements made by those around them (Yeager and Dweck, 2012).

Based on these brief descriptions of growth and fixed mindsets, we can already begin to see which mindset may be more beneficial and positively associated with higher academic achievement and teaching satisfaction. But do we have any proof to show that our individual mindsets may be positively or negatively influential? And if so, how can we increase the likelihood that the positive influences and outcomes are seen in the classroom?

To answer this, we turn to numerous research studies that have examined mindsets, specifically those that note the positive impact associated with a growth mindset and the negative impact of a fixed mindset. However, before we discuss those studies, it is important to note the main neuroscientific concept that supports the idea of a 'growth mindset': neuroplasticity. Neuroplasticity is the brain's ability to change and adapt in order to learn (Dubinsky and Miyasaki, 2010; Münte et al., 2002). As new information is learned and strategies are used to reinforce that learning, new synapses form and strengthen (Draganski et al., 2006). This supports the principle underpinning growth mindset – that intelligence and other psychological attributes are malleable.

Research on the impact that mindsets have on students' academic achievement mostly report changes in academic performance seen in students who take part in growth mindset interventions versus students who do not. These improvements, found in different academic testing measures, give greater support to the legitimacy of the principle behind neuroplasticity, which is that the brain can change. Joshua Aronson et al. (2002) examined college students and the impact that participation in a growth mindset intervention had on them and found that students who were exposed to the intervention group made gains in academic achievement, whereas the control group, which did not receive a growth mindset intervention, experienced no changes in academic achievement. During an examination of younger students, this time seventh graders (12- to 13-year-olds), Lisa Blackwell et al. (2007) found that after applying a growth mindset and study skills intervention to students who were experiencing declining grades, deterioration not only stopped but actually began to improve. This particular study included teaching students about neuroplasticity and synaptic plasticity to inform them that by applying effort and continued focus on specific areas for improvement, to different academic situations, their brains could actually change and grow (Blackwell et al., 2007). In another study on seventh graders, Catherine Good et al. (2003) applied a growth mindset intervention to one group of students and compared it to a control group of students who did not receive the intervention. Findings showed that both mathematics and reading achievement test scores for the students in the growth mindset intervention group were higher than those of students in the control group (a 4.5-point gain in mathematics and a 4-point gain in reading). Through the use of a growth mindset intervention, it was also found that students could increase their resilience (Yeager et al., 2013).

As mentioned earlier, the neuroscience behind mindset research revolves around neuroplasticity. Growth mindset individuals, who are putting effort into learning something, accepting and using challenges to better understand concepts and taking on and applying feedback in a positive manner, experience changes on a neural level. As they learn, new neural networks form (effort to learn something new). The strength between synaptic connections change in response to their experiences and stimuli (accepting challenges, applying feedback, positivity), and new connections between neurons are created (neural level changes, memories forming; Segev, 2006). However, how do individuals come to possess a growth mindset? While it was stated that a potential intervention to promote a growth mindset was to inform and educate students about neuroplasticity, perhaps a deeper underlying psychological process is occurring and can be further examined by teachers (and researchers) within their students to build and maintain growth mindsets. One such potential process we will look at briefly is that of self-efficacy. The connections between this process and both mindsets and motivation are of the upmost importance.

Found within social cognitive theory, self-efficacy, as defined by Albert Bandura (1977), is an individual's belief in his or her ability to perform a task. Self-efficacy has been found to influence not only willingness to engage in or avoid certain behaviours but also the amount of effort an individual exerts (Zimmerman et al., 1992). Additionally, Albert Bandura (1986) reported that self-efficacy beliefs impacted thought patterns, responses and actions and are positively related to positive motivational patterns. As such, self-efficacy is a mechanism associated with higher performance. Interestingly, higher self-efficacy has been found to correlate with higher academic achievement (Bandura et al., 1996; Komarraju and Nadler, 2013; Lent et al., 1984; Turner et al., 2009) and influenced academic goals that students set for themselves (Zimmerman et al., 1992), and lower self-efficacy was found in students who believe that intelligence is fixed (Komarraju and Nadler, 2013). Further, self-efficacy theory states that when individuals believe that they can be successful performing a task, they are more likely to engage in performance-enhancing behaviours (Bandura, 1992), and empirical evidence has found that self-efficacy is positively correlated with motivation and academic attainment (Zimmerman, 2000). Doesn't this sound like an ideal pupil? Willing to engage, avoiding negative behaviours, engaging in performance-enhancing behaviours, exerting high levels of effort, setting higher academic goals and having more academic motivation? Where can I get a classroom full of these types of students?

While we may not have classrooms like this *yet* (keep this small word in mind for later in this chapter), we may not be too far off from building and fostering them. According to Albert Bandura (1986), an individual's self-efficacy beliefs can impact thought patterns, responses and actions (Schunk, 1990), and students' self-efficacy beliefs may be influenced by a number of different sources. Research has found that the four main sources of information used when developing self-efficacy beliefs are mastery experiences, vicarious experiences, verbal persuasion and emotional/physiological states (Bandura, 1977). Within the educational context, all these sources can be used by teachers to promote and encourage positive self-efficacy beliefs in their students (Bandura, 1997; Pajares, 1996; Shell et al., 1995) and themselves (Henson, 2001).

Additionally, a teacher's own self-efficacy is linked to both positive teaching behaviours and student attainment (Henson, 2001), and it is important to professional satisfaction that teachers believe in their ability to positively influence students and help them learn. To further understand those sources of information, we will quickly describe them here, with an example of how they could be used in the classroom to build both students' and teachers' self-efficacy.

Mastery experiences

In the educational setting, students are introduced to information that is brand new and previously learned. When faced with academic demands, a student's self-efficacy beliefs can influence his or her performance (Bandura, 1997; Pajares, 1996). Of the four main sources of information that influence self-efficacy beliefs, mastery experiences have the biggest impact (Bandura, 1997). Students' beliefs that they can accomplish academic demands are shaped by how they did on past academic tasks (Schunk et al., 1987). These past performances do not necessarily have to be subject or task specific, as past experiences from other subjects and academic tasks can influence self-efficacy beliefs as well (Lane et al., 2003). Findings from a study conducted by John Lane et al. (2004) found support for this, as they studied 205 postgraduate students and found that there was a relationship between past performance accomplishments and academic performance. They suggest that encouraging students to perceive their past academic performances in a positive way may positively impact self-efficacy expectations. Thus, perhaps by placing emphasis on past academic tasks that are completed successfully, teachers can influence students' self-efficacy beliefs and reassure them that they possess the tools needed to successfully accomplish future academic tasks. It may also be beneficial for teachers to regularly revisit previously learned concepts, allowing students the opportunity to experience mastery throughout the learning process.

Teachers may also increase their own self-efficacy beliefs through mastery experiences. One such way of building this 'mastery database' for teachers is through the delivery of teacher training courses that allow teachers the opportunity to try various teaching techniques, with successful outcomes, before applying the techniques later on in the classroom (Bray-Clark and Bates, 2003). Teachers may also use personal reflection after lessons to evaluate what went well (or what did not go so well) and how those techniques, both positive and negative, may be applied or adjusted in the future.

Vicarious experiences

A vicarious experience is one that occurs through the observation of others performing and achieving a task (Usher and Pajares, 2006). There are two potential sources of vicarious experiences for students: their teachers and their peers. Seeing their teacher or their peers succeed at an academic task can influence their own belief that they are capable to succeed at that task (Bandura, 1986). Therefore, in the classroom environment, it becomes important for students to see other students succeeding. Creating opportunities for students to demonstrate and accomplish different tasks in front of their peers may foster these vicarious experiences and thus allow students who are unsure about their own capabilities to see their peers succeed. This can be done by, for instance, having students complete problems on the board or having time built into lessons in which peer-to-peer teaching can occur.

Additionally, it is important for teachers to see other teachers succeeding. The implementation of teacher mentoring programmes, allowing teachers to 'sit in' on other teachers, and opportunities for sharing teaching success stories may be beneficial ways to boost positive vicarious experiences for teachers and other staff members.

Verbal persuasion

Verbal persuasion can encompass any form of feedback given from one person to another. Encouraging constructive and positive feedback about a student's work ethic and ability to accomplish a task can have a positive impact on that student's self-efficacy beliefs (Pajares et al., 2007), while negative feedback can have the opposite effect. Verbal persuasion, as a type of praise, is important, and a study conducted by Huy Phuong Phan (2011) found that students who reported receiving forms of verbal persuasion had increases in their self-efficacy beliefs for both mathematics and science. Research conducted by Frank Pajares et al. (2007) also found that verbal persuasion was correlated with writing self-efficacy. Teachers may use this source of self-efficacy in classrooms by providing verbal feedback to students and taking advantage of any opportunities that arise to praise and deliver positive feedback to students, in both verbal and written deliveries (Schunk, 1995). In relation to promoting growth mindsets within students, it is also important to place an emphasis on feedback that supports hard work and taking on challenges with a positive outlook.

Teachers may also benefit from verbal persuasion. Senior management should not shy away from praising teachers for their work, highlighting their accomplishments and delivering positive feedback throughout the school year. By giving teachers the opportunity to receive not only constructive feedback but also professional praise, a supportive and positive culture within the school can be fostered, and with these increased feelings of support and positivity in the workplace, teachers' individual classrooms may also see a benefit. For example, teachers with positive attitudes about teaching were found to have students that had higher self-esteem.

With this in mind, it is important to note that the 'credibility, trustworthiness, and expertise' (Mohamadi et al., 2011, 427) of the teacher (or persuader) can influence the amount of persuasion experienced (Bandura, 1997). The development of the perception of credibility, trustworthiness and expertise between a teacher and his or her students or between a teacher and a supervisor or member of senior management can be done in numerous ways. Some of these may include building rapport, using positive and supportive language and demonstrating knowledge through modelling or the delivery of instructions.

Emotional/physiological states

An individual's emotional and physiological states can deliver a wealth of information back to them as they determine whether they are capable of accomplishing a task. For instance, arousal may be experienced both emotionally and physiologically in the form of anxiety and increased heart rate. With this in mind, it is how those emotional and physical reactions are perceived that determines whether we feel positively capable or negatively unprepared.

If the emotional or physiological state is deemed to be negative, performance on a task may be inhibited (Bandura, 1997). However, if those states are deemed positive (e.g. you may experience arousal and increased heart rate as exciting), the level of performance can increase (Bandura, 1997). Teachers may help students reframe negative emotional and physiological states into positive ones by acknowledging the state the student is in as positive and associating it with what is needed to meet a task's demands. An example of this may be preparing students to take exams. If you have a student who feels nervous or anxious prior to and during an exam, you can reassure the student that those feelings and physical sensations are normal and that they feel that way because the exam matters to them. This attention given to the importance that the student feels about the exam can then be linked to the hard work that the student has put in to prepare for the exam, and that increased arousal has been linked to better performance outcomes and improved focus (for further information on this, see the 'inverted-U theory'; Yerkes and Dodson, 1908). Greater understanding of the sources of information that can influence self-efficacy beliefs and the role that self-efficacy can play in the development and maintenance of a growth mindset can help teachers to better examine how they run their classrooms and identify strategies that can be employed to boost their students' and their own self-efficacy beliefs.

From the perspective of teachers, understanding their own emotional and physiological states may help them to better understand themselves or their teaching style. It may also enable them to identify areas of their teaching that are positive or areas that need additional attention. By taking time to reflect on how you feel, both emotionally and physically, you may also be able to more quickly identify when burnout is approaching and apply mechanisms to potentially help reduce the severity of the burnout. Reflection can take place at any time: after specific classes, at the end of the school day, during school breaks, over the summer months and so on.

Before we move on, I would be remiss to not discuss the literature that criticises growth mindset research and its application. That being said, it is important to keep in mind that when dealing with psychology, there are vast numbers of variables, each of which can change outcomes, perspectives and applications. When examining the potential influence of having a growth mindset, in respect to academic attainment, a recent study funded by the Education Endowment Foundation reported that students taught by educators who had taken part in the Changing Mindset Project had no additional academic improvements compared to a control group. Implications of this study reported that only using a growth mindset intervention to boost attainment may not be the best option. This could support an argument that providing direct growth mindset training to students (rather than teachers to students) may be more beneficial for academic achievement (Rienzo et al., 2015). Carol Dweck acknowledges some limitations herself, arguing that the impact of growth mindset interventions may only be fully realised once a certain culture can be attained in the classroom (Severs, 2019).

> There was evidence that growth mindset had been tested and shown to work in ways that were meaningful to students – OK, that was the evidence, but the evidence did not speak to how to implement it in the classroom. That part was not yet evidence-based. Research takes place over many years. We continue to probe and validate and extend it
>
> *[Dweck, 2019 as quoted in Severs, 2019].*

We have now discussed what a mindset is and how the type of mindset a student has may influence his or her academic achievement, and we have gotten a glimpse into the neuroscience and psychology behind it – neuroplasticity and self-efficacy. What we have not yet discussed is how the mindset of a teacher may impact students (Stevens and White, 1987). There may be positive impacts, such as building resilience (Beilock et al., 2010; Brooks and Goldstein, 2008), or negative impacts, such as influencing negative attitudes towards certain subjects (Omolara and Adebukola, 2015). While we have mentioned that cultivating and maintaining a classroom that is both positive and in line with the promotion and development of a growth mindset within students are important, it is also imperative that teachers set high but, more importantly, realistic aspirations for their students.

Let's examine this briefly through goal setting. Goals benefit from being specific, measurable, attainable, relevant and time sensitive (Rubin, 2002). Emphasis should be placed on their attainability. As evidenced by a research study conducted by Kou Murayama et al. (2016), when unrealistically high aspirations were placed onto children by their parents, academic achievement was negatively influenced. One way to make sure that the goals being set for your students are reasonable and attainable is to build rapport with your students. Get to know your students prior to the development of a goal, closely monitor how your students are doing as they work towards that goal and don't be afraid to make changes! The goal-setting process should be flexible and, most importantly, allow students (and teachers) to see that progress is being made, keeping both parties

,motivated and positive. Goals that are 'too big, too fast' can leave students and teachers feeling excessive pressure to perform – an experience that is not good for anyone involved. Thus, while it is great to have a growth mindset as a teacher and believe that your students are capable of high academic achievement, it is also important to set appropriate goals for your students and yourself as a teacher, to help eliminate unwanted and excessive pressure to perform.

Motivation

It does not matter how slowly you go, as long as you do not stop.

– Confucius[1]

Motivation is defined in the *Oxford English Dictionary* as 'a reason or reasons for acting or behaving in a particular way'. This understanding of motivation could lead us to assume, in educational settings, that every act or behaviour that a student (or teacher) exhibits is motivated by some reason(s). For instance, a student who revises and a student who does not are both motivated by something to act in their respective ways. With regard to motivation and mindset, an interesting 'chicken or egg' question emerges: does one come first and influence the other, or is one just a consequence of the other?

In an attempt to answer this revolving and debatable question, this section will briefly describe the role that all the following have on an individual's overall motivation and academic achievement: achievement goals or goal orientations, motivational climate and intrinsic/extrinsic motivation. Achievement goal theory attempts to understand what behaviour a student displays when approaching his or her academic work and the motivation behind it (Dweck and Leggett, 1988; Meece and Holt, 1993; Wolters, 2004). Within this theory, there are four main goal orientations: mastery approach, mastery avoidance, performance approach and performance avoidance (Elliot and McGregor, 2001). This can be outlined as follows:

- *Mastery approach.* A student's goal is to learn as much as he or she can. Students like to overcome challenges; they wish to increase their understanding; and they are intrinsically motivated.
- *Mastery avoidance.* A student's goal is to learn so he or she is not deemed to be a 'failure'. Students do not want to be embarrassed by not understanding; they are motivated by a fear of failure.
- *Performance approach.* A student's goal is to outperform his or her peers and prove to others that he or she is capable. Students are motivated to demonstrate superior ability over their peers.
- *Performance avoidance.* A student's goal is to not look like he or she is incompetent or 'less able' than his or her peers. Students are motivated to avoid looking inadequate in comparison with their peers.

Within achievement goal theory, research has been conducted around its relationship with motivation, cognition and achievement in academic settings (Wolters, 2004). In a study conducted by Andrew Elliot et al. (1999), it was found that college students who adapted a performance approach orientation had higher self-reported effort and persistence (Wolters, 2004). When examining secondary school pupils, a mastery goal orientation was found to be more highly correlated with effort and persistence when performing an academic task than were performance goal orientations (Miller et al., 1996). With regard to the types of learning strategies used by different goal orientations, research has found that those who employed mastery goal orientations reported using more adaptive learning strategies than those who had performance goal orientations (Elliot and McGregor, 2001; Pintrich and DeGroot, 1990; Wolters et al., 1996). When examining academic achievement, a difference in age seems to have emerged in the research. University students who adopted a performance approach goal orientation tended to have high course achievement (Church et al., 2001), whereas another study found that younger students who possessed a performance goal orientation had lower grades than classmates who had a mastery goal orientation (Skaalvik, 1997).

While the type of goal orientation a student has is important, the academic environment in which students perceive themselves to be is also important. The motivational climate, also sometimes referred to as the 'goal structure' (Ames and Archer, 1988), examines the influence the environment may have on students' motivation and goal orientations. Some of the types of environmental variables that may be taken into consideration are the types of achievement goals that are emphasised by the teacher, the school or educational governing body, the type of assignments used to specify attainment levels, the way that students are grouped and how grade feedback is given (Ames, 1992; Urdan, 1997; Wolters, 2004). Two main types of goal structures are found in the research, and to remain consistent with the terminology, we will use the terms more closely related to goal structure research in education. The two goal structures are 'mastery goal structure' and 'performance goal structure' (Dweck, 1986; Nicholls, 1984; Midgley et al., 1998). These are outlined as follows:

- *Mastery goal structure.* An educational environment that places an emphasis on the importance of learning, hard work and the view that success can be achieved through the successful application of hard work.
- *Performance goal structure.* An educational environment that places an emphasis on high achievement, outperforming others and being extrinsically rewarded when success is achieved.

As with the achievement goal theory and goal orientations, research has been conducted on the impact of the goal structure and motivational climate on motivation, cognition and academic achievement (Wolters, 2004). Carole Ames and Jennifer Archer (1988) researched the impact of goal structure on the challenge preferences of adolescents, finding that when a mastery goal structure was perceived by students, they reported a greater preference for challenging academic tasks. In the same study, it was found that a perceived mastery goal structure was correlated with adolescents' use of learning strategies (Ames and Archer, 1988). Mastery goals have also been found to influence effort and persistence (Grant and Dweck, 2003), perceived academic ability and academic performance in junior high school students (Wolters et al., 1996).

This introduction to achievement goal theory, goal orientations and goal structures has hopefully begun to paint a more thorough picture of the types of variables that might influence a student's motivation in the classroom. Another factor that ties everything together is intrinsic and extrinsic motivation. Intrinsically motivated individuals perform tasks because they enjoy them (Berlyne, 1960). Extrinsically motivated individuals perform tasks because there is some sort of reward associated with completing the task successfully (Ryan and Deci, 2000). Research has shown that extrinsic rewards can reduce an individual's intrinsic motivation (Wiersma, 1992), thus resulting in the conclusion that reward-based incentives are harmful in the long run and result in diminished motivation and personal enjoyment over time (Deci, 1971), even if incentives may boost persistence in certain educational settings such as games (O'Rourke, et al., 2014). In a society that seems focused on using extrinsic enticements to motivate individuals (i.e. money, trophies, public recognition, etc.), it becomes imperative that intrinsic motivation be fostered in the classroom (Ryan and Deci, 2000; Tanaka and Murayama, 2014), especially when research has found that placing an emphasis on building intrinsic motivation within students is linked to a number of positive results, such as work quality, productivity, academic performance, persistence on assignments and overall health and well-being (Deci and Ryan, 2002; as stated in Murayama et al., 2016).

Having discussed how students may be motivated (or unmotivated) to do well in the classroom, it is now time to turn the magnifying glass onto teachers. Why do some teachers enjoy going to work every day, whereas other teachers find themselves dragging their feet? There are, of course, many reasons for this difference. The factors influencing teacher enjoyment and motivation can range from the purely altruistic (preparing the future generation) to the purely self-driven (wages and summer holidays). Other factors may involve feeling supported (or not supported) by their departments, the culture fostered by the leadership team and school districts and personal reasons. That being said, burnout is one of the most reported reasons for why teachers have gone from having a 'pep in their step' entering their school building to dragging each foot as though it were trapped in cement.

Burnout, as described by Christina Maslach (2003), takes place when a person experiences stress for a long period of time, resulting in emotional exhaustion, feelings of being disconnected and an absence of feelings of accomplishment. In the context of the teaching profession, various situations and repeated stressors, from both within and outside the classroom, can lead to a teacher experiencing burnout, and it is important to keep in mind that it is not uncommon. Burnout, however, can influence a teacher's presence, engagement and enthusiasm in the classroom, leading to a potentially negative impact on student learning and attainment.

Common solutions to handling burnout have included training teachers with stress-reduction techniques and holding teacher in-service workshops to develop support among teachers. However, as Barry Farber (1982) described, these solutions tend to fall short and only result in short-term solutions. Schools as a whole should aim to have individualised and group-based workshops available to teachers throughout a school year, not just one-off sessions. Schools should also be aware of the needs of each teacher; personalised options of support for teachers could be potentially valuable, as well as having additional support counselling opportunities available. Once again, self-reflection is an important practice for teachers to undertake. Being aware of their emotions and physical feelings can help them monitor whether burnout is occurring or likely to occur; if so, interventions to boost motivation and professional satisfaction can be used.

Practical application strategies (implications for practice)

It is one thing to read about theories or variables that may influence a student's academic achievement, but it is another thing to attempt to put different strategies into action. There are many possible strategies that teachers could employ to help students reach their highest academic achievement levels. Unfortunately, there is not enough room in this chapter to discuss them all. Instead, this chapter discusses six strategies that can be applied by teachers to help promote and foster a growth mindset and high motivation levels in their students and themselves.

Feedback/language

Objective: to create a positive climate for motivation and growth mindset. Mentioned throughout this chapter is the importance of the feedback and language used by teachers and students to cultivate positive mindsets and motivation. Dweck (2000) suggested a number of different techniques that could be used to develop a growth mindset in students; two of these are feedback and language. 'Feedback' is information that is delivered to students from their teachers, peers and themselves. It is usually delivered in the form of critique or praise. In order for critique to lead to improvement, evidence suggests that the way students are critiqued should be constructive and encouraging, with an emphasis on success being accomplished through hard work and the application of different strategies to find paths that lead to success (Dweck and Elliot, 1988; Dweck and Leggett, 1988).

The type of language we use as teachers and the type of language our students use are interconnected. If a teacher praises students with labels such as 'smart' or 'intelligent', students begin to associate personal value to those particular words (Baumeister et al., 1990; Butler, 1987). This could potentially lead them to believe that if they get something wrong, they are not 'smart' and attribute a setback to their lack of ability, thus resulting in negative motivational influence (Bell et al., 1994) and learned helplessness (Dweck and Leggett, 1988). Positivity in the language used by both parties is needed to foster and maintain growth mindsets in educational settings. This, in turn, relates to verbal persuasion as a source of self-efficacy, which is given both by external sources (teachers) and by internal sources (students). Ways of promoting positive language from both external and internal sources include the 'power of "yet"' and 'self-affirmations'. These are outlined in the following table:

The power of 'yet'	Self-affirmations
✔ Based on the work of Carol Dweck, with an emphasis placed on the importance of experiencing failure. ✔ Failures allow students to learn from their mistakes, apply different solutions to problems and see progression throughout the year. Teachers can reinforce positive language by applying 'yet' to the end of negative thoughts. Student: 'I can't do this' Teacher: 'You can't do this, yet!' ✔ Implies that students may not have succeeded this time, but with continued practice, hard work and determination, they will succeed at some point in the future. ✔ Helps to reframe negative thoughts to more positive ones. ✔ Students and teachers alike can add this simple word to their vocabulary. Teacher: 'This class doesn't understand what I'm teaching … yet!'	✔ Self-affirmations are positive statements, quotes, words, beliefs and qualities about oneself. ✔ What we say to ourselves is often more powerful than what others say to us. ✔ Saying negative things about ourselves to ourselves can result in negative emotions, behaviours and attitudes that become ingrained. ✔ We can train the brain to be more positive. ✔ Self-affirmations can work both by writing them down and by speaking them out loud. ✔ They may help people remember their own resourcefulness in challenging situations (Sherman and Hartson, 2011), change their assessments of daily stressors (Schmeichel and Vohs, 2009), see increased academic achievement (Cohen et al., 2006, 2009; Purdie-Vaughns et al., 2009) and even improve attention (Koole et al., 1999). ✔ Should be used daily – by students and teachers alike!

Goal setting/reinforcement

Objective: to increase and maintain motivation and positive mindset. One strategy that fits within both building a growth mindset and fostering and maintaining motivation is that of goal setting. Goal setting is nothing new, and many schools and teachers already have some sort of goal-setting intervention in place. But it is worth asking whether goal setting is being carried out effectively and efficiently. Within the educational setting, there is potential for goals to be set in a number of different areas and with the influence of many different people. If not monitored carefully, students and teachers can potentially have too many goals, set by too many people, thus devaluing and detracting from the goals that are personally set and most important to the individual.

A consequence of excessive goal setting is that students can end up setting goals not because they want to accomplish them but because they are told to set them. This can turn a valuable tool into a chore, thereby turning it from a positive experience and effective process into a negative experience and an ineffective process. It is a bit like when you get home from school and in your mind you had sorted out how you were going to go about doing your homework, and then one of your parents tells you to do your homework, so you would do absolutely everything except your homework!

I am not implying that goal setting is not important in many facets of life and that many goals can't be in motion at once. Goals can and should be made, examined, re-examined and accomplished daily. But the challenge becomes how to teach someone else to set goals without setting the goals for them. How do you make it fun? How do you keep students interested? Two strategies that can be used to answer those questions are: '"SMART" targets' and 'positive reinforcement'. These are outlined in the following table:

'SMART' targets	Positive reinforcement
✔ Believed to be attributed to Doran (1981) ✔ S – Specific (Ask: What do you want to achieve, where, how, when, why?) ✔ M – Measurable (Identify: What will be seen and felt when the goal is reached and along the way?) ✔ A – Achievable/attainable (Ask: Do you have resources in place to accomplish the goal?) ✔ R – Realistic/relevant (Ask: Is this goal really what I want? What is the objective?) ✔ T – Timely (Create a plan: Smaller goals to achieve along the way with deadlines – but stay flexible.) ✔ Create opportunities for your students to set their own goals, monitor their progression and learn how to adapt to timelines. ✔ Goal setting can help students achieve results, maintain focus and build confidence. ✔ There are many different goal-setting frameworks that can be used; SMART is a simple way for teachers to use goal setting with younger students or larger classrooms.	✔ Reinforcement can be used to strengthen positive behaviours and weaken negative ones. ✔ Positive behaviours/actions should be reinforced immediately after they occur – used often but then thinned out over time. ✔ Encourage the promotion of intrinsic motivation – not extrinsic (avoid over-using tangible rewards). ✔ How to help support intrinsic motivation: ■ Ask your students what motivates them and what they are passionate about. ■ Praise students for both their accomplishments and their perseverance. ■ Set not only individual goals but also class goals. ■ Give students choices: how they do assignments, optional assignments. ■ Allow for group interaction: peer-to-peer teaching, group projects and class discussions. ■ Avoid punishments – don't threaten to do or take away something from the class or individual student. ■ Allow students time to self-reflect at the end of the day, week, term, etc.

Neuroscience education/classroom environment

Objective: to inform students about the brain and their potential to learn and grow. As mentioned earlier in this chapter, growth mindset interventions have included teaching students and teachers about the brain. Neuroscience research has provided us with valuable knowledge about how the brain works, what the brain is capable of and how to get the most out of it. This information, when presented to students, may help them begin to grasp the complexity of that organ floating inside their heads. For example, when information is delivered in the form of a growth mindset intervention, students with a fixed mindset may begin to question their particular belief that intelligence is finite by further understanding neuroplasticity and how it supports the claim that abilities can change over time. Or students who do not think they are capable of achieving good marks on their end-of-year exams may benefit from learning about how neural connections are strengthened through continued use and practice to aid them during revision. Growth mindset interventions that include the use of neuroscience research can be found online.[2]

Additionally, a teacher might use visual stimulators to help drum home some points about neuroscience, positive language habits and an intrinsically motivated classroom environment. Posters, decorations, previously completed assignments and achievement charts are just some of things teachers could have in their classroom environment. However, keep in mind that depending on the age group you are teaching, the visual environment you provide should be appropriate for your students. (Fisher, Godwin, and Seltman, 2014) Ultimately, learning the basics of the brain and using visual stimulators within the classroom may help your students throughout the academic year. These points are illustrated in the following table:

Learning the basics of the brain	Visual stimulators
✔ Growth mindset interventions incorporate teaching students about neuroscience (Aronson et al., 2002).	✔ Create a visual environment within your classroom to help reinforce information students have learned.
✔ Teaching students about how neuroscience findings show how challenges (and failures) allow for opportunities to learn was linked to increased grade point averages (Paunesku et al., 2015).	✔ Positive and motivational posters can help remind students to use positive language with themselves and others.
✔ A study that discussed neuroplasticity with students found that students' motivation improved, impacted academic achievement and increased brain activity (Sarrasin et al., 2018).	✔ Beware: Visual stimulators should be appropriate for the age and level of your students.
	✔ Younger students may benefit from fewer visual distracters.
✔ Help students understand just how powerful their brains are.	✔ Allow students to be a part of the classroom environment by giving them assignments that will be used to decorate the classroom.

Conclusion

This chapter has provided descriptions of mindset and motivation and how they relate to the classroom setting for both students and teachers. Underlying psychological processes have been discussed, including self-efficacy theory (sources of self-efficacy), achievement goal theory, goal orientations theory, burnout and the role of neuroplasticity. While research aimed at finding support for the influence of a growth mindset on academic achievement is mixed, the overall idea behind it and the differing types of interventions produced so far seem to be an area of research worth further exploration. Research into motivation has provided us with a solid groundwork in the educational setting, with achievement goal theory and goal orientation providing insights into what may motivate students and how to help support and grow intrinsic motivation. It is important to note the interplay between mindset and motivation and that both work with each other, with a growth mindset having been found to have positive influences on a student's motivation and academic performance (Blackwell et al., 2007; Dweck, 2009).

It is not lost on me, nor should it be on you, that there is a myriad of factors that influence a student's academic achievement and a teacher's professional satisfaction. Truth be told, the topics of mindsets and motivation are too large to have been thoroughly examined and described in this chapter alone. However, it is my hope that by beginning to further understand the role that both mindsets and motivation can play in the classroom, for both teachers and students, you can begin to understand how important and influential these areas are.

The existing literature provides many more practical applications, interventions and strategies that you can use and weave among your personal approach to teaching that could benefit your students' attainment and enjoyment of your subject. Mindset and motivation are by no means the only two areas that should be focused on, and these two topics will not be the sole areas that make or break your students' potential academic attainment. But they just might help – and that makes them worth a try!

Notes

1 Confucius (1997). *The Analects of Confucius* (trans. by C. Huang, p. 283). Oxford, UK: Oxford University Press.
2 For further information about growth mindset interventions that use neuroscience research and information, visit mindsetworks.com.

References

Ames, C. (1992). Classrooms: goals, structures, and student motivation. *Journal of Educational Psychology, 84*(3), 261–71.

Ames, C., and Archer, J. (1988). Achievement goals in the classroom: students' learning strategies and motivation processes. *Journal of Educational Psychology, 80* (3), 260–67.

Aronson, J., Fried, C. B., and Good, C. (2002). Reducing the effects of stereotype threat on African American college students by shaping theories of intelligence. *Journal of Experimental Social Psychology, 38*(2), 113–25.

Bandura, A. (1977). Self-efficacy: toward a unifying theory of behavioral change. *Psychological Review, 84*(2), 191–215.

Bandura, A. (1986). The explanatory and predictive scope of self-efficacy theory. *Journal of Social and Clinical Psychology, 4*(3), 359–73.

Bandura, A. (1992). Exercise of personal agency through the self-efficacy mechanism. *Self-Efficacy: Thought Control of Action, 1*, 3–37.

Bandura, A. (1997). *Self-efficacy: The Exercise of Control*. London: Macmillan.

Bandura, A., Barbaranelli, C., Caprara, G. V., and Pastorelli, C. (1996). Multifaceted impact of self-efficacy beliefs on academic functioning. *Child Development, 67*(3), 1206–22.

Baumeister, R. F., Hutton, D. G., and Cairns, K. J. (1990). Negative effects of praise on skilled performance. *Basic and Applied Social Psychology, 11*(2), 131–48.

Beilock, S. L., Gunderson, E. A., Ramirez, G., and Levine, S. C. (2010). Female teachers' math anxiety affects girls' math achievement. *Proceedings of the National Academy of Sciences, 107*(5), 1860–63.

Bell, S. M., McCallum, R. S., Bryles, J., et al. (1994). Attributions for academic success and failure: an individual difference investigation of academic achievement and gender. *Journal of Psychoeducational Assessment, 12*(1), 4–13.

Berlyne, D. E. (1960). *Conflict, Arousal, and Curiosity*, McGraw-Hill series in psychology. New York: McGraw-Hill Book Company.

Blackwell, L. S., Trzesniewski, K. H., and Dweck, C. S. (2007). Implicit theories of intelligence predict achievement across an adolescent transition: a longitudinal study and an intervention. *Child Development, 78*(1), 246–63.

Bray-Clark, N., and Bates, R. (2003). Self-efficacy beliefs and teacher effectiveness: implications for professional development. *Professional Educator, 26*(1), 13–22.

Brooks, R., and Goldstein, S. (2008). The mindset of teachers capable of fostering resilience in students. *Canadian Journal of School Psychology, 23*(1), 114–26.

Butler, R. (1987). Task-involving and ego-involving properties of evaluation: effects of different feedback conditions on motivational perceptions, interest, and performance. *Journal of Educational Psychology, 79*(4), 474–82.

Church, M. A., Elliot, A. J., and Gable, S. L. (2001). Perceptions of classroom environment, achievement goals, and achievement outcomes. *Journal of Educational Psychology, 93*(1), 43–54.

Cohen, G. L., Garcia, J., Apfel, N., and Master, A. (2006). Reducing the racial achievement gap: a social-psychological intervention. *Science, 313*(5791), 1307–10.

Cohen, G. L., Garcia, J., Purdie-Vaughns, V., et al. (2009). Recursive processes in self-affirmation: intervening to close the minority achievement gap. *Science, 324*(5925), 400–3.

Confucius. (1997). *The Analects of Confucius* (trans. C. Huang). Oxford, UK: Oxford University Press.

Deci, E. L. (1971). Effects of externally mediated rewards on intrinsic motivation. *Journal of Personality and Social Psychology, 18*(1), 105–15.

Deci, E. L., and Ryan, R. M. (2002). Overview of self-determination theory: an organismic dialectical perspective. In *Handbook of Self-determination Research* (pp. 3–33). Rochester, NY: University of Rochester Press.

Doran, G. T. (1981). There's a SMART way to write management's goals and objectives. *Management Review, 70*(11), 35–36.

Draganski, B., Gaser, C., Kempermann, G., et al. (2006). Temporal and spatial dynamics of brain structure changes during extensive learning. *Journal of Neuroscience, 26*(23), 6314–17.

Dubinsky, R. M., and Miyasaki, J. (2010). Assessment: efficacy of transcutaneous electric nerve stimulation in the treatment of pain in neurologic disorders (an evidence-based review). Report of the Therapeutics and Technology Assessment Subcommittee of the American Academy of Neurology. *Neurology, 74*(2), 173–76.

Dweck, C.S. (1986). Motivational processes affecting learning. American Psychologist, 41, 1040–1048.

Dweck, C. (2009). Who will the 21st-century learners be? *Knowledge Quest, 38*(2), 8–10.

Dweck, C. (2016). What having a 'growth mindset' actually means. *Harvard Business Review, 13*, 213–26.

Dweck, C. S. (2000). *Self-theories: Their Role in Motivation, Personality, and Development*. New York: Psychology Press.

Dweck, C. S. (2006). *Mindset: The New Psychology of Success*. New York: Random House.

Dweck, C. S. (2007). The perils and promises of praise. *Kaleidoscope: Contemporary and Classic Readings in Education, 12*, 34–39.

Dweck, C. S. (2010a). Even geniuses work hard. *Educational Leadership, 68*(1), 16–20.

Dweck, C. S. (2010b). Mind-sets. *Principal Leadership, 10*(5), 26–29.

Dweck, C. S., and Leggett, E. L. (1988). A social-cognitive approach to motivation and personality. *Psychological Review, 95*(2), 256–73.

Elliot, E.S., and Dweck, C.S. (1988). Goals: An approach to motivation and achievement. Journal of Personality and Social Psychology, 54(1), 5–12.

Elliot, A. J., and McGregor, H. A. (2001). A 2 × 2 achievement goal framework. *Journal of Personality and Social Psychology, 80*(3), 501–19.

Elliot, A. J., McGregor, H. A., and Gable, S. (1999). Achievement goals, study strategies, and exam performance: a mediational analysis. *Journal of Educational Psychology, 91*(3), 549–63.

Farber, B. A. (1982). *Teacher Burnout: Assumptions, Myths, and Issues*. Chicago: Spencer Foundation.

Fisher, A. V., Godwin, K. E., and Seltman, H. (2014). Visual environment, attention allocation, and learning in young children: when too much of a good thing may be bad. *Psychological Science*, 25(7), 1362–70.

Ford, H. (1947). *Reader's Digest*, 54, 64.

Good, C., Aronson, J., and Inzlicht, M. (2003). Improving adolescents' standardized test performance: an intervention to reduce the effects of stereotype threat. *Journal of Applied Developmental Psychology*, 24(6), 645–62.

Grant, H., and Dweck, C. S. (2003). Clarifying achievement goals and their impact. *Journal of Personality and Social Psychology*, 85(3), 541153.

Henson, R. K. (2001). *Teacher Self-efficacy: Substantive Implications and Measurement Dilemmas*. Paper presented at the Annual Meeting of Educational Research Exchange, College Station, TX.

Komarraju, M., and Nadler, D. (2013). Self-efficacy and academic achievement: why do implicit beliefs, goals, and effort regulation matter? *Learning and Individual Differences*, 25, 67–72.

Koole, S. L., Smeets, K., Van Knippenberg, A., and Dijksterhuis, A. (1999). The cessation of rumination through self-affirmation. *Journal of Personality and Social Psychology*, 77(1), 111–25.

Lane, J., Lane, A., and Cockerton, T. (2003). Prediction of postgraduate performance from self-efficacy, class of degree and cognitive ability test scores. *Journal of Hospitality, Leisure, Sport and Tourism Education*, 2(1), 113–18.

Lane, J., Lane, A. M., and Kyprianou, A. (2004). Self-efficacy, self-esteem and their impact on academic performance. *Social Behavior and Personality: An International Journal*, 32(3), 247–56.

Lent, R. W., Brown, S. D., and Larkin, K. C. (1984). Relation of self-efficacy expectations to academic achievement and persistence. *Journal of Counseling Psychology*, 31(3), 356–62.

Maslach, C. (2003). *Burnout: The Cost of Caring*. Los Altos, CA: Institute for the Study of Human Knowledge.

Meece, J. L., and Holt, K. (1993). A pattern analysis of students' achievement goals. *Journal of Educational Psychology*, 85(4), 582–90.

Midgley, C., Kaplan, A., Middleton, M., et al. (1998). The development and validation of scales assessing students' achievement goal orientations. *Contemporary Educational Psychology*, 23(2), 113–31.

Miller, R. B., Greene, B. A., Montalvo, G. P., et al. (1996). Engagement in academic work: the role of learning goals, future consequences, pleasing others, and perceived ability. *Contemporary Educational Psychology*, 21(4), 388–422.

Mohamadi, F. S., Asadzadeh, H., Ahadi, H., and Jomehri, F. (2011). Testing Bandura's theory in school. *Procedia-Social and Behavioral Sciences*, 12, 426–35.

Münte, T. F., Altenmüller, E., and Jäncke, L. (2002). The musician's brain as a model of neuroplasticity. *Nature Reviews Neuroscience*, 3(6), 473–78.

Murayama, K., Pekrun, R., Suzuki, M., et al. (2016). Don't aim too high for your kids: parental overaspiration undermines students' learning in mathematics. *Journal of Personality and Social Psychology*, 111(5), 766–79.

Nicholls, J.G. (1984). Achievement motivation: Conceptions of ability, subjective experience, task choice, and performance. *Psychological Review, 91*, 328–346.

O'Rourke, E., Haimovitz, K., Ballweber, C., Dweck, C.S. and Popovic, Z. (2014). Brain points: a growth mindset incentive structure boosts persistence in an educational game. In *Proceedings of the SIGCHI Conference on Human Factors in Computing Systems* (pp. 3339–48). New York: ACM.

Omolara, S. R., and Adebukola, O. R. (2015). Teachers' attitudes: a great influence on teaching and learning of social studies. *Journal of Law, Policy and Globalization, 42*, 131–7.

Pajares, F. (1996). Self-efficacy beliefs in academic settings. *Review of Educational Research, 66*(4), 543–78.

Pajares, F., Johnson, M. J., and Usher, E. L. (2007). Sources of writing self-efficacy beliefs of elementary, middle, and high school students. *Research in the Teaching of English, 42*(1), 104–20.

Paunesku, D., Walton, G. M., Romero, C., et al. (2015). Mind-set interventions are a scalable treatment for academic underachievement. *Psychological Science, 26*(6), 784–93.

Phan, H. P. (2011). Interrelations between self-efficacy and learning approaches: a developmental approach. *Educational Psychology, 31*(2), 225–46.

Pintrich, P. R., and DeGroot, E. (1990). Quantitative and qualitative perspectives on student motivational beliefs and self-regulated learning. In *Proceedings of the Annual Meeting of the American Educational Research Association* (Vol. 128). Boston.

Purdie-Vaughns, V., Cohen, G. L., Garcia, J., et al. (2009). Improving minority academic performance: how a values-affirmation intervention works. *Teachers College Record*, 1–4.

Rienzo, C., Rolfe, H., and Wilkinson, D. (2015). *Changing Mindsets: Evaluation Report and Executive Summary*. London: Education Endowment Foundation.

Rubin, R. S. (2002). Will the real SMART goals please stand up. *Industrial-Organizational Psychologist, 39*(4), 26–27.

Ryan, R. M., and Deci, E. L. (2000). Intrinsic and extrinsic motivations: classic definitions and new directions. *Contemporary Educational Psychology, 25*(1), 54–67.

Sarrasin, J. B., Nenciovici, L., Foisy, L. M. B., et al. (2018). Effects of teaching the concept of neuroplasticity to induce a growth mindset on motivation, achievement, and brain activity: A meta-analysis. *Trends in Neuroscience and Education, 12*, 22–31.

Schleider, J. L., Abel, M. R., and Weisz, J. R. (2015). Implicit theories and youth mental health problems: a random-effects meta-analysis. *Clinical Psychology Review, 35*, 1–9.

Schmeichel, B. J., and Vohs, K. (2009). Self-affirmation and self-control: affirming core values counteracts ego depletion. *Journal of Personality and Social Psychology, 96*(4), 770–82.

Schunk, D. H. (1990). Goal setting and self-efficacy during self-regulated learning. *Educational Psychologist, 25*(1), 71–86.

Schunk, D. H. (1995). Self-efficacy and education and instruction. InJ. E. Maddux (Eds.), Self-Efficacy, Adaptation, and Adjustment, Plenum Series in Social/Clinical Psychology. Boston: Springer.

Schunk, D. H., Hanson, A. R., and Cox, P. D. (1987). Peer-model attributes and children's achievement behaviors. *Journal of Educational Psychology*, *79*(1), 54–61.

Segev, I. (2006). What do dendrites and their synapses tell the neuron? *Journal of Neurophysiology*, *95*(3), 1295–97.

Severs, J. (2019). Carol Dweck: where growth mindset went wrong. Available at www.tes.com/news/carol-dweck-where-growth-mindset-went-wrong.TES.

Shell, D. F., Colvin, C., and Bruning, R. H. (1995). Self-efficacy, attribution, and outcome expectancy mechanisms in reading and writing achievement: grade-level and achievement-level differences. *Journal of Educational Psychology*, *87*(3), 386–98.

Sherman, D. K., and Hartson, K. A. (2011). Reconciling self-protection with self-improvement. In M. D. Alicke and C. Sedikides (Eds.), *Handbook of Self-enhancement and Self-protection* (p. 128). New York: Guildford Press.

Skaalvik, E. M. (1997). Self-enhancing and self-defeating ego orientation: relations with task and avoidance orientation, achievement, self-perceptions, and anxiety. *Journal of Educational Psychology*, *89*(1), 71–81.

Stevens, R., and White, W. (1987). Impact of teachers' morale on the classroom. *Perceptual and Motor Skills*, *65*(3), 767–70.

Tanaka, A., and Murayama, K. (2014). Within-person analyses of situational interest and boredom: interactions between task-specific perceptions and achievement goals. *Journal of Educational Psychology*, *106*(4), 1122–34.

Turner, E. A., Chandler, M., and Heffer, R. W. (2009). The influence of parenting styles, achievement motivation, and self-efficacy on academic performance in college students. *Journal of College Student Development*, *50*(3), 337–46.

Urdan, T. C. (1997). Examining the relations among early adolescent students' goals and friends' orientation toward effort and achievement in school. *Contemporary Educational Psychology*, *22*(2), 165–91.

Usher, E. L., and Pajares, F. (2006). Sources of academic and self-regulatory efficacy beliefs of entering middle school students. *Contemporary Educational Psychology*, *31*(2), 125–41.

Wiersma, U. J. (1992). The effects of extrinsic rewards in intrinsic motivation: a meta-analysis. *Journal of Occupational and Organizational Psychology*, *65*(2), 101–14.

Wolters, C. A. (2004). Advancing achievement goal theory: using goal structures and goal orientations to predict students' motivation, cognition, and achievement. *Journal of Educational Psychology*, *96*(2), 236–50.

Wolters, C. A., Shirley, L. Y., and Pintrich, P. R. (1996). The relation between goal orientation and students' motivational beliefs and self-regulated learning. *Learning and Individual Differences*, *8*(3), 211–38.

Yeager, D. S., and Dweck, C. S. (2012). Mindsets that promote resilience: when students believe that personal characteristics can be developed. *Educational Psychologist*, *47*(4), 302–14.

Yeager, D. S., Trzesniewski, K. H., and Dweck, C. S. (2013). An implicit theories of personality intervention reduces adolescent aggression in response to victimization and exclusion. *Child Development, 84*(3), 970–88.

Yerkes, R. M., and Dodson, J. D. (1908). The relation of strength of stimulus to rapidity of habit-formation. *Journal of Comparative Neurology and Psychology, 18*(5), 459–82.

Zimmerman, B. J. (2000). Self-efficacy: an essential motive to learn. *Contemporary Educational Psychology, 25*(1), 82–91.

Zimmerman, B. J., Bandura, A., and Martinez-Pons, M. (1992). Self-motivation for academic attainment: the role of self-efficacy beliefs and personal goal setting. *American Educational Research Journal, 29*(3), 663–76.

7

Using an executive function–focused approach to build self-regulation, metacognition and motivation in all learners

Laurie Faith, Bettina Hohnen, Victoria Bagnall and Imogen Moore-Shelley

Introduction

Did you know that in addition to their intellectual and creative capacity, humans must use a set of higher-order cognitive skills to meet the demands of their environment (Banich, 2004)? If you are a psychologist, you almost certainly know that these cognitive skills, called 'executive functions', explain over half of all variation in school performance (Visu-Petra et al., 2011) and predict academic functioning beyond indexes of language or intellectual ability (Blair and Razza, 2007; Duckworth and Seligman, 2005; Espy et al., 2004). You may be aware that executive functioning skills (EFSs) are significant for occupational functioning (Daly et al., 2015), marital stability (Eakin et al., 2004) and interpersonal skills (Denson et al., 2011). You probably also know that specific dysfunction to these skills, such as challenges with organisation, attention or working memory, are common among learners with a wide range of disabilities and disadvantages. Most psychologists are aware that weak executive functions are co-morbid with acquired cognitive impairment (Gioia and Isquith, 2004), attention deficit/hyperactivity disorder (ADHD) and autism (Ozonoff and

Jensen, 1999), fetal alcohol syndrome (Fryer et al., 2007) and learning disabilities (Elliott, 2003; Stein and Krishnan, 2007). More recently, research shared at academically oriented and clinical conferences has revealed that weak development of EFSs is further exacerbated by over-exposure to screens, lack of exercise, improper sleep or nutrition, sickness (Swing et al., 2010), low socio-economic status and high levels of familial stress (Southern Education Foundation, 2015). If you are a psychologist, you probably know these facts about EFSs.

While it is not surprising that most psychologists from neurological to clinical domains are intimately acquainted with the science of EFSs, it is rather stunning that most teachers are not. Up to their eyeballs in students with executive functioning challenges, many have only heard the term 'executive functioning' in passing or while flipping through a psychologist's report. Having worked with thousands of teachers from across North America and in the United Kingdom, however, we can confirm that teachers' lack of exposure to this information is almost always exceeded by an urgent desire to learn more.

This chapter provides an overview of EFSs in the context of primary and secondary school-aged development and outlines an approach for building EFSs that is currently being used in both primary and secondary schools in the United Kingdom and Canada. Our goal is to equip a diverse team of caring adults – from teachers to parents to one-on-one coaches – with the key concepts, knowledge, skills and tangible resources necessary to ensure optimal EFS development in every child.

Defining executive functions

Scientific interest in executive functioning began long before the phenomenon was named and defined. As far as we know, doctors in the 1940s were the first to delineate the *executive* functions of the brain while noticing their absence in patients recovering from traumatic injury to the frontal lobe (Ratiu and Talos, 2004). The conspicuous lack of attention, inhibition and general self-control they observed was further studied throughout the 1970s and 1980s (e.g. Posner and Snyder, 1975) and continues to be a subject of fascination to this day. With the help of sophisticated neuroimaging equipment, the fact that observable self-regulatory behaviour is driven by the complex network of brain circuitry centralized in the prefrontal cortex and subcortical structures of the brain has been firmly established (Collette et al., 2016). For example, when performing tasks requiring planning, response inhibition or working memory, such as a speedy card game, the dorsolateral prefrontal cortex appears active (Alvarez and Emory, 2006). When arousing energy for routines of daily hygiene, such as getting out of bed on time, eating a good breakfast and brushing one's teeth, the anterior cingulate cortex is more active (Lezak et al., 2004). In this way, generally, EFSs are regarded as the behavioural manifestation of the frontal lobe or prefrontal cortex of the brain.

Currently, there is no universally accepted definition of executive functioning, although most agree that it is an umbrella term describing a family of distinct but inter-related cognitive processes. To conceptualise EFSs vis-à-vis other cognitive skills, you can also imagine a vast orchestra of perceptual, spatial, linguistic and mathematical 'players' being timed, sequenced, planned and modulated by an EFS 'conductor'. In this role, EFSs enable goal-directed behaviour and mediate responses to novel or complex situations (Hughes, 2011). Disagreement arises concerning the number of distinct EFSs, but many believe that there are three broad categories: inhibitory control, working memory and cognitive flexibility (Diamond, 2013; Miyake et al., 2000). Inhibitory control involves selective attention, cognitive inhibition, resisting temptations or stopping impulsive action. Working memory involves holding information in the mind for short periods of time while acting on that content – like a mental workspace. Cognitive flexibility involves seeing things from different perspectives and shifting and adapting to changed circumstances (Miyake et al., 2000). More recent frameworks flesh out the individual skills more fully. For example, in a series of books offering practical advice for parents and teachers, Peg Dawson and Richard Guare (2008, 2012, 2018) break down EFSs into eleven inter-related skills outlined and described in Table 7.1. This scheme is useful as it offers a more nuanced, wider vocabulary and descriptive framework for EFSs.

A developmental perspective on executive functioning skills

Most developmental EFS research has focused on children with neuro-developmental impairment, such as children diagnosed with ADHD or autism spectrum disorder. Recently, however, EFSs have been increasingly recognised by researchers, clinicians and parents as a key aspect of all children's development, impacting on almost all aspects of functioning in school, at home and in the community. As noted earlier, functional and structural brain imaging studies support the claim that EFSs are a function of the prefrontal cortex (PFC). The PFC has a protracted developmental trajectory, continuing to develop into early adulthood (Hughes, 2011); thus, EFSs also follow a staged development, with more complex executive functioning tasks, such as problem solving, reaching maturity in late adolescence or early adulthood (e.g. Romine and Reynolds, 2005). Although the fundamentals of EFSs are likely to emerge in the first year of life (Johnson and de Haan, 2015), rapid improvements occur during preschool and early school years (Carlson and Moses, 2001; Zelazo, Craik and Booth, 2004), a period when the PFC undergoes significant development as the result of synaptic pruning and myelination. There is then a second period of enhanced PFC development during the adolescent years (Blakemore, 2012). The principles of developmental plasticity support the idea that the areas of the brain in flux are most susceptible to the environment during which time experience is most influential (Fox et al., 2010). This has led to the now-well-accepted theory that adolescence is a critical period for the development of EFSs (Blakemore and Choudhury, 2006).

Table 7.1 Executive function skills.

Skill	Definition
Response inhibition	The capacity to think before you act; this ability to resist the urge to say or do something allows your child the time to evaluate a situation and how his or her behaviour might impact it.
Working memory	The ability to hold information in memory while performing complex tasks. It incorporates the ability to draw on past learning or experience to apply to the situation at hand or to project into the future.
Emotional control	The ability to manage emotions to achieve goals, complete tasks or control and direct behaviour.
Sustained attention	The capacity to keep paying attention to a situation or task despite distractibility, fatigue or boredom.
Task initiation	The ability to begin projects without undue procrastination in an efficient or timely fashion.
Planning and prioritisation	The ability to create a roadmap to reach a goal or to complete a task. It also involves being able to make decisions about what's important to focus on and what's not important.
Organisation	The ability to create and maintain systems to keep track of information or materials.
Time management	The capacity to estimate how much time one has, how to allocate it and how to stay within time limits and deadlines. It also involves a sense that time is important.
Goal-directed persistence	The capacity to have a goal, follow through to the completion of the goal and not be put off by or distracted by competing interests.
Flexibility	The ability to revise plans in the face of obstacles, setbacks, new information or mistakes. It relates to an adaptability to changing conditions.
Metacognition	The ability to stand back and take a bird's-eye view of yourself in a situation to observe how you problem solve. It also includes self-monitoring and self-evaluative skills (e.g. asking yourself, 'How am I doing?' or 'How did I do?').

Source: The scheme and definitions in this table are taken from Dawson and Guare (2008). Reprinted with permission of Guilford Press.

As with most cognitive skills, EFSs show strong heritability. Indeed, behavioural genetics studies suggest that they are some of the most heritable cognitive skills whose genetic effects are independent of general intelligence and perceptual speed (Friedman et al., 2008). It has long been recognised that environmental conditions in the prenatal and early-childhood periods are instrumental in the development of EFSs. For example, adversity such as poverty, domestic violence, neglect, childhood abuse and substance abuse in utero appear to negatively impact the development of EFSs (Blair et al., 2008).

Are executive functioning skills trainable?

As our knowledge of neuroscience increases, particularly our understanding of 'neuroplasticity' in the brain, the possibility of counteracting or even reversing early EFS vulnerability is compelling. Could we intervene during the enhanced windows of development during the preschool and teenage years? Evidence of the 'trainability' of these skills, however, remains muddy. Early reports of the effectiveness of computerised training such as CogMed to strengthen working memory were promising and quickly became popular. Questions about the generalisability of the positive effects of such training have, however, arisen (Diamond and Ling, 2016; Shipstead et al., 2012). For example, while a child may improve at the working memory demands of a computerised training task, these improvements may not be observed in their everyday performance, such as in a math lesson. Learning to play a video simulation more effectively is not the goal. There is no easy solution.

'Add-on' classroom curriculums such as Promoting Alternative Thinking Strategies (PATHS) which emphasize self-control, managing feelings and interpersonal problem solving have been shown to improve inhibitory control and cognitive flexibility (Riggs et al., 2006). These require teachers to order special materials, receive special training and designate blocks of time. Thankfully, experts agree that a surprisingly diverse array of more *everyday* activities can improve children's EFSs (Diamond and Lee, 2011). For example, steadily increasing challenge in a structured, stimulating, social and happy environment such a well-run classroom or a sports or activity program supports the development of EFSs (Diamond, 2014). This message is validating for teachers because so many of their daily efforts revolve around these goals. In familial contexts, the mechanisms that support the growth of EFSs include scaffolded problem solving; modelled, mindful verbal reflection on thinking; and a sensitive engagement style that permits children to have a sense of agency and impact (Carlson, 2003). As with so many enriching childhood experiences, these lessons, special activities, high-functioning classrooms and calm parenting are either costly in terms of time and money or require considerable emotional demands on adults.

It is worth considering in which socio-economic contexts and geographical regions these crucial resources may be more or less available. Our mandate regarding EFSs therefore should be the same as for any disability or learning challenge. We must continue to work towards positive, structured, stimulating and supportive classrooms and family experiences, but we must also invest in approaches that build student self-advocacy and the ability to work around limitations.

A self-regulating 21st-century workforce

As technology advances, the economy transforms and communication media draw us closer together in time and space, the way we raise and educate young people must change, too. With technology serving up information faster than we can process it, schools must focus not only on the delivery of information but also on its *handling*. Accordingly, higher-order critical thinking, problem solving, communication and collaboration have gone from being enrichment activities for especially capable students to being basic life skills required by everyone (Framework for 21st-Century Learning; Bellanca, 2017). From a pedagogical perspective, these skills are associated with 'self-regulated learning' (SRL), an approach to learning in which students are active agents who tackle novel challenges by first planning and strategising, then performing planned approaches and finally reflecting on their success (Pintrich, 2000; Winne, 2010; Zimmerman, 2001).

This process relies heavily on EFSs. For example, metacognition is used to perceive challenges; planning and prioritising are used to develop plans and create strategies; task initiation, response inhibition, time management and goal-directed persistence are used to perform plans and strategies; and flexibility and metacognition are used to evaluate and adapt strategies on final reflection. In many ways, EFSs are the raw materials for self-regulated learning.

Much is known about the centrality of SRL to success at school and in life. SRL is demonstrated by the highest-achieving students (Nota et al., 2004; Pintrich, 2000; Purdie and Hattie, 1996; Schraw et al., 2006; Zimmerman, 2008; Zimmerman and Martinez-Pons, 1986, 1998), and metacognitive skilfulness is not only the most important predictor of learning performance in school but is also a necessary skill for managing the non-routine challenges of a rapidly changing world (Veenman, 2008; Wang et al., 1990). The connection between SRL and academic success holds up across a broad demographic spectrum, benefitting both the speakers of non-native languages and those with socio-economic vulnerability (McClelland and Wanless, 2012). Because EFSs comprise the raw materials of strategic and self-regulated work, we have a strong social and economic argument for gearing public education towards their optimisation.

Building EFSs at home, school and with a coach

We have collaborated with teachers, parents and coaches across North America and the United Kingdom to understand the most feasible way to deliver EFS and SRL support to children and young people. The solutions we have developed can be applied in schools, at home and with a one-on-one coach and have several higher- and lower-intensity options for different contexts. This range of approaches is grounded, to greater and lesser extents, in three key components, which are displayed in Figure 7.1: using EFS literacy to reframe challenges, an intentionally applied self-regulated learning protocol and process-oriented feedback (Faith, 2018). We will briefly explain each of these components and then explain the way they may work at home, at school and in a one-on-one coaching relationship.

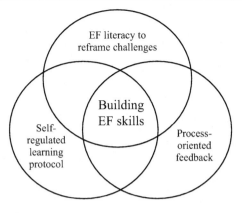

Figure 7.1 Building executive functioning skills.

Using executive functioning literacy to reframe challenges

All children struggle from time to time. When they believe that their challenges are caused by fixed factors that cannot be controlled (Baird et al., 2009; Majorano et al., 2017), they may feel discouraged, experience low academic self-efficacy and self-esteem and adopt maladaptive self-regulatory patterns such as avoidance and distraction (Elliott and Dweck, 1988). This phenomenon has been referred to as a 'fixed mindset' (Dweck, 2006, 11) and occurs, for example, when children assume that they cannot solve a math problem because they are not clever enough. We believe that this pattern can be disrupted in two ways: by helping students to see that many of their challenges are due to very actionable and common obstacles and by training them to look for and act on sources of control.

We believe in re-characterising learning challenges. By increasing a child's or young adult's awareness of EFSs and embedding a shared lexicon of EFSs, teachers, parents and coaches can discuss challenges clearly and precisely. Based on this shared knowledge, adults and children have the opportunity to perceive different reasons for their challenges. For example, we may reassure them as follows: 'This challenge is tricky. Your obstacle may simply be organisation or attention to detail'. Or they may reflect: 'I was not successful because I didn't ask for clearer instructions, not because I'm not clever'. Teachers and adults can normalise everyday difficulties further by modelling this reframing in their own self-assessment. For example, a teacher might say, 'This card game is hard for me. It's that old response inhibition' or 'I had a terrible night's sleep, and my working memory is struggling. Can you repeat what you just said? I missed the last half'. Learning challenges that are connected to lagging EFSs seem less mysterious and insurmountable and more like something we can use strategy to tame.

This process of finding control relates to a powerful motivational intervention: 'attributional retraining' (AR). AR works by changing one's ideas about the potential causes for failure to factors that can be controlled. In studies spanning elementary, secondary, special education and college-age students, shifting the locus of cause for difficulty at school away from innate, internal and fixed factors such as character or intelligence consistently boosts performance (Andrews and Debus, 1978; Chapin and Dyck, 1976; Dweck, 1975). These findings are most pronounced for students with performance worries (Van Overwalle and de Metsenaere, 1990; Wilson and Linville, 1985) and poor past performance (Menec et al., 1994; Perry et al., 2010). Weiner's (1985, 1995, 2006) theory of attribution laid the groundwork for several randomised field and laboratory studies showing that correcting students' attributional schema changes their expectation of success, reduces debilitating emotions such as shame and hopelessness, increases positive emotions such as hope and pride and thus makes possible a strategic approach to overcome obstacles (Hall et al., 2004, 2007; Haynes et al., 2006; Menec et al., 1994).

Using a knowledge of EFSs, students can respond to challenges that seem fixed with a greater sense of power and control. Thus, even a challenge associated with a learning disability, for example, can be re-attributed to also being a challenge of goal-directed persistence (for which a student needs to advocate for access to technology), organisation (for which a student needs to keep personal copies of anchor charts and other visual supports) or difficulties with emotional control (for which a student needs to stay calm in the face of frustration). In this way, any student can find ways to be adaptive and get in the habit of moving obstacles from the 'impossible' pile to the 'I can control this' pile. They may discover that in addition to having a challenging learning disability, they are also extraordinarily organized and persistent; EFS literacy allows learners to identify EFS strengths that can be harnessed for academic success.

Using an intentionally applied self-regulated learning protocol: barriers and strategies protocol

Humans are subject to a number of mental shortcuts, thinking errors and biases that cause us to jump to conclusions and misdiagnose challenges (Katz and Dack, 2013). In a year 4 mathematics class in a UK school, for example, where the pupils are typically 8–9 years of age, we may quickly assume that a struggling student needs to practice times tables. Or we may happen upon a group of disagreeing year 8 students, where the pupils are typically 12–13 years of age, and immediately recommend that they all take three deep breaths. We may not only have been wrong in both cases, but our suggestions may also have been directly counterproductive. Perhaps the student struggling with mathematics simply didn't know how to begin. Or what if the year 8s were actually desperate for another five minutes to finish their discussion? In both cases, the children may have retreated, rolled their eyes, huffed and puffed or otherwise expressed frustration with our misdiagnosis and subsequent intervention. Sound familiar? It happens all the time. A protocol, by contrast, forces us to suspend our snap judgements in favour of a disciplined and rational set of procedures.

Our protocol is based on a well-researched goal-striving approach called 'mental contrasting with implementation intentions' (MCII). Within MCII, users are prompted to vividly imagine, first, the positive outcome associated with what they would like to achieve. Then they are asked to consider what exactly might stand in the way of that goal and what specific strategies they might use to be successful. This type of premeditation is often referred to as 'if-then planning', where individuals deliberately connect a challenging contingency to the response they will use. Its chief mechanism is the use of a mental contrast, through which one's goals are considered opposite one's specific obstacles. Creating mental contrast, when accompanied by the formation of an if-then plan, has been shown to boost success in goal achievement by helping individuals to act more quickly (Gollwitzer and Brandstatter, 1997), deal more effectively with cognitive demands and execute planned strategies with less effort (Brandstatter et al., 2001).

We have worked with teachers, teacher's assistants, psychologists, coaches and parents to develop and fine-tune the 'barriers and strategies protocol' (BSP). In a myriad of contexts – individually, small group or whole class – it forces adults out of their routine responses with children for long enough to slow down, see things that are otherwise missed and discover the most productive ways forward. It is very simple: when students struggle, instead of swooping in to misdiagnose and improperly intervene, it asks an adult facilitator to open a discussion about the specific obstacles faced and then co-create strategies to be successful. In an EFS-literate context, students may refer to EFSs by name, though this is not necessary. This process is designed to be quick and snappy; it can occur at any time of the day, as often as it is needed. The following is an example of how a simple BSP might sound:

FACILITATOR: You seem to be having difficulty with these math problems. What are your obstacles? What is difficult about this task?

PARTICPANT(S): Rushing and forgetting to do certain steps.

FACILITATOR: Rushing. I'm writing that down. What else?

PARTICPANT(S): It is hard because the numbers get all jumbled up.

FACILITATOR: Getting all disorganised. I'm writing that down. Anything else?

(Further discussion during which facilitator elicits other obstacle ideas and jots them on a T-chart with 'Barriers' on one side and 'Strategies' on the other.)

FACILITATOR: What strategies can we use to overcome these obstacles?

(Discussion, during which facilitator charts a variety of strategy ideas for the student/s.)

FACILITATOR: You have suggested several strategies that might work. I am very interested to see which strategy you choose and use.

Process-oriented feedback

Having been empowered in both the diagnosis of challenge and the prescription of solution, students are then encouraged to 'choose and use' a strategy they think will be most suitable for them. The facilitator's role as provider of feedback is therefore quite straightforward: to emphasise, with feedback, the types of strategies that were previously discussed. They may say, 'Tell me how your strategies are working' or 'I see you've circled the key words' or 'You talked about making a list before starting the problem; I don't see that happening yet' or even 'I see someone using a strategy that we didn't even talk about; drawing the problem before you start will probably help a lot!'. This approach emphasises student competence and autonomy. These are key determinants of student motivation and engagement (Andrade, 2010; Black and Wiliam, 2009; Deci and Ryan, 2000; Mouratidis et al., 2010; Reeve, 1998; Reeve et al., 1999; Zimmerman and Martinez-Pons, 1986) which are known to predict academic engagement and success (Benware and Deci, 1984; Grolnick and Ryan, 1987; Hofferber et al., 2014; Miserando, 1996; Zimmerman and Martinez-Pons, 1986).

Providing process-oriented feedback corrects an environment of feedback that may otherwise be rather confusing and unhelpful. Accepting feedback graciously is hard for anyone, but children often receive it with a foggy sense of what was expected in the first place from an adult who may not understand their perspective, equipped with only emerging emotional regulation. Sometimes this stressful event takes place in front of peers. Qualitative studies show that in classrooms, feedback tends to follow patterns of rewarding or punishing, approving or disapproving and providing specific academic or creative help (Tunstall and Gipps, 1996). So, in addition to the discomfort related to timing, context and intent of feedback, the content of it often communicates a loss of confidence, conveys displeasure, appropriates student thinking or repeats ineffective teaching. Our approach makes feedback and assessment more fair, transparent and useful and reduces teacher intrusion on the creative and intellectual aspects of student work.

Education

Although it may have been simpler to design a series of free-standing lessons on self-regulated learning, we knew better. The best approach to building non-cognitive skills is to integrate them into meaningful daily activities (Diamond and Lee, 2011; Farrington et al., 2012). Our approach, therefore, was designed and redesigned to be straightforward and efficient enough to navigate the implementation gap and thrive within the daily pedagogy of real classrooms. This was an uphill battle. Research suggests that despite the existence of hundreds of interventions that aim to foster more strategic and capable learning (Boer et al., 2013), a cohesive impact on classroom practice has yet to be observed (Dignath-van Ewijk et al., 2013; Kistner et al., 2010; Spruce and Bol, 2015). Even the most-well-trained teachers do not engage students in formal SRL as often as they say they would like to (Spruce and Bol, 2015). Many teachers feel that it requires constant individual attention, competes with curricular demands and requires an unattainable number of strategy ideas (Winne, 2010).

Researchers studying the effectiveness of SRL often conduct their studies in highly controlled environments. It is no surprise, therefore, that their results far exceed what has been achieved by real teachers who are juggling many more demands and priorities in their typical classrooms (Dignath et al., 2008; Hattie et al., 1996). The small amount of SRL-type teaching that has been observed is often delivered implicitly rather than explicitly (Kistner et al., 2010), meaning that students will have a chance to watch a teacher model a strategy or receive instructions to use a strategy but are not being prepared to evaluate challenges, plan strategies and monitor success for themselves. In creating our approach, we were aiming for a self-regulated learning practice that could survive in a real classroom (Quigley et al., 2018).

Sending an approach into a classroom is like shooting it into space. You can never quite anticipate how it will interact with the environment, and there is always a chance that it will disintegrate on contact. Over the years, the teaching communities we have worked with have pioneered our approach under a variety of names: EFs2theRescue Pedagogy, Executive Skills Feedback and Assessment, #EF4ALL, and finally, Activated Learning (AL). Indeed, the context of each of these communities was rich with unique features, both positive and negative, that shaped the nature of the classroom approach. On the one hand, classrooms possess rich social networks that can be leveraged and enjoyed. This allowed us to communalise our approach so that a single teacher could facilitate it among his or her entire class at one time. On the other hand, classrooms suffer from a relentless shortfall of time and resources, which forced us to figure out the smallest possible version of the approach that would still work. For example, we have found that in some cases it can prove challenging for teachers to establish EFS literacy. Regardless, most could apply the BSP and orient their feedback more toward process, and these seem to be the most essential factors.

AL is similar to other interventions that call for the direct teaching of learning strategies, such as facilitated planning (Naglieri and Pickering, 2003) or Lynn Meltzer's 'Drive to Thrive' (Meltzer, 2010), but AL is unique because of its timing, key teaching mechanism, themes of instruction, context and follow-up. It is a viable, teacher-friendly pedagogy that aims to optimise the performance of every student and make it possible to deliver a challenging 21st-century curriculum (see Table 7.2).

In classrooms, AL aims to intervene on a downward spiral of teacher-student interaction that is often initiated by students' weak EFSs. When teachers become overwhelmed by off-task, inattentive or disruptive student behaviour, they often fall into 'cascades' of over-simplification in which best practices are abandoned and replaced with safer lessons that are more didactic and controlled (Klusmann et al., 2008; Muller et al., 2011; Yong and Yue, 2007). As the classroom becomes more deprived of work that is creative, engaging and meaningful, students respond poorly, and the phenomenon intensifies (Blase, 1986). With increasing intensity, these students demonstrate poor EFSs, which are overwhelming for classroom teachers and hard to relate to and work with. Their maladaptive

Table 7.2 Features of AL.

Time commitment	Trigger: Teacher recognises that the class is having difficulty, is stuck or otherwise needs a lot of help to progress. Duration: Five to ten minutes. Frequency: One to three times per day, as needed.
Central teaching mechanism	Whole-class discussion in which teacher charts students' ideas about specific obstacles to performance and strategies to overcome those obstacles (BSP).
Themes of instruction	Self-knowledge, self-acceptance and other acceptance, self-compassion and other compassion, a strategising stance, teamwork and a growth mindset. Discovering the factors that can be controlled.
Follow-up	Students are encouraged to 'choose and use' suitable strategies. Teacher does 'notice and name', providing ongoing descriptive feedback on student choice of and use of strategy. Teacher conducts ongoing assessment of student use of strategy.

behaviours are often mistaken for symptoms of poor character (Gaier, 2015), and they often seem intentional (Elik et al., 2010). A paradox familiar to any teacher is the student who seems to put in very little effort and tolerate novel tasks poorly but who complains of boredom and acts out. AL offers an alternate response.

In addition to the benefits associated with a more feasible classroom practice, the benefits of communalising SRL are considerable. Conducting the BSP in a social context stimulates a sense of relatedness and a belonging that are associated with motivation (Deci and Ryan, 2000). As students discuss barriers and strategies, they gain substantive insight into their differences and similarities. We often hear students say, 'I do that too!' or 'I'm going to try X's strategy' or 'I thought I was the only one'. The communalisation of self-regulated learning advances a classroom culture in which, for any given learning task, there is no one specific challenge and no one correct approach. This emphasis on diversity 'creates spaces for multiple zones of proximal development' (Perry et al., 2017, 372), even within classrooms with kaleidoscopically varied abilities, experiences, backgrounds and cultures. Thus, when a learning challenge arises, the processes of both diagnosis and prescription are no longer tethered to the limited experience of one teacher. Rather, within an open large-group conversation, students are free to declare learning statuses that may occupy intersectional coordinates so remote from that of the teacher that they would never have been suspected. This process allows students, in their fullness, to feel a sense of belonging in a classroom alongside classmates and teachers to whom they feel connected. This full articulation of myself and yourself, in a context in which a safe and productive interaction has been facilitated, is a recipe for connectedness and a sense of belonging.

In the home

Parents who care about their children's learning and are keen to do the right thing to support the development of positive skills and good habits are vital partners in the education of young people. We have quickly understood the potential power of our approach for strengthening EFSs if embedded in a child's life at home as well as at school. Self-understanding, self-compassion, explicit problem solving and planning and monitoring for success can then become part of a child's everyday life. Moreover, EFSs are essential to take part in family life (e.g. sitting at the dinner table or following instructions from parents), including fulfilling daily routines (e.g. getting ready in the morning). Failure to engage in executive functioning effectively is often the underlying cause of tensions and stresses that can erode positive parent-child relationships over time.

Metacognition and reframing behaviour in the home

Step one is re-characterising behaviour by increasing awareness of EFSs (both parent and child awareness) and embedding a shared lexicon for these skills at home. We encourage parents to tap into their child's creativity to label and characterise these skills and to begin to notice when they have and have not been activated at home. Additionally, we encourage parents to focus on their child's emotional experiences and actively extend their child's emotional lexicon to recognise a broader range of emotions, modelling acceptance of all. Evidence from neuroscience suggests that just naming emotions reduces their potency at the brain level (Torre and Lieberman, 2018), and when young people are shown what underlies their behaviour, they can begin to have a mastery of it.

Part of this approach is to give parents (and children) a new lens for seeing behaviour. The 'iceberg model' of behaviour can be used for both emotions and EFSs, where the behavioural manifestations are merely the tip of the iceberg (French and Bell, 1979; Selfridge and Sokolik, 1975). The rich information about the meaning and cause of the behaviour is below the surface and cannot be seen. For example, a child forgetting that he or she had homework to do until 10 p.m. is seen as a planning issue, or a boy who hits his sister when she gets a treat is seen as having an emotional issue (jealousy) as well as having poor EFSs (response inhibition). The aim is for the parent and child to identify the emotions or EFSs that are lacking, and once those needs are seen to and the skills are strengthened, the behaviour can be adapted.

Developing empathy in the parents is key here, helping parents to 'get in the pit' with their child when things go wrong and see difficulties from the child's perspective (Brown, 2013). While poor behaviour is never accepted and boundaries are very clearly delineated, understanding the behaviour becomes the first task. Once the underlying emotional driver of the behaviour and/or EFS weakness is identified, strategies can be put in place to manage those issues. Everyday challenges or transgressions become an opportunity for deeper understanding and problem solving. This is far more effective and instructive for long-term success at managing the stresses of everyday life. In the moment, parents, of course, need to take charge and get things done, but later there is time for discussion and creative problem solving to do things differently next time.

Everyday routines and difficult moments at home

As we learn more about neuroplasticity, we realise that day-to-day experiences are the driving forces behind learning (on neuroplasticity; see de Graaf-Petera and Hadders-Algra, 2006). Experiences build brain circuits so that whatever we spend our time doing becomes embedded in the brain. Research in the area of mindset shows that changing parental beliefs about how children learn can change their language and behaviour around their child's learning (Moorman and Pomerantz, 2010). Similarly, we believe that teaching parents how important 'doing' is to building brains will help them to see the importance of embedding good EFS habits at home. Tasks such as laying the table, working out the route and timing to the airport, baking a cake and tidying the bedroom may seem trivial feats to master, but the benefits to the development of EFSs are enormous. In this way, EFSs are built and developed every day by doing simple tasks and chores.

Our approach is also applied to solve the most challenging aspects of family life. Most parents are able to identify repeated times during the day or week when things just do not go to plan and someone has an emotional meltdown (parent and/or child). These instances cause daily stress and ultimately can erode positive relationships and reduce a parent's ability to be responsive and warm, which we know to be care-giving qualities that are fundamental to emotional well-being in children (Sroufe, 1995). This is where the EFS protocol comes into play, in a similar manner to the self-regulated learning approach reviewed earlier. Always at a time when the young person is in his or her 'rational brain' and never when someone has 'lost it' or are highly emotional, parents are encouraged to discuss these moments of difficulty and set a goal to change things. After discussing the benefits of a different outcome (e.g. 'Wouldn't it be great to have extra time to play when your homework is done?'), the mental contrasting technique is used to identify obstacles that might get in the way of success (e.g. 'You might feel hungry and irritable straight after school'). Young people are encouraged to try problem-solving strategies next time for greater success (e.g. 'How about I make a clear plan at the beginning of the evening after a snack?').

We encourage parents to identify a specific time each day to talk through goals, obstacles and strategies, reviewing and reflecting on how things went and making new plans for next time if needed. The key to success is for parents to fine-tune their communication skills so that these sessions are non-blaming and non-judgemental. Some of the skills used in the coaching model are needed, such as listening with curiosity, validating and reflecting back. Open-ended questions are key to ensure that the young person, rather than the parent, comes up with the plan, giving the young person autonomy and ownership. In this way, EFSs are strengthening just when the brain circuits are ripe and ready for development.

We encourage parents to also identify their own EFS strengths and weaknesses (we all have them) and identify their own goals to work on alongside their child. There are many benefits to this. Along with normalising difficulties, it is humbling for adults to realise their own struggles. More importantly, modelling is the most powerful form of behaviour (Bandura, 1976), and the sharing of difficulties builds strength in relationships.

Developmental considerations at home

It is never too young to start embedding EFS-strengthening rituals in home life, but the parental role will change. Younger children need a lot more support and scaffolding, and the approach to training EFSs needs to be engaging and fun, as well as applied to everyday life (e.g. packing a school bag). There is no doubt that habits that are established early on can set a child up for life. At the same time, we know that the connections from the prefrontal cortex that houses EFSs are naturally strengthening in the teenage brain (Blakemore, 2012), and one of the developmental tasks of the teenage years is to gain independence from parents and adults (Hohnen et al., 2019). As children grow, parental communication and intervention need to change. Telling teens what to do without listening and respecting their opinions is known to be far less effective for behaviour change (Yeager et al., 2018) because of the inherent teen drive for autonomy and independence.

Coaching

We believe that our approach, which consists of the three areas outlined earlier – using executive functioning literacy to reframe challenges, a self-regulated learning protocol and process-oriented feedback – can support all young people to strengthen their EFSs. Our ideal is that this is executed in universally designed mainstream learning spaces and reinforced at home. However, not all children's brains develop evenly, and for some young people, executive function challenges hamper academic progress, well-being and mental health to such a degree that additional support and reinforcement are needed. Just as with other types of individual difference, such as dyslexia, a targeted and initially intensive intervention may be required to strengthen EFSs for some young people.

Historically, when trying to impart a skill that has not been consolidated in mainstream education, schools and parents turn to one-on-one teaching or tutoring. One might assume that the same would be true of developing EFSs;

however, the teaching of EFSs is not the most effective method of improving executive functions in a one-on-one setting (Dawson and Guare, 2012).

Drawing on our professional experience, we have found that an executive function coaching approach that centres around the same tripartite framework of using executive functioning literacy to reframe challenges, a self-regulated learning protocol and process-oriented feedback is the optimal one-on-one approach. Indeed, research in the field of ADHD coaching that focuses on supporting people to strengthen the weak EFSs supports our professional findings (Field et al., 2013; Parker et al., 2009; Prevatt and Yelland, 2015; Richman et al., 2014; Swartz et al., 2005; Zwart and Kallemeyn, 2001). Two American educational psychologists, Peg Dawson and Richard Guare, have written extensively on the application of coaching to support students to develop EFSs (Dawson and Guare, 2012). The next section describes some of the ways a coaching approach supports young people to develop EFSs and what the advantages are to a more didactic teaching approach.

Metacognition in a coaching relationship

Coaching involves using open-ended questioning techniques and active listening to help a person to set goals and identify actions and solutions they need to take to reach their potential. Unlike many teaching or therapeutic approaches, the coach is not the expert; instead, the relationship between the coach and the client is a partnership, and the coach supports the client to find his or her own solutions that maximise his or her potential (The Coaching and Mentoring Network, 2019). EFS and ADHD coaching also incorporate psycho-educational techniques where the coach shares information with the client about executive functioning in order to help the client to better understand his or her challenges (Field et al., 2013; Merriman and Codding, 2008; Parker and Boutelle, 2009; Prevatt and Yelland, 2015; Richman et al., 2014; Swartz et al., 2005; Zwart and Kallemeyn, 2001).

Unlike traditional coaching, executive function coaches do not completely veer away from advice or instruction. Rather, the coach will only offer advice on strategies after a young person is EFS literate and has been encouraged to set his or her own goals and to reflect on how he or she could overcome EFS barriers. For example, while working with a client who has identified time management as an issue, a coach may help him or her explore how he or she can manage his or her time better, but the coach will only step in and offer specific resources and strategies after first gently encouraging the client to come up with his or her own strategies. This scaffolded approach to guiding reflection and goal setting is particularly important for young people who struggle with executive function challenges and who often have difficulties with metacognition. Their EFS challenges mean that they find it difficult to see how their current habits are impacting their lives and those of people around them (Fernandez-Duquea et al., 2000). They can therefore benefit from a skilled adult who can help them to self-reflect and work towards realistic goals (Zimmerman, 2001). By patiently asking open-ended questions, coaches support clients to develop their meta-cognitive skills.

When supporting a student with weak metacognition, it is tempting to jump in with ready-made solutions and strategies. Slowly questioning and coaching seems to take forever. As efficient as a more heavy-handed approach would seem, consider the ways in which it is short-sighted. In fact, young people who struggle with metacognition need even more support to develop and practice their metacognitive skills. In the absence of a professional, they will struggle to become independent learners who can generate their own strategies in the face of everyday executive function obstacles. This is corroborated by studies showing that more didactic models for teaching strategies are less effective at changing student performance in the context of real life (Byron and Parker, 2002; Wedlake, 2002).

Motivation and self-efficacy in a coaching relationship

A patient and open-minded executive function coach, when working with a willing young person, can discover and affirm a wide variety of personal strategies for success. In this way, coaches work with clients to unveil previously hidden sources of skill and ability, thus boosting the self-determination and self-efficacy that underlie motivation (Getzel and Thoma, 2006). Indeed, motivation is key if the child or young adult being coached is to effectively change his or her habits, reach goals and strengthen EFSs (Prochaska and Velicer, 1997; Wolters, 2003). Studies also show that the application of EFSs is context dependent and that students are better able to use their executive functions if they are interested in the activity or the outcome (Barkley, 1997). Therefore, the level of personal relevance and agency experienced by child or young person being coached cannot be ignored. They are key factors in the success of coaching.

Goal setting in a coaching relationship

Since motivation is critical to the development of EFSs, collaborative work with a young person to set meaningful goals can be very effective. Studies have repeatedly shown that setting realistic goals to work towards improves motivation and increases successful outcomes (Locke and Latham, 2002). However, when young people are asked to work towards goals set by someone else, they are less likely to make progress, even if the person setting the goals is a person they trust and respect (Schunk, 2003).

Personally meaningful goals that are set within a coaching relationship can be particularly effective. When goals are set and verbalised to another party, their impact on outcomes is significantly improved (Paniauga, 1992). This technique is dubbed 'correspondence training', and in 2004, a literature review of thirty-three empirical studies with younger children and adolescents with disabilities surmised that the evidence supporting this technique was promising and recommended further research (Bevill-Davis et al., 2004). After helping young people to set meaningful goals, they can use a BSP to anticipate obstacles and create feasible strategies for success.

Habit setting in a coaching relationship

Goal setting and use of the BSP are not enough. Young people with EFS challenges often struggle with sustained attention and goal-directed persistence. Left to their own devices, the young people we encounter often lose focus, get disheartened and disengage as soon as they meet an unexpected obstacle. Therefore, after setting goals and creating strategy plans, it is important that coaches follow up regularly to ensure that their clients are on track. While it may only take a few minutes to check in, this support may provide just the troubleshooting and encouragement required for success. Failing to provide this ongoing support, by contrast, may leave coaches in the much less advantageous position of trying to reengage a young person who feels ashamed and discouraged after having dropped the ball and broken your verbal contract (Dawson and Guare, 2012).

Coaching also offers an opportunity for young people to practice EFSs in authentic daily contexts. This is important because the transfer effects of non-context-specific executive function training are narrow (Cortese et al., 2015; Diamond and Ling, 2016). The connection is simple: if we want children and young adults to independently apply new EFSs in the context of their own learning and studying, they need to practise applying new EFSs in the context of their own learning and studying (Field et al., 2013; Merriman and Codding, 2008; Parker and Boutelle, 2009; Prevatt and Yelland, 2015; Richman et al., 2014; Zwart and Kallemeyn, 2001).

Putting it all together: school, home, and coaching

It is no surprise that limitations in EFSs often remain and that the children we work with often navigate school and life challenges with different levels of success. Consider, for example, Joe, Ami, Tao and Dev (Figure 7.2). This group of typical year 4 children is just the kind you would likely meet as you walk down the corridor of a school. As they stand in line at the water fountain, each one has different memories about home and school experiences, they will act out different emotions and can anticipate very different report cards at the end of term. The amount of shading in the figure of each student represents the degree to which each of them either meets or fails to meet the EFS demands of his or her life and education. There are differences in EFS capacity among children, and some are not equipped to meet the goals that have been set for them.

The ability of each of these children to meet the EFS demands of his or her environment is based on the support and enrichment each receives at home, in

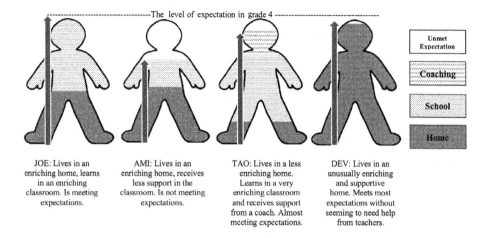

Figure 7.2 How children in the same grade meet expectations differently based on the different sources of executive functioning support and enrichment they receive.

school and in coaching relationships. While Joe receives adequate support between both school and home to manage the executive function demands of his year 4 classroom, you can see that Ami, while coming from a similarly nurturing home, is not receiving quite enough support at school to meet expectations. Tao, by contrast, represents a child who, despite receiving considerably less support at home, can almost meet the expectations of his year group because of extra classroom support and the help of a one-on-one coach. And don't we all know a student like Dev, whose home is so enriching and nurturing that he seems to sail through school with ease? The next time you walk by a group of children in your school hallway, perhaps you will regard them as if looking through an EFS lens. From this perspective, we can appreciate the many ways that a child's performance is dictated by his or her EFSs but also the many opportunities that exist at home, school and through coaching to provide essential support and guidance.

Conclusion

To conclude, we would like to remind you that when home, school and coaches work together, much can be done to support and develop EFSs in all children. While the efficacy of our approach in its entirety has yet to be firmly established, its potential benefits are alluring. As well as directly teaching strategic skills, it demystifies a child's experience, increases positive attributions and emotions and rehearses adaptive responses to challenge. Most importantly, it places struggling children and young adults into supportive relationships with parents, peers, teachers and coaches who will endorse their capability and appreciate their individuality. At the societal level, this approach has the potential to reduce disparity between groups in society and improve well-being for all. We hope our discussion has provided you with the key concepts, knowledge, skills and tangible resources you will need to colour the children you care for all the way up to the top. Working as a team, parents, educators and coaches can ensure that every child not only succeeds, but thrives.

References

Alvarez, J. A., and Emory, E. (2006). Executive function and the frontal lobes: a meta-analytic review. *Neuropsychology Review, 16*(1), 17–42.

Andrade, H. (2010). Students as the definitive source of formative assessment. In H. Andrade and G. Cizek (Eds.), *Handbook of Formative Assessment* (pp. 90–105). New York: Routledge.

Andrews, G. R., and Debus, R. L. (1978). Persistence and the causal perception of failure: modifying cognitive attributions. *Journal of Educational Psychology, 70,* 154–66.

Baird, G. L., Scott, W. D., Dearing, E., and Hamill, S. K. (2009). Cognitive self-regulation in youth with and without learning disabilities: academic self-efficacy, theories of intelligence, learning vs. performance goal preferences, and effort attributions. *Journal of Social and Clinical Psychology, 28,* 881–908.

Bandura, A. (1976). *Social Learning Theory.* London: Pearson.

Banich, M. (2004). *Cognitive Neuroscience and Neuropsychology* (2nd ed.). New York: Houghton Mifflin.

Bellanca, J. (2017). 21st-Century skills. In K. Peppler (Ed.), *The SAGE encyclopedia of out-of-school learning* (Vol. 1, pp. 793–8). Thousand Oaks, CA: SAGE Publications.

Barkley, R. (1997). *ADHD and the Nature of Self Control.* New York: Guildford Press.

Benware, C. A., and Deci, E. L. (1984). Quality of learning with an active versus passive motivational set. *American Educational Research Journal, 21,* 755–65.

Bevill-Davis, A., Clees, T. J., and Gast, D. L. (2004). Correspondence training: a review of the literature. *Journal of Early and Intensive Behavioural Intervention, 1,* 17–26.

Black, P., and Wiliam, D. (2009). Developing the theory of formative assessment educational assessment. *Evaluation and Accountability, 21*(1), 5–31.

Blakemore, S. J. (2012). Development of the social brain in adolescence. *Journal of the Royal Society of Medicine, 105*(3), 111–16.

Blakemore, S. J., and Choudhury, S. (2006). Development of the adolescent brain: implications for executive function and social cognition. *Journal of Child Psychology and Psychiatry 47*(3–4), 296–312.

Blair, C., and Razza, R. P. (2007). Relating effortful control, executive function, and false belief understanding to emerging math and literacy ability in kindergarten. *Child Development, 78*(2), 647–63. doi:10.1111/j.1467-8624.2007. 01019.x.

Blair, C., Granger, D. A., Kivlighan, K. T., et al.(2008). Maternal and child contributions to cortisol response to emotional arousal in young children from low-income, rural communities. *Developmental Psychology, 44,* 1095–109.

Blase, J. (1986). A qualitative analysis of sources of teacher stress: consequences for performance. *American Educational Research Journal, 23*(1), 13–40.

Boer, H., Donker-Bergstra, A., Kostons, D., et al. (2013). *Effective Strategies for Self-regulated Learning: A Meta-analysis.* Groningen, Netherlands: University of Groningen.

Brandstatter, V., Lengfelder, A., and Gollwitzer, P. (2001). Implementation intentions and efficient action initiation. *Journal of Personality and Social Psychology, 81,* 946–60.

Brown, B. (2013). *The Power of Vulnerability.* Royal Soceity of Arts, London. Available at https://youtu.be/sXSjc-pbXk4.

Byron, J., and Parker, D. R. (2002). College students with ADHD: new challenges and directions. In L. C. Brinckerhoff, J. M. McGuire, and S. F. Shaw (Eds.), *Postsecondary Education and Transition for Students with Learning Disabilities* (2nd ed., pp. 335–87). Austin, TX: PRO-ED.

Carlson, S. (2003). Executive function in context: development, measurement, theory, and experience. *Monographs of the Society for Research in Child Development, 68,* 138–51.

Carlson, S. M., and Moses, L. J. (2001). Individual differences in inhibitory control and children's theory of mind. *Child Development, 72,* 1032–53.

Chapin, M., and Dyck, D. (1976). Persistence in children's reading behavior as a function of n length and attributional retraining. *Journal of Abnormal Psychology, 85,* 511–15.

Collette, F., Hogge, M., Salmon, E., and Van der Linden, M. (2006). Exploration of the neural substrates of executive functioning by functional neuroimaging. *Neuroscience, 139,* 209–21. doi:10.1016/j.neuroscience.2005.05.035.

Cortese, S., Ferrin, M., Brandeis, D., et al. (2015). Cognitive training for attention-deficit/hyperactivity disorder: meta-analysis of clinical and neuropsychological outcomes from randomized controlled trials. *Journal of the American Academy of Child and Adolescent Psychiatry, 54*(3), 164–74. doi:10.1016/j. jaac.2014.12.010.

Daly, M., Delaney, L., Egan, M., and Baumeister, R. F. (2015). Childhood self-control and unemployment throughout the life span: evidence from two British cohort studies. *Psychological Science, 26*(6), 709–23. doi:10.1177/ 0956797615569001.

Dawson, P., and Guare, R. (2008). *Smart but Scattered.* New York: Guilford Press.

Dawson, P., and Guare, R. (2012). *Coaching Students with Executive Skills Deficits.* New York: Guilford Press.

Dawson, P., and Guare, R. (2018). *Executive Skills in Children and Adolescents: A Practical Guide to Assessment and Intervention* (3rd ed.). New York: Guilford Press.

Deci, E., and Ryan, R. (2000). The 'what' and 'why' of goal pursuits: human needs and self-determination of behavior. *Psychological Inquiry, 11*(4), 227–68.

de Graaf-Petera, V. B., and Hadders-Algra, M. (2006). Ontogeny of the human central nervous system: what is happening when? *Early Human Development, 82*(4), 257–66.

Denson, T. F., Pederson, W. C., Friese, M., et al. (2011). Understanding impulsive aggression: angry rumination and reduced self-control capacity are mechanisms underlying the provocation–aggression relationship. *Personality and Social Psychology Bulletin, 37,* 850–62.

Diamond, A. (2013). Executive functions. *Annual Review of Psychology, 64,* 135–68. doi:10.1146/annurev-psych-113011-143750.

Diamond, A. (2014). Want to optimize executive functions and academic outcomes? Simple, just nourish the human spirit. *Minnesota Symposia on Child Psychology, 37,* 205–32.

Diamond, A., and Lee, K. (2011). Interventions shown to aid executive function development in children 4 to 12 years old. *Science (New York), 333*(6045), 959–964. doi:10.1126/science.1204529

Diamond, A., and Ling, D. S. (2016). Conclusions about interventions, programs, and approaches for improving executive functions that appear justified and those that, despite much hype, do not. *Developmental Cognitive Neuroscience, 18,* 34–48.

Dignath, C., Buettner, G., and Langfeldt, H. (2008). How can primary school students learn self-regulated learning strategies most effectively? A meta-analysis on self-regulation training programmes. *Educational Research Review, 3*(2), 101–29.

Dignath-van Ewijk, C., Dickhäuser, O., and Büttner, G. (2013). Assessing how teachers enhance self-regulated learning: a multiperspective approach. *Journal of Cognitive Education and Psychology, 12,* 338–58.

Duckworth, A. L., and Seligman, M. E. P. (2005). Self-discipline outdoes IQ in predicting academic performance of adolescents. *Psychological Science, 16*(2), 939–44.

Dweck, C. (2006). *Mindset: The New Psychology of Success.* New York: Random House.

Dweck, C. S. (1975). The role of expectations and attributions in the alleviation of learned helplessness. *Journal of Personality and Social Psychology, 31,* 674–85.

Eakin, L., Minde, K., Hechtman, L., et al. (2004). The marital and family functioning of adults with ADHD and their spouses. *Journal of Attention Disorders, 8,* 1–10.

Elik, N., Wiener, J., and Corkum, P. (2010). Preservice teachers' open-minded thinking dispositions, readiness to learn, and attitudes towards learning and behavioral difficulties in students. *European Journal of Teacher Education, 33*(2), 127–46.

Elliott, E. S., and Dweck, C. S. (1988). Goals: an approach to motivation and achievement. *Journal of Personality and Social Psychology, 54*, 5–12.

Elliott, R. (2003). Executive functions and their disorders: imaging in clinical neuroscience. *British Medical Bulletin, 65*(1), 49–59.

Espy, K. A., McDiarmid, M. M., Cwik, M. F., et al. (2004). The contribution of executive functions to emergent mathematic skills in preschool children. *Developmental Neuropsychology, 26*(1), 465–86.

Faith, L. (2018). EFs 2the Rescue pedagogy. In P. Dawson and D. Guare (Eds.), *Executive Skills in Children and Adolescents* (3rd ed., Vol. 3, pp. 206–25). New York: Guilford Press.

Farrington, C., Roderick, M., Allensworth, E., et al. (2012). *Teaching Adolescents to Become Learners. The Role of Noncognitive Factors in Shaping School Performance: A Critical Literature Review.* Chicago: University of Chicago Consortium on Chicago School Research.

Fernandez-Duquea, D., Bairdb, J. A., and Posner, M. I. (2000). Executive attention and metacognitive regulation. *Consciousness and Cognition, 9*(2), 288–307.

Field, S., Parker, D. R., Sawilowsky, S., and Rolands, L. (2013). Assessing the impact of ADHD coaching services on university students' learning skills, self-regulation, and well-being. *Journal of Postsecondary Education and Disability, 26* (1), 67–81.

Fox, S. E., Levitt, P., and Nelson, C. A., 3rd. (2010). How the timing and quality of early experiences influence the development of brain architecture. *Child Development, 81*(1), 28–40.

French, W. L., and Bell, C. H. (1979). *Organization Development.* Englewood Cliffs, NJ: Prentice-Hall.

Friedman, N. P., Miyake, A., Young, S. E., et al. (2008). Individual differences in executive functions are almost entirely genetic in origin. *Journal of Experimental Psychology: General, 137*(2), 201–25. doi:10.1037/0096-3445.137.2.201.

Fryer, S. L., Tapert, S. F., Mattson, S. N., et al. (2007). Prenatal alcohol exposure affects frontal-striatal BOLD response during inhibitory control. *Alcoholism: Clinical and Experimental Research, 3*(18), 1415–24.

Gaier, S. (2015). Understanding why students do what they do: using attribution theory to help students succeed academically. *Research and Teaching in Developmental Education, 31*(2), 6–19.

Getzel, E., and Thoma, C. A. (2006). Voice of experience: what college students with learning disabilities and attention deficit/hyperactivity disorders tell us are important self-determination skills for success. *Learning Disabilities: A Multidisciplinary Journal, 14*(1), 33–40.

Gioia, G. A., and Isquith, P. K. (2004). Ecological assessment of executive function in traumatic brain injury. *Developmental Neuropsychology, 25*, 135–58.

Gollwitzer, P., and Brandstatter, V. (1997). Implementations and effective goal striving. *Journal of Personality and Social Psychology, 73*, 186–99.

Grolnick, W. S., and Ryan, R. M. (1987). Autonomy in children's learning: an experimental and individual difference investigation. *Journal of Personality and Social Psychology, 52*(5), 890–98.

Hall, N. C., Hladkyj, S., Perry, R. P., and Ruthig, J. C. (2004). The role of attributional retraining and elaborative learning in college students' academic development. *Journal of Social Psychology, 144*, 591–612.

Hall, N. C., Perry, R. P., Goetz, T., et al. (2007). Attributional retraining and elaborative learning: improving academic development through writing-based interventions. *Learning and Individual Differences, 17*, 280–90.

Hattie, J., Biggs, J., and Purdie, N. (1996). Effects of learning skills interventions on student learning: a meta-analysis. *Review of Educational Research, 66*(2), 99–136.

Haynes, T. L., Ruthig, J. C., Perry, R. P., et al. (2006). Reducing the academic risks of over-optimism: the longitudinal effects of attributional retraining on cognition and achievement. *Research in Higher Education, 47*, 755–79.

Hofferber, N., Eckes, A., and Wilde, M. (2014). Effects of autonomy supportive vs. controlling teachers' behaviour on students achievements. *European Journal of Educational Research, 3*(4), 177–84.

Hohnen, B., Gilmour, J., and Murphy, T. (2019). *The Incredible Teenage Brain: Everything You Need to Know to Unlock a Teenager's Potential*. London: JKP.

Hughes, C. (2011). Changes and challenges in 20 years of research into the development of executive functions. *Infant and Child Development, 20*(3), 251–71. doi:10.1002/icd.736.

Johnson, M. H., and de Haan, M. (2015) *Developmental Cognitive Neuroscience: An Introduction* (4th edition). Wiley-Blackwell.

Katz, S., and Dack, L. (2013). *Intentional Interruption: Breaking Down Learning Barriers to Transform Professional Practice*. Thousand Oaks, CA: Corwin Press.

Kistner, S., Rakoczy, K., Otto, B., et al. (2010). Promotion of self-regulated learning in classrooms: Investigating frequency, quality, and consequences for student performance. *Metacognition and Learning, 5*(2), 157–71. doi:10.1007/s11409-010-9055-3.

Klusmann, U., Kunter, M., Trautwein, U., et al. (2008). Teachers' occupational well-being and quality of instruction: the important role of self regulatory patterns. *Journal of Educational Psychology, 100*(3), 702–15.

Lezak, M. D., Howieson, D. B., and Loring, D. W. (2004). *Neuropsychological Assessment* (4th ed.). New York: Oxford University Press.

Locke, E. A., and Latham, G. P. (2002). Building a practically usefule theory of goal setting and task modification. *American Psychologist, 57*, 705–17.

Majorano, M., Brondino, M., Morelli, M., and Maes, M. (2017). Quality of relationship with parents and emotional autonomy as predictors of self concept and loneliness in adolescents with learning disabilities: the moderating role of the relationship with teachers. *Journal of Child and Family Studies, 26*, 690–700.

McClelland, M. M., and Wanless, S. B. (2012). Growing up with assets and risks: the importance of self-regulation for academic achievement. *Research in Human Development, 9*(4), 278–97.

Meltzer, L. (2010). *Promoting Executive Function in the Classroom*. New York: Guilford Press.

Menec, V. H., Perry, R. P., Struthers, C. W., et al. (1994). Assisting at-risk college students with attributional retraining and effective teaching. *Journal of Applied Social Psychology, 24*, 675–701.

Merriman, D. E., and Codding, R. S. (2008). The effects of coaching on mathematics homework completion and accuracy of high school students with attention-deficit/hyperactivity disorder. *Journal of Behavioral Education, 17*, 339–55.

Miserando, M. (1996). Children who do well in school: individual differences in perceived competence and autonomy in above-average children. *Journal of Educational Psychology, 88*, 203–14.

Mikaye, A., Friedman, N. P., Emerson, M. J., et al. (2000). The unity and diversity of executive functions and their contributions to complex "frontal lobe" tasks: a latent variable analysis. *Cognitive Psychology, 41*(1), 49–100.

Moorman, E. A., and Pomerantz, E. M. (2010). Ability mindsets influence the quality of mothers' involvement in children's learning: an experimental investigation. *Developmental Psychology, 46*(5), 1354–62.

Mouratidis, A., Lens, W., and Vansteenkiste, M. (2010). How you provide corrective feedback makes a difference: the motivating role of communicating in an autonomy-supporting way. *Journal of Sport and Exercise Psychology, 32*, 619–37.

Muller, S., Gorrow, T., and Fiala, K. (2011). Considering protective factors as a tool for teacher resiliency. *Education, 131*(3), 545–55. Available at www.salisbury.edu/directories/single.asp?username=SMMULLER.

Naglieri, J. A., and Pickering, E. (2003). *Helping Children Learning: Instructional Handouts for Use in School and Home*. Baltimore: Brookes.

Nota, L., Soresi, S., and Zimmerman, B. J. (2004). Self-regulation and academic achievement and resilience: a longitudinal study. *International Journal of Educational Research, 41*, 198–215.

Ozonoff, S., and Jensen, J. (1999). Brief report: specific executive function profiles in three neurodevelopmental disorders. *Autism and Developmental Disorders, 29*, 171–77.

Paniauga, F. A. (1992). Verbal– non-verbal correspondence training with ADHD children. *Behaviour Modification, 16*, 226–52.

Parker, D. R., and Boutelle, K. (2009). Executive function coaching for college students with learning disabilities and ADHD: a new approach for fostering self-determination. *Learning Disabilities Research and Practice, 24*(4), 204–15.

Perry, N. E., Yee, N., Mazabel, S., et al. (2017). Using self-regulated learning as a framework for creating inclusive classrooms for ethnically and linguistically diverse learners in Canada. In N. J. Cabrera and B. Leyendecker (Eds.), *Handbook on Positive Development of Minority Children and Youth*. Berlin: Springer.

Perry, R. P., Stupnisky, R. H., Hall, N. C., et al. (2010). Bad starts and better finishes: attributional retraining and initial performance in competitive achievement settings. *Journal of Social and Clinical Psychology, 29*(6), 668–700.

Pintrich, P. R. (2000). Multiple goals, multiple pathways: the role of goal orientation in learning and achievement. *Journal of Educational Psychology*, *92*, 544–55.

Posner, M. I., and Snyder, C. R. R. (1975). Attention and cognitive control. In R. L. Solso (Ed.), *Information Processing and Cognition: The Loyola Symposium* (pp. 205–23). Hillsdale, NJ: Erlbaum Associates.

Prevatt, F., and Yelland, S. (2015). An empirical evaluation of ADHD coaching in college students. *Journal of Attention Disorders*, *19*, 666–77.

Prochaska, J. O., and Velicer, W. F. (1997). The transtheoretical model of health behavior change. *American Journal of Health Promotion*, *12*(1), 38–48.

Purdie, N., and Hattie, J. (1996). Cultural differences in the use of strategies for self-regulated learning. *American Educational Research Journal*, *33*(4), 845–71.

Quigley, A., Muijs, D., and Stringer, E. (2018). *Metacognition and Self-Regulated Learning Guidance Report*. London: Education Endowment Fund.

Ratiu, P., and Talos, I. F. (2004). Images in clinical medicine: the tale of Phineas Gage. *New England Journal of Medicine*, *351*(23), e21.

Reeve, J. (1998). Autonomy support as an interpersonal motivating style: is it teachable? *Contemporary Educational Psychology*, *23*, 312–30.

Reeve, J., Bolt, E., and Cai, Y. (1999). Autonomy-supportive teachers: how they teach and motivate students. *Journal of Educational Psychology*, *91*(3), 537–48.

Richman, E. L., Radenmacher, K. N., and Maitland, T. L. (2014). Coaching and college success. *Journal of Postsecondary Education and Disability*, *27*(1), 33–52.

Riggs, N. R., Greenberg, M. T., Kusche, C. A., and Pentz, M. A. (2006). The mediational role of neurocognition in the behavioral outcomes of a social-emotional prevention program in elementary school students: effects of the PATHS curriculum. *Preventions Science*, *7*(1), 91–102.

Romine, C. B., and Reynolds, C. R. (2005). A model of the development of frontal lobe functioning: findings from a meta-analysis. *Applied Neuropsychology*, *12*(4), 190–201.

Schraw, G., Crippen, K. J., and Hartley, K. (2006). Promoting self-regulation in science education: metacognition as part of a broader perspective on learning. *Research in Science Education*, *36*, 111–39.

Schunk, D. H. (2003). Self-efficacy for reading and writing: influence of modeling, goal setting, and self-evaluation. *Reading and Writing Quarterly*, *19*, 159–72.

Selfridge, R., and Sokolik, S. (1975). A comprehensive view of organizational management. *MSU Business Topics*, *23*(1), 46–61.

Shipstead, Z., Hicks, K. L., and Engle, R. W. (2012). CogMed working memory training: does the evidence support the claims? *Journal of Applied Research in Memory and Cognition*, *1*, 185–93.

Spruce, R., and Bol, L. (2015). Teacher beliefs, knowledge, and practice of self-regulated learning. *Metacognition and Learning*, *10*(2), 245–77.

Sroufe, L. A. (1995). *Emotional Development: The Organisation of Emotional Life in the Early Years*. New York: Cambridge University Press.

Stein, J. A., and Krishnan, K. (2007). Nonverbal learning disabilities and executive function: the challenges of effective assessment and teaching. In L. Meltzer

(Ed.), *Executive Function in Education: From Theory to Practice* (pp. 106–32). New York: Guilford Press.

Swartz, S. L., Prevatt, F., and Proctor, B. E. (2005). A coaching intervention for college students with attention deficit/hyperactivity disorder. *Psychology in the Schools, 42*, 647–56.

Swing, E. L., Gentile, D. A., Anderson, C. A., and Walsh, D. A. (2010). Television and video game exposure and the development of attention problems. *Pediatrics, 126*(2), 214–21. doi:10.1542/peds.2009-1508.

The Coaching and Mentoring Network. (September 2019). *What Are Coaching and Mentoring?* London. Available at https://new.coachingnetwork.org.uk/infor mation-portal/what-are-coaching-and-mentoring/

Torre, J. B., and Lieberman, M. D. (2018). Putting feelings into words: affect labelling as implicit emotion regulation. *Emotion Review, 10*(2), 116–24.

Tunstall, P., and Gipps, C. (1996). Teacher feedback to young children in formative assessment: a typology. *British Educational Research Journal, 22*(4), 389–404.

Van Overwalle, F., and de Metsenaere, M. (1990). The effects of attribution-based intervention and study strategy training on academic achievement in college freshmen. *British Journal of Educational Psychology, 60*, 299–311.

Veenman, M. V. J. (2008). Giftedness: predicting the speed of expertise acquisition by intellecual ability and metacognitive skillfulness of novices. In M. F. Shaughnessy, M. V. J. Veenman, and C. Kleyn-Kennedy (Eds.), *Meta-cognition: A Recent Review of Research, Theory, and Perspectives* (pp. 207–20). Hauppauge, NY: Nova Science Publishers.

Visu-Petra, L., Cheie, L., Benga, O., and Miclea, M. (2011). Cognitive control goes to school: the impact of executive functions on academic performance. *Procedia: Social and Behavioral Sciences, 11*, 240–44.

Wang, M. C., Haertel, G. D., and Walberg, H. J. (1990). What influences learning? A content analysis of review literature. *Journal of Educational Research, 84*, 30–43.

Wedlake, M. (2002). Cognitive remediation therapy for undergraduates with ADHD. *ADHD Report, 10*(5), 11–13, 16.

Weiner, B. (1985). An attributional theory of achievement motivation and emotion. *Psychological Review, 92*, 548–73.

Weiner, B. (1995). *Judgments of Responsibility: A Foundation for a Theory of Social Conduct.* New York: Guilford Press.

Weiner, B. (2006). *Social Motivation, Justice, and the Moral Emotions: An Attributional Approach.* Mahwah, NJ: Lawrence Erlbaum Associates.

Wilson, T. D., and Linville, P. W. (1985). Improving the performance of college freshmen with attributional techniques. *Journal of Personality and Social Psychology, 49*, 287–93.

Winne, P. H. (2010). Bootstrapping learner's self-regulated learning. *Psychological Test and Assessment Modelling, 52*(4), 472–90.

Wolters, C. A. (2003). Regulation of motivation: evaluating an under emphasized aspect of self-regulated learning. *Educational Psychologist, 38*, 189–205.

Yeager, D. S., Dahl, R. E., and Dweck, C. S. (2018). Why interventions to influence adolescent behavior often fail but could succeed. *Perspectives on Psychological Science, 13*(1), 101–22.

Yong, Z., and Yue, Y. (2007). Causes for burnout among secondary and elementary school teachers and preventive strategies. *Chinese Education and Society, 40*(5), 78–85. doi:10.2753/CED1061-1932400508.

Zelazo, P. D., Craik, F. I., and Booth, L. (2004). Executive function across the life span. *Acta Psycholoica, 115*, 167–84.

Zimmerman, B. (2008). Investigating self-regulation and motivation: historical background, methodological developments, and future prospects. *American Educational Research Journal, 45*(1), 166–83.

Zimmerman, B. J. (2001). Theories of self- regulated learning and academic achievement: an overview and analysis. In B. J. Zimmerman and D. H. Schunk (Eds.), *Self Regulated Learning and Academic Achievement* (pp. 1–37). Hillsdale, NJ: Erlbaum Associates.

Zimmerman, B. J., and Martinez-Pons, M. (1986). Development of a structured interview for assessing students' use of self-regulated learning strategies. *American Educational Research Journal, 23*(4), 614–28.

Zimmerman, B. J., and Martinez-Pons, M. (1998). Construct validation of a strategy model of student self-regulated learning. *Journal of Educational Psychology, 80*(3), 284–90.

Zwart, L. M., and Kallemeyn, L. M. (2001). Peer-based coaching for college students with ADHD and learning disabilities. *Journal of Postsecondary Education and Disability, 15*(1), 1–15.

Well-being

8

Sleepy teens in the classroom

Frances Le Cornu Knight

Introduction

We are all too aware of the negative effects of a poor night's sleep. When I ask talk attendees to share some insights, they frequently report being irritable and easy to snap, feeling generally fatigued and less motivated, and finding it more difficult to concentrate and bring things to mind. And yet, whilst we are aware of these negative consequences, we often do not budget for sleep in the way we should. These common phenomena are now the point of rigorous research, and results consistently confirm that insufficient sleep leads to a whole host of undesirable physical, cognitive and behavioural outcomes. In this chapter, I focus on the role sleep has to play in promoting the optimal conditions for learning and healthy development during adolescence.

Sleep is a wonderful thing. It provides a window of opportunity for our brains to take a break from the relentless sensory, social and intellectual processing of the waking world. It provides our minds with space to reflect and recharge. Because sleep has been preserved through evolution and still makes up such a large portion of our lives (roughly a third), we can safely assume that there must be some fundamental function(s) of sleep. Indeed, there are many theories on the functions of sleep, and I advocate a combined approach. Sleep allows us to recharge our energy stores at a time when traditionally a lack of light would constrain activities. Sleep promotes growth and physical repair, both of which occur predominantly at night. The onset of deep sleep, or slow-wave sleep (SWS), signals the release of human growth hormone (HGH), which prompts physical growth across early development and physical repair across all ages. More recently, it has been discovered that the brain is also cleansed during sleep: cerebrospinal fluid is flushed throughout the brain during sleep and takes with it the neurotoxins that naturally build up as a by-product of daily functioning. Perhaps the most important function of sleep in the context of education is the established role that sleep has to play in memory consolidation and therefore learning.

Through this chapter, I present evidence, mechanisms and recommendations from research on three topics advocating the importance of sleep in the context of secondary education: 'Sleepy teens: what's going on?', 'Sleep and academic performance' and 'Sleep, health and well-being'. In order to aid my explanations and hopefully your understanding, I have also included a box titled, 'The biology of the sleep-wake cycle', which aims to be an accessible explanation of the biological systems governing our sleep regulation.

Sleepy teens: what's going on?

Lazy teens?

When I give sleep education talks in secondary schools, I like to begin by asking the students two questions: 'Who here likes sleep?' and 'Who feels like they get enough sleep?'. In answer to the first question, a sea of hands enthusiastically shoots up, along with happy murmurs throughout the audience. In answer to the second question, the majority of those hands sink down, with only a few proudly proclaiming that they are happy with their sleep. Despite sleep being viewed as a cherished activity, it seems that teenagers (like most adults) are not prioritising it. Chronic and habitual sleep deprivation in our teenage population is a growing problem worldwide. The National Sleep Foundation (NSF) recommends that adolescents aged 14–17 years should get between eight and ten hours of sleep per night, and children aged 6–13 should get between nine and eleven hours (NSF, 2015). At these ages, eight hours or less a night is deemed as the marker for insufficient sleep (NSF, 2006). And yet, a recent meta-analysis of forty-one studies of adolescent sleep from across the globe (Gradisar et al., 2011) and another study of 9,251 teenagers across Europe (Leger et al., 2012) both conclude that there is a strong negative relationship between age and sleep duration such that older adolescents increasingly report fewer than eight hours sleep per night on weekdays. This reduction in sleep duration is not mirrored by a reduced need for sleep. Indeed, in a longitudinal study, Mary Carskadon et al. (1983) fixed teenagers' time in bed at ten hours and found that the need for sleep remained stable across adolescents aged 10–17 years, with participants sleeping for an average of nine hours and twenty minutes. And so we observe teenagers who are increasingly difficult to wake in the mornings, fatigued throughout the day and playing catch up on the weekends, trying to recuperate the sleep they have missed during the school week by sleeping later into the day on weekends.

So what is going on? Why are our teenagers getting less sleep? This is not a straightforward question to answer. There is a host of wider psychosocial explanations for the increasing sleep loss in modern teenagers which are likely working in combination. For example, adolescence is typically a period in which teenagers are granted more freedom; bedtimes transition from being parentally governed to self-controlled. At the same time, teenagers experience increased academic and social obligations, which have the potential to delay bedtimes (Carskadon et al., 2004; Crowley et al., 2007). Students report staying up later to talk with friends or finish their homework (Adam et al., 2007); during exam periods, students often sacrifice sleep in favour of additional revision time and cramming. Such revision tactics have been shown to be counterintuitive, leading to reduced performance, and are discussed in more detail later in the chapter.

A contemporary point of concern is the proliferation of mobile technology, allowing the modern teenager to watch entertainment, play games and interact with peers around the clock. The attractive allure of social networking sites (which are specifically designed to hook the user) is particularly tempting for adolescents. Hormonal changes prompt teenagers to explore peer relations with greater fervour. And yet, the region of the brain that governs decision making and self-control, namely the frontal lobe, is one of the last to develop, continuing maturation into the early twenties. The result is that post-pubescent teenagers are increasingly drawn to social media sites, without having the necessary powers of reasoning and impulse control to self-regulate their screen-time (Blakemore and Choudhury, 2006). Indeed, in a 2013 survey of adolescents aged 12–17 years, 82% reported that they owned either a mobile phone or a tablet, and 74% of those had access to the internet (Madden et al., 2013). Sue Adams et al. (2013) report that excessive social media consumption before bedtime leads to delayed sleep onset and shorter total sleep time (TST). Furthermore, in a recent UK study, electronic media use and caffeine before bed were found to be strong predictors of poor sleep, which, in turn, was found to negatively affect academic performance (Dimitriou et al., 2015).

Electronic media (e.g. entertainment and games) and social media are particularly intrusive of sleep for three key reasons.

1. Entertainment and games are designed to increase arousal states, meaning that users are more 'geared up', making it more difficult to settle into sleep.
2. Social media can increase anxieties driven by the pressures of unrelenting peer relations and fear of missing out: increased anxiety and stress induce the release of the hormone cortisol (see Box 8.1), which is directly intrusive of sleep.
3. The bright light that many electronic devices omit suppresses the release of the hormone melatonin, which typically acts as a signal for sleepiness.

Hence, using mobile technology around bedtime delays sleep, not only by engaging in these activities later into the evening, but also by increasing arousal states and suppressing the feeling of sleepiness such that once the activity is terminated, the teenager is less likely to feel tired. Furthermore, underlying these

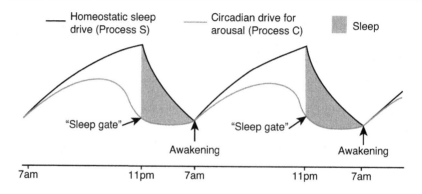

Figure 8.1 Biology of the sleep-wake cycle. (Courtesy of Luke Mastin.)

psychosocial factors is a biological shift during adolescence that helps to promote the engagement of activities such as these further into the evening.

Box 8.1 The biology of the sleep-wake cycle

In order to fully understand the concepts presented across this chapter, here I provide a brief description of the biological underpinnings of the sleep-wake cycle. According to the two-process model, first described by Alexander Borbély (1982), two distinct drives exist that govern sleep and wakefulness. The first is a circadian drive (Figure 8.1, curved line), which is sensitive to external light exposure and so entrains our sleep-wake cycle to daily rise and fall of the sun. The circadian drive (circadian, translating to *circa*, 'roughly', and *dies*, 'a day') promotes wakefulness during daylight hours and sleep in the absence of light. This is achieved in part by prompting the release of a wake-promoting hormone, cortisol, upon waking and the release of a sleep-promoting hormone, melatonin, as light withdraws. Working in tandem, the second drive is the homeostatic drive, which is sensitive to internally occurring 'sleep pressure' that builds through wakeful hours and is released during sleep. The homeostatic drive (Figure 8.1, steep line) incrementally favours sleep more as hours of wake extend and favours waking more as the hours of sleep increase. These two systems are distinct but work together to regulate an individual's sleep-wake cycle according to the external environment and internal needs. As the circadian drive dips due to the receding light level, homeostatic sleep pressure will typically be high as a result of a day's wakeful activity, so external and internal factors promote sleep.

The perfect storm: biological shifts, school starts and social jetlag

In an interesting review of adolescent sleep research, Mary Carskadon (2011) describes a 'perfect storm' of psychosocial factors interacting with a biological shift in the sleep-wake cycle during adolescence, leading to short and ill-timed sleep. Carskadon points out that whilst research consistently shows that bed and sleep times get later across adolescence, school times remain fixed or get earlier, and consequently, sleep duration diminishes. She provides compelling evidence to suggest that this reduction is not explained by a reduced *need* for sleep but instead by a biologically driven shift towards later sleep times being at odds with rigid societal expectations. In order to fully understand the significance of this biological shift and emphasise its impact on adolescence, please refer to Box 8.1.

During adolescence or, more precisely, during puberty, these systems undergo substantial change. Puberty sees a reduction in the sensitivity to diminishing light levels (the circadian drive) and a delay in the accumulation of sleep pressure (the homeostatic drive) such that older adolescents are less biologically prepared for sleep until later into the evening than their pre-pubescent peers and even adults (Jenni et al., 2005). For example, Crowley et al. (2014) monitored the sleep-wake cycles of ninety-four adolescents aged between 9 and16 years across a two-and-a-half-year period, taking measures of evening melatonin release, as an index of internal bodily preparation for sleep. The researchers found that whilst externally governed waking times became earlier as the adolescents transitioned from middle to high school, the release of melatonin and thus sleep onset shifted later as a function of age, leading to a reduction in nightly sleep duration across adolescence. Importantly, this study highlights that the delay in sleep timings during adolescence is a result of developmental changes in the biological drive for sleep rather than simply being a result of psychosocial factors. Interestingly, once those adolescents left high school and were therefore in control of their own morning routines (aged 18–19 years), wake times shifted later, resulting in an extension of sleep duration. This further supports the proposal that shorter sleep duration in older school-aged adolescents reflects the mismatch between biologically governed delayed sleep patterns and early school start times rather than a reduced need for sleep.

The resulting short sleep during the school week leads to a connected phenomenon known as 'social jetlag', in which sleep-deprived adolescents are sleeping in later on the weekends in order to recuperate the sleep that they have missed during the week. This phenomenon has been termed 'social jetlag' because, akin to common jetlag, periodically shifting the sleep-wake routine puts the body (which tries to establish consistent routines) in a continual state of flux. In 2006, the National Sleep Foundation performed a large-scale review of 1,602 teenagers' sleep-wake cycles across weekdays and weekends. On weekdays, the average bedtime shifted later by around one and a half hours from

11–18 years of age (from 22:31–00:45), whilst rise times became earlier by ten minutes (from 6:42–6:31). As a result, total sleep time between these ages dropped from 8.4 hours to 6.9 hours on weekdays. If this finding reflected a true reduction in the need for sleep, a similar pattern would be observed in weekend sleep-wake cycles. This was not the case. The report found that weekend wake times became later as participants aged, leading to an extension of sleep durations over weekend, from 8.4–9 hours. When teenagers' sleep was unconstrained by school start times on the weekends, this led to a sleep extension of up to an hour for teens aged 11–14 years and a two-hour extension for teens aged 16–18 years. An important point to note here is that teenagers are not sleeping later on the weekend because they are lazy but because their biological drive for sleep occurs later in the day. To put this into context, imagine on a typical day being told that you must fall asleep at 8 p.m.; whilst in our busy lives this might sound attractive, most of us would struggle. As a consequence of this delay in sleep preparation, teenagers must sleep later into the morning to compensate.

Social jetlag during adolescence is a well-replicated result. And much like typical jetlag or shift working, larger degrees of social jetlag have been associated with a host of educational and wider health implications (see Crowley et al., 2014), such as reduced attentional capacity, greater incidence of risky behaviours (such as alcohol and nicotine consumption) and an increased risk of depression and obesity (discussed in the coming sections).

Delayed school start times

Owing to the dearth of emerging research suggesting that teenage sleep debt results from early school starts, specialist bodies in America (home to the prominent leaders in this line of research) have begun forceful public health campaigns advocating for delayed school start times. The American Academy of Pediatrics (Adolescent Sleep Working Group, Committee on Adolescence, and Council on School Health, 2014), the Centers for Disease Control and Prevention (Wheaton et al., 2016) and the American Academy of Sleep Medicine (Watson et al., 2017) have all promoted delayed school start times on the basis of a link between short sleep times in adolescents and increased car accidents, as well as an increased risk of behavioural and emotional problems. A number of schools have responded by implementing later start times, resulting in a variety of positive outcomes.

In the United Kingdom recently, a naturalistic investigation came about through a change in local administration, which lead to a delay in school start times in one UK borough, from 8:50 to 10:00 a.m. Two years later, another change in local administration saw the earlier start of 8:50 a.m. reinstated. This unique scenario created an A-B-A intervention design, allowing for the comparison of educational outcomes between these periods, and the results were persuasive. Paul Kelley et al. (2017) report that during the two-year intervention period, absence due to illness dropped by 50%, and value-added scores associated with students making good academic progress improved by 12%. When reverting back to the earlier start time, the value-added scores for those students were retained at the one-year follow-up; however, student illness again increased by 30%. These findings suggest that earlier start times might be impeding the progression of some students and furthermore are associated with real negative health implications.

Similar results have been reported in a range of cross-sectional studies that compare one school which has implemented a delayed school start to another school which has not. A note of warning must be added here: these studies can be problematic given that school performance can vary widely from the outset. Karl Minges and Nancy Redeker (2016) provide a clear systematic review of six strictly experimental studies of delayed school start times. In each of these studies, the extension of sleep from which teenagers benefit directly parallels the duration of delay; for example, if the school start is delayed by thirty minutes, students extend their sleep by roughly thirty minutes (Boergers et al., 2014); if the school start is delayed by an hour, sleep is extended by roughly an hour (Lufi et al., 2011). Recently, Frances Knight and Amy Fancourt (in preparation) found that delaying the school start time by two hours led to an average sleep extension of 1.3 hours, pointing to an upper limit. These findings suggest that current school start times are causing teenagers to be habitually deprived of sleep: if students were obtaining sufficient sleep during the week, a delay in school times would not result in an extension of sleep. Across the six studies, observations were also made of a reduction in depressed moods and improved motivation (Owens et al., 2010), reduced daytime sleepiness and caffeine consumption (Boergers et al., 2014) and improved attentional capacity (Knight and Fancourt, in preparation; Lufi et al., 2011; Vedaa et al., 2012). One study even saw a state-wide reduction in incidents of car crashes caused by teenage drivers (Danner and Phillips, 2008). Most studies report a reduction in daytime sleepiness, which in turn, is associated with increases in students' motivation to learn, attentional capacity and overall academic achievement (Li et al., 2013). These studies make a very convincing case for optimal sleep conditions producing the optimal conditions for learning.

The next section will dig a little deeper into the relationship between sleep and academic performance, looking into the nuances and underlying mechanisms of this relationship.

Sleep and academic performance

Sleep and academic achievement

If we accept that the modern teenager is typically in a state of insufficient sleep and that one of the principal causes of this is the structure of the school system, then we should consider the effects of this poor sleep on learning and academic achievement. For a moment, bring to mind the ambience among your teenage students in your first class in the morning and compare that to the atmosphere of an afternoon class. The difference is stark. One might readily conclude that sleepy teens make less engaged and less motivated learners. It is perhaps unsurprising, then, that good sleep is one of the key predictors for academic achievement (Gomes et al., 2011). Recently, Mari Hysing et al. (2015) performed a large-scale investigation into the association between sleep and academic performance. The authors surveyed 7,798 Norwegian adolescents aged 16–19 years and found that a range of sleep parameters was significantly associated with poor academic performance, measured using grade-point average (GPA), even after adjusting for a range of socio-demographic factors that typically predict success (e.g. age, sex, parental education and family affluence). Of particular note is the authors' report that students obtaining between seven and nine hours of sleep significantly outperformed students obtaining less than seven hours of sleep *or* those obtaining more than nine hours (across those with GPA scores of 4.0, 3.4 and 3.9, respectively). Similarly, they found that students who went to bed between 22:00 and 23:00 had the best GPA (4.0); these students outperformed those who went to sleep later in a linear fashion (i.e. the later the sleep time, the lower the GPA) but also outperformed those who went to bed earlier than 22:00. The large representative sample used in this study implies that these results are highly generalisable across borders.

From a research perspective, GPA is an efficient way to operationalise 'academic performance'; however, many would argue that academic success goes far beyond the final average grade to encompass factors such as concentration, attention, motivation and receptivity to learning. Indeed, an earlier review of 449 Dutch pupils aged 9–14 years found that better quality of sleep was associated with increased levels of motivation, receptivity to the teacher, positive student self-image and greater emotional regulation (Meijer et al., 2000). In a sample of slightly younger pupils, aged 7–11 years, Reut Gruber et al. (2014) reported that objectively measured better sleep efficiency is associated with better performance on core topics such as mathematics and English, as well as learning French as a second language. Conversely, Adams et al. (2013) concluded that sacrificing sleep for revision actually reduces school performance in terms of understanding the material covered in class and struggling on assignments. Moreover, whilst sleep deprivation negatively affects task performance, it is not always met with an overt realisation of this fact. In an experimental study, June Pilcher and Amy Walters (1997) required forty-four college students to complete a critical thinking activity after either twenty-four hours of sleep deprivation or after approximately eight hours of sleep. Unsurprisingly, those who were deprived of sleep performed worse than those who slept; surprisingly, however, when asked to rate their perceived performance, sleep-deprived students rated themselves significantly higher than the students who had eight hours of sleep. These results are concerning as they suggest that students are not explicitly aware of the negative impact poor sleep might have on their school performance.

The association between sleep and academic performance is well established (see Dewald et al., 2010), and the reasons for this association are no doubt multifaceted. The next two sections will consider the role sleep has to play in memory consolidation specifically and cognitive function more generally, both being essential for classroom learning.

Sleep, memory consolidation and learning

Perhaps the most compelling argument for the beneficial effects of sleep for academic performance is the mechanism of sleep-dependent memory consolidation. We now know that a good night's sleep stimulates the consolidation of newly acquired information into stable, long-lasting memories. There are various ways of demonstrating this effect. Typically in this research, participants are split into two groups and given a memory task to perform: the sleep group receive training in the evening and are tested the next morning following a night's sleep, and the wake group receive their training in the morning and are tested following the same amount of restful wakefulness. Using this paradigm, a breadth of research persuasively demonstrates that the sleep group outperform the wake group on a wide range of memory tasks.[1]

Neuroscientific research demonstrates that during sleep, when the brain is freed from the busy functioning of the waking hours, newly acquired information taken on through the day is reactivated and redistributed through the brain (Born and Wilhelm, 2012). During the day, novel information is initially encoded within the hippocampus, a region of the brain that acts as an effective but rudimentary and temporary memory store. During sleep, the hippocampus communicates this information to the neocortex, the region of the brain that is associated with higher-order thought processes. This process can be thought of as a sort of filing system through which the new memory traces are redistributed around regions of the brain that store related information. Memories that are initially weak become consolidated into stable, long-lasting memories. This process of sleep-dependent memory consolidation is fundamental to learning. In adults, sleep-dependent memory consolidation has been evidenced across a range of different memory tasks from word-pair learning to memorising short stories and remembering hidden object locations and finger-tapping sequences. Furthermore, the process of filing novel information with existing relevant memories during sleep is so effective that it can lead to the learning of new insights (Wagner et al., 2004). It is perhaps for this reason that when people have a difficult decision to make, they are often advised to 'sleep on it'.

Over the past two decades, researchers have become interested in how sleep-dependent memory consolidation develops across childhood and adolescence. In a seminal study, Steffen Gais et al. (2006) demonstrated that English-speaking teenage boys' ability to recall newly learnt German vocabulary was significantly improved when sleep followed learning compared to the same period of time awake. In a series of experiments, these authors confirmed that this sleep-dependent learning occurred irrespective of fatigue, time of day and interference during waking intervals, and furthermore, the memory enhancement was retained two nights later. More recently, sleep has been shown to improve memory in children and teens on a range of declarative memory tasks such as novel word learning (Henderson et al., 2012), novel non-word pairs and rule learning (Ashworth et al., 2014), picture recognition (Prehn-Kristensen et al., 2011) and emotion recognition (Prehn-Kristensen et al., 2013). Furthermore, sleep has been shown to facilitate the detection of hidden insights to a greater degree than a waking period in children, and this sleep-related enhancement effect is greater in children than that observed in adults (Wilhelm et al., 2013). One suggestion for why this might be is that children spend more time in SWS, a depth of sleep that is particularly important for this process of memory consolidation. This suggestion is supported by the observation that sleep-dependent memory consolidation in children and adolescents is correlated with SWS such that the more time spent in SWS, the larger is the memory-enhancement effect (Backhaus et al., 2008; Prehn-Kristensen et al., 2011; Wilhelm et al., 2013). Likewise, research has shown that this memory enhancement is disrupted following a full night's sleep deprivation (Wilhelm et al., 2013), although it should be noted that other reports suggest that adolescent declarative memory consolidation is fairly robust to sleep restriction of a few hours (Kopasz et al., 2010).

Sleep and cognitive functions

Classroom learning requires a broader set of faculties than simply memorising information. In order for students to encode the information in the first instance, they must pay attention to the dialogue and digest its meaning; they must call upon previously learnt material and make new links; they must flexibly and intelligently use this information to answer questions and participate in class discussions; and they must maintain concentration and suppress the range of environmental distracters that are likely to be present. The broad range of capabilities a student must employ to achieve academic success is underscored by a range of cognitive functions which may also be affected by poor sleep. Here I focus on attention, working memory (the ability to hold and manipulate task-dependent information in memory) and speed of processing (the speed at which a person can understand and react to information he or she receives).

Aside from memory, attention is perhaps one of the most crucial capacities for learning. Think of times that you have slept particularly badly; the next day you most probably found holding focus on a task much more difficult. Indeed, studies in which habitually good sleep is restricted often demonstrate increased attentional lapses (Louca and Short, 2014; Peters et al., 2009) and increased mean reaction times (Sadeh et al., 2003). In an elegantly designed study, June

Lo et al. (2016) restricted the sleep of thirty adolescents (aged 15–19 years), allowing them five hours of time in bed (TIB) for five consecutive nights, and compared their functioning to that of a control group of twenty-six students who were allowed nine hours of TIB. Teenagers in both groups were also assessed during a baseline period and a 'recovery period', each three days in length, in which all teens were allowed nine hours TIB. The participants' nocturnal sleep and daytime sleepiness were assessed along with a battery of cognitive tasks, measuring sustained attention, working memory and speed of processing (using a mental arithmetic task and a symbol digit modality task). Over the course of the sleep restriction period, those in the sleep-restricted group demonstrated a dramatic cumulative decrease in sustained attention capacity and speed of processing. Working memory capacity, subjective sleepiness and mood were also negatively affected. Whilst most variables rebounded to normal performance during the recovery period, speed of processing and subjective sleepiness remained low. It is perhaps not surprising that when we restrict teenagers' sleep, they perform worse on a range of cognitive tasks, but when we consider this experimental evidence in the context of the established teenage sleep debt, it paints a stark picture of how modern teenagers may be functioning on a daily basis.

People often ask whether sleep-deprived teenagers would benefit from taking naps during the day to fresh them. In answer to this question, the same group of researchers (Lo et al., 2017) performed a similar study providing students with daytime napping opportunities. In an attempt to mimic the social jetlag observed between weekdays and weekends, fifty-seven students (aged 15–19 years) had their sleep restricted to five hours TIB for five consecutive days, with two recovery days, followed by a further three days of sleep restriction. Half the students were given the opportunity for a one-hour nap during the day. As observed earlier, sleep-restricted students who were not allowed naps demonstrated a dramatic cumulative deterioration in sustained attention capacity. However, whilst morning sustained attention performance was similarly poor between the nap and no-nap groups, post-nap performance rebounded for the nap group so that it was similar to control performance. Concerningly, the deterioration in sustained attention showed a marked accelerated progression for both groups in the second round of sleep restriction and to a greater degree for those in the no-nap group. This finding suggests that whilst the weekend recovery periods might serve as short-term respite for students who are habitually under-slept on weeknights, they are not enough to ameliorate negative effects in the subsequent school week. Taken together, these findings point to the potential short-term benefits of napping for sleep-deprived students; however, it is necessary to add a few words of caution. Firstly, it is important to note that whilst the daily one-hour nap served to reduce performance degradation, it was not enough to eliminate it on a longer-term basis. Secondly, a major concern in promoting daytime napping centres on the disruption it might cause for nocturnal sleep: those who nap during the day might feel less ready for sleep at night. Attempting to improve habitual noctur-nal sleep during the week should be our first, and most successful, line of attack. Indeed, studies that extend teenagers' sleep duration by delaying school start times provide compelling evidence of improvements in sustained attention level, impulsivity and rate of performance (Lufi et al., 2011) and fewer atten-tional lapses and quicker response times (Vedaa et al., 2012).

Sleep, health and well-being

Sleep and mental health

One of the most established associates with insufficient sleep in the adolescent population is poor mental health. Good sleep is commonly found to predict better emotional regulation, fewer depressive symptoms and better quality of life and well-being.[2] Large-scale correlational studies (e.g. Short et al., 2013) consistently show that insufficient sleep duration is associated with increased experience of anxiety and depressive symptoms, as well as general fatigue during the day. In a review of the sleep habits and mood of 741 Australian school-aged teenagers (aged 12–19 years), Monika Raniti et al. (2017) conclude that the observed population-wide increase in depressive symptoms across ado-lescence is in part explained by the mediating role of progressively shorter sleep duration across this age group. In review of 750 Californian teens (aged 14–15 years), Andrew Fuligni and Christina Hardway (2006) found that shorter sleep duration is directly related to the experience of stressful demands (from family, school and friends) on the previous day. In turn, adolescents who had slept poorly the night before reported higher levels of anxiety and, to a lesser degree, depressive symptoms. This important point highlights the cyclical nature of these relationships: stressful daily demands make for worse sleep, and worse sleep produces more highly anxious teens, who are less able to cope with stress-ful situations. Corroborating these naturalistic findings, in response to experi-mentally restricted sleep (e.g. Baum et al., 2014), teenagers report that they are more tense/anxious, hostile and irritable, and their parents report that they are less able to regulate their own emotions. Michelle Short and Mia Louca (2015) suggest that female students (aged 14–18 years) show greater vulnerability to sleep-related increases in anxiety and depression following sleep restriction com-pared to their male counterparts. In addition, shorter sleep duration is also con-sistently linked with increased risky behaviours. In a self-report questionnaire of 242 adolescents aged 14–17 years, Keryn Pasch et al. (2010) report that shorter sleep duration during the week was associated with increased depressive symp-toms and increased alcohol use.

Mental health in the adolescent population is a growing concern in the modern world. We are observing students who appear to be more anxious and less able to cope with the daily stresses of modern living. Many attribute this to the increasing social burden introduced by social media: the unrelenting pressure to present themselves as attractive, popular and happy individuals on a moment-by-moment basis is fostering an environment of continual self-assessment. From the sleep perspective, the proliferation of mobile technology is also damaging in its intrusion into the night-time hours that would previously have been reserved for restorative sleep. Teenagers who now feel a social obligation to stay online 24/7 perhaps do not realise that substituting their sleeping hours for such activities might be compounding the anxieties they feel as a result of this burden.

Taking a positive spin on these findings, we might conclude that improving sleep is an effective and healthy remedy in ameliorating the mental issues that are increasingly reported in the modern teenager. Indeed, Julia Dewald-Kaufmann et al. (2014) have shown that a three-week sleep intervention that demonstrates modest improvements in sleep duration significantly reduces depressive symptoms in teenagers with chronically reduced sleep. Recently in the United Kingdom, Frances Knight and Amy Fancourt (in preparation) have found that the sleep extension that follows a delayed school start serves to reduce levels of anxiety and depression in teenaged girls aged 16–17 years.

Sleep and general health

Through this section, it is important to note that the consequences of poor sleep often have complex relationships with the causes; one often exacerbates the other. Take, for example, the relationship between caffeine and poor sleep. Late or excessive caffeine consumption during the day, particularly in the afternoon or evening, leads to difficulty falling asleep later that night and more disrupted sleep once it is achieved. As a consequence of a poor night's sleep, we find ourselves reaching more readily for the coffee pot, so if the cycle begins, it is difficult to break. Because many of the large-scale studies are cross-sectional in nature, it can be difficult to tease out the direction of these relationships.

One established relationship between sleep and general health factors is the link between poor sleep and an increased prevalence of obesity (Seicean et al., 2007). In a sample of teenagers aged 11–16 years, one study claims that for every hour of sleep that is lost, an 80% increase in the likelihood to be classified as obese is observed (Gupta et al., 2002). There are two potential reasons for the link between sleep and obesity: sedentary behaviours and diet. As with sleep and caffeine, the association between sleep and exercise is another example of a reciprocal relationship. We know that exercise during the day improves sleep quality at night.[3] Sleep, in turn, restores energy levels so that someone who is well slept is more likely to exercise. Similarly, sedentary behaviours (such as spending hours in front of the television) reduce the need for sleep and therefore make sleep more difficult to achieve. Consequently, without achieving a deep, satisfying sleep through the night, the individual feels more fatigued during the day, thus increasing the engagement with sedentary behaviours.

Supporting this cycle, a recent study of 8,640 teenagers aged 13–16 years found that the three biggest risk factors for obesity were sleeping for fewer than 7.75 hours a night, watching television for more than two hours a day and parental obesity (incorporating genetic and parenting factors; Liou et al., 2010). The relationship between insufficient sleep and specific food choices in adolescents is yet to be established through formal investigation; however, there is some research to suggest that poor sleepers consume more carbohydrates (Al-Disi et al., 2010) and are more likely to snack and consume more fatty foods overall (Weiss et al., 2010). A potential biological mechanism for increased snacking and seeking out more calorie-rich foods is that insufficient sleep interrupts the typical balance of hormones that signal hunger and satiety (e.g. ghrelin and insulin; Al-Disi et al., 2010; Matthews et al., 2012). Obesity itself increases the likelihood of experiencing a range of more serious health issues later in life, such as increased risk for diabetes, cardiovascular disease and cancer, and individuals who are obese in their teenage years are more likely to struggle with their weight later in life (Biro and Wien, 2010). Therefore, promoting healthy sleeping habits among teenagers has the potential to have a knock-on beneficial effect on larger general health issues.

Recommendations

Delayed school start times

Teenagers across the globe are increasingly reporting fewer hours sleep than is recommended. Through adolescence, increasing social and academic demands come at a time when young people are given more control over their own bedtimes and bedtime activities, thus consuming more of their evening hours. This is compounded by the fact that the technology that allows them to fulfil these obligations has the effect of suppressing their desire to sleep despite their need for sleep. Underlying these intrusive psychosocial factors, a biological shift helps to promote engagement in evening activities. With rigid school times necessitating early rise times, this perfect storm of factors that push sleeping hours later into the evening means that as teenagers age, their window of opportunity for sleep notably diminishes on weeknights.

In light of these findings, the most effective recommendation would be to alter the societal expectation for teenagers to maintain early wake times by delaying school starts so that they are more in line with their biological clocks. The evidence compellingly suggests that doing so would result in a dramatic increase in nightly sleep duration, as well as a reduction in social jetlag. As a result of optimising sleep, it is likely that we would also see improvements in academic performance as well as wider health and well-being among our teens.

However, it should be noted that delaying school start times is not an easy task to achieve. School start times have been fixed for many decades and are typically constrained by a range of important external factors, including parental working patterns dictating school drop-offs as well as the time at which teachers (who are often parents too) are able to get to, and leave, work around their own school drop-offs. Therefore, it is perhaps more practical to recommend that we educate teenagers in the importance of obtaining sufficient sleep in an attempt to encourage them to prioritise it.

Sleep education for teens

What should this sleep education entail? Firstly, it should include the facts about obtaining adequate sleep on a habitual basis, prompting students to reflect on their actual sleep in the context of their need for sleep. Teenagers should be educated about the intrusive effects of bedtime electronic media use. I recommend that teenagers are strongly encouraged not to have mobile phones in their bedrooms at night: this is a recommendation that is easier said than done, but once adopted, the positive effects will be easily apparent. Secondly, teenagers should be made explicitly aware of the established benefits sleep has in providing the optimal conditions for academic success. Teenagers should be educated on sleep's role in memory consolidation as a compelling mechanism for educational success. And whilst it might not come as a shock to any teenager that insufficient sleep makes it more difficult to maintain focus, explicitly pointing teenagers to this fact using scientific evidence might encourage them to prioritise sleep during weeknights. For students who are notably sleep deprived, a midday nap might serve to refresh attentional function. However, this strategy should be adopted with caution so as to avoid disrupting or displacing nocturnal sleep.

Thirdly, sleep education should highlight the benefits of good sleep for important wider mental and physical health factors, as well as the negative reciprocal relationship between poor sleep, anxiety and reduced ability to cope with the potentially stressful demands of modern living. Finally, sleep education for teenagers should highlight that those with good sleep habits lead healthier lifestyles. Sufficient sleep affords better appetite control, leaving teens less likely to crave fatty snacks and carbohydrates, as well as providing more energy and more motivation to exercise, veering away from sedentary activities. Given that modern teens (or teens in general) are typically more focused on their self-image than any other age group, promoting the health benefits of good sleep might also serve as a persuasive avenue of endorsement.

Conclusions

We live in an era in which a shrinking jobs market is forcing higher competition among applicants, and school grades are an important first indicator of performance. Teenagers appear to be increasingly aware of the importance of leaving school with a strong academic record and therefore should be striving to create the optimal conditions to achieve their full academic potential. In addition to academic pressures, the teenage years can be a fraught landscape of complex and changing peer relations and self-evaluation. Maintaining a good baseline of mental well-being and emotional stability is key to navigating these complex demands. Convincingly, evidence points to sleep in providing these optimal conditions for academic performance, well-being and wider physical health. Whilst much of the evidence reviewed in this chapter has focussed on the negative impact of poor sleep, the key take-home message is to promote an activity that most teenagers relish. Sleep is important, so be selfish, claim back some time and prioritise it.

Notes

1 For a comprehensive and accessible review of the research evidencing sleep-dependent memory consolidation in both adults and children, with some developmental differences discussed, see Wilhelm et al. (2012).
2 For a thorough review, see Chaput et al. (2016)
3 Note that. exercise immediately prior to sleep interrupts sleep by increasing arousal levels.

References

Adam, E. K., Snell, E. K., and Pendry, P. (2007). Sleep timing and quantity in ecological and family context: a nationally representative time-diary study. *Journal of Family Psychology, 21*(1), 4.

Adams, S. K., Daly, J. F., and Williford, D. N. (2013). Article commentary: adolescent sleep and cellular phone use – recent trends and implications for research. *Health Services Insights, 6*, HIS–S11083.

Adolescent Sleep Working Group, Committee on Adolescence and Council on School Health. (2014). School start times for adolescents. *Pediatrics, 134*(3), 642–49. doi:10.1542/peds.2014-1697.

Al-Disi, D., Al-Daghri, N., Khanam, L., et al. (2010). Subjective sleep duration and quality influence diet composition and circulating adipocytokines and ghrelin levels in teen-age girls. *Endocrine Journal, 57*(10), 915–23.

Ashworth, A., Hill, C. M., Karmiloff-Smith, A., and Dimitriou, D. (2014). Sleep enhances memory consolidation in children. *Journal of Sleep Research, 23*(3), 304–10.

Backhaus, J., Hoeckesfeld, R., Born, J., et al. (2008). Immediate as well as delayed post learning sleep but not wakefulness enhances declarative memory consolidation in children. *Neurobiology of Learning and Memory, 89*(1), 76–80.

Biro, F. M., and Wien, M. (2010). Childhood obesity and adult morbidities. *American Journal of Clinical Nutrition, 91*(5), 1499S–505S.

Blakemore, S. J., and Choudhury, S. (2006). Development of the adolescent brain: implications for executive function and social cognition. *Journal of Child Psychology and Psychiatry, 47*(3–4), 296–312.

Boergers, J., Gable, C. J., and Owens, J. A. (2014). Later school start time is associated with improved sleep and daytime functioning in adolescents. *Journal of Developmental and Behavioral Pediatrics, 35*, 11e7.

Borbély, A. A. (1982). A two process model of sleep regulation. *Human Neurobiology, 1*(3), 195–204.

Born, J., and Wilhelm, I. (2012). System consolidation of memory during sleep. *Psychological Research, 76*(2), 192–203.

Carskadon, M. A. (2011). Sleep in adolescents: the perfect storm. *Pediatric Clinics, 58*(3), 637–47.

Carskadon, M. A., Acebo, C., and Jenni, O. G. (2004). Regulation of adolescent sleep. *Annals of the New York Academy of Sciences, 1021*, 276–91.

Carskadon, M. A., Orav, E. J., and Dement, W. C. (1983). Evolution of sleep and daytime sleepiness in adolescents. In C. Guilleminault and E. Lugaresi (Eds.), *Sleep/Wake Disorders: Natural History, Epidemiology, and Long-Term Evolution* (pp. 201–16). New York: Raven Press.

Chaput, J. P., Gray, C. E., Poitras, V. J., et al. (2016). Systematic review of the relationships between sleep duration and health indicators in school-aged children and youth. *Applied Physiology, Nutrition, and Metabolism, 41*(6), S266–82.

Crowley, S. J., Acebo, C., and Carskadon, M. A. (2007). Sleep, circadian rhythms, and delayed phase in adolescence. *Sleep Medicine, 8*(6), 602–12.

Crowley, S. J., Van Reen, E., LeBourgeois, M. K., et al. (2014). A longitudinal assessment of sleep timing, circadian phase, and phase angle of entrainment across human adolescence. *PLoS One, 9*(11), e112199.

Danner, F., and Phillips, B. (2008). Adolescent sleep, school start times, and teen motor vehicle crashes. *Journal of Clinical Sleep Medicine, 4*(6), 533–35.

Dewald, J. F., Meijer, A. M., Oort, F. J., et al. (2010). The influence of sleep quality, sleep duration and sleepiness on school performance in children and adolescents: a meta-analytic review. *Sleep Medicine Reviews, 14*(3), 179–89.

Dewald-Kaufmann, J. F., Oort, F. J., and Meijer, A. M. (2014). The effects of sleep extension and sleep hygiene advice on sleep and depressive symptoms in adolescents: a randomized, controlled trial. *Journal of Child Psychology and Psychiatry, 55*(3), 273–83.

Dimitriou, D., Le Cornu Knight, F., and Milton, P. (2015). The role of environmental factors on sleep patterns and school performance in adolescents. *Frontiers in Psychology, 6*, 1717.

Gais, S., Lucas, B., and Born, J. (2006). Sleep after learning aids memory recall. *Learning and Memory, 13*(3), 259–62.

Gomes, A. A., Tavares, J., and de Azevedo, M. H. P. (2011). Sleep and academic performance in undergraduates: a multi-measure, multi-predictor approach. *Chronobiology International, 28*(9), 786–801.

Gradisar, M., Gardner, G., and Dohnt, H. (2011). Recent worldwide sleep patterns and problems during adolescence: a review and meta-analysis of age, region, and sleep. *Sleep Medicine, 12*(2), 110–18.

Gruber, R., Somerville, G., Enros, P., et al. (2014). Sleep efficiency (but not sleep duration) of healthy school-age children is associated with grades in math and languages. *Sleep Medicine, 15*(12), 1517–25.

Gupta, N. K., Mueller, W. H., Chan, W., and Meininger, J. C. (2002). Is obesity associated with poor sleep quality in adolescents? *American Journal of Human Biology, 14*(6), 762–68.

Henderson, L. M., Weighall, A. R., Brown, H., and Gareth Gaskell, M. (2012). Consolidation of vocabulary is associated with sleep in children. *Developmental Science, 15*(5), 674–87.

Hysing, M., Harvey, A. G., Linton, S. J., et al. (2016). Sleep and academic performance in later adolescence: results from a large population-based study. *Journal of Sleep Research, 25*(3), 318–24.

Jenni, O. G., Achermann, P., and Carskadon, M. A. (2005). Homeostatic sleep regulation in adolescents. *Sleep, 28*(11), 1446–54.

Kelley, P., Lockley, S. W., Kelley, J., and Evans, M. D. (2017). Is 8:30 am still too early to start school? A 10:00 am school start time improves health and performance of students aged 13–16. *Frontiers in Human Neuroscience, 11*, 588.

Kopasz, M., Loessl, B., Valerius, G., et al. (2010). No persisting effect of partial sleep curtailment on cognitive performance and declarative memory recall in adolescents. *Journal of Sleep Research, 19*(1 Part I), 71–79.

Leger, D., Beck, F., Richard, J. B., and Godeau, E. (2012). Total sleep time severely drops during adolescence. *PLoS One, 7*(10), e45204.

Li, S., Arguelles, L., Jiang, F., et al. (2013). Sleep, school performance, and a school-based intervention among school-aged children: a sleep series study in China. *PLoS One, 8*(7), e67928.

Liou, Y. M., Liou, T. H., and Chang, L. C. (2010). Obesity among adolescents: sedentary leisure time and sleeping as determinants. *Journal of Advanced Nursing, 66*(6), 1246–56.

Lo, J. C., Lee, S. M., Teo, L. M., etal. (2017). Neurobehavioral impact of successive cycles of sleep restriction with and without naps in adolescents. *Sleep, 40*(2).

Lo, J. C., Ong, J. L., Leong, R. L., et al. (2016). Cognitive performance, sleepiness, and mood in partially sleep deprived adolescents: the need for sleep study. *Sleep, 39*(3), 687–98.

Louca, M., and Short, M. A. (2014). The effect of one night's sleep deprivation on adolescent neurobehavioral performance. *Sleep, 37*(11), 1799–1807.

Lufi, D., Tzischinsky, O., and Hadar, S. (2011). Delaying school starting time by one hour: some effects on attention levels in adolescents. *Journal of Clinical Sleep Medicine, 7*(2), 137–43.

Madden, M., Lenhart, A., Cortesi, S., and Gasser, U. (2013). *Teens and Mobile Apps Privacy*. Pew Internet and American Life Project, Washington, DC. Available at http://pewinternet.org/Reports/2012/Teens-and-Privacy.aspx.

Matthews, K. A., Dahl, R. E., Owens, J. F., et al. (2012). Sleep duration and insulin resistance in healthy black and white adolescents. *Sleep*, *35*(10), 1353–58.

Meijer, A. M., Habekothe, H. T., and Den Wittenboer, V. (2000). Time in bed, quality of sleep and school functioning of children. *Journal of Sleep Research*, *9* (2), 145–53.

Minges, K. E., and Redeker, N. S. (2016). Delayed school start times and adolescent sleep: a systematic review of the experimental evidence. *Sleep Medicine Reviews*, *28*, 86–95.

National Sleep Foundation. (2006). Sleep in America poll summary findings. NSF, Washington, DC. Available at www.sleepfoundation.org/site/c.huIXKj M0IxF/b.2419037/k1466/2006_Sleep_in_America_Poll.htm.

National Sleep Foundation. (2015). *Sleep Health: The Journal of the National Sleep Foundation*.

Owens, J. A., Belon, K., and Moss, P. (2010). Impact of delaying school start time on adolescent sleep, mood, and behavior. *Archives of Pediatrics and Adolescent Medicine*, *164*(7), 608–14.

Pasch, K. E., Laska, M. N., Lytle, L. A., and Moe, S. G. (2010). Adolescent sleep, risk behaviors, and depressive symptoms: are they linked? *American Journal of Health Behavior*, *34*(2), 237–48.

Peters, J. D., Biggs, S. N., Bauer, K. M., et al. (2009). The sensitivity of a PDA-based psychomotor vigilance task to sleep restriction in 10-year-old girls. *Journal of Sleep Research*, *18*(2), 173–77.

Prehn-Kristensen, A., Göder, R., Fischer, J., et al. (2011). Reduced sleep-associated consolidation of declarative memory in attention-deficit/ hyperactivity disorder. *Sleep Medicine*, *12*(7), 672–79.

Prehn-Kristensen, A., Munz, M., Molzow, I., et al. (2013). Sleep promotes consolidation of emotional memory in healthy children but not in children with attention-deficit hyperactivity disorder. *PLoS One*, *8*(5), e65098.

Sadeh, A., Gruber, R., and Raviv, A. (2003). The effects of sleep restriction and extension on school-age children: what a difference an hour makes. *Child Development*, *74*(2), 444–55.

Seicean, A., Redline, S., Seicean, S., et al. (2007). Association between short sleeping hours and overweight in adolescents: results from a US suburban high school survey. *Sleep and Breathing*, *11*(4), 285–93.

Vedaa, Ø., West Saxvig, I., Wilhelmsen-Langeland, A., et al. (2012). School start time, sleepiness and functioning in Norwegian adolescents. *Scandinavian Journal of Educational Research*, *56*(1), 55–67.

Wagner, U. et al. (2004). Sleep inspires insight. *Nature*, *427*(6972), 352.

Watson, N. F., Martin, J. L., Wise, M. S., et al. (2017). Delaying middle school and high school start times promotes student health and performance: an

American Academy of Sleep Medicine position statement. *Journal of Clinical Sleep Medicine, 13*(4), 623–25.

Weiss, A., Xu, F., Storfer-Isser, A., et al. (2010). The association of sleep duration with adolescents' fat and carbohydrate consumption. *Sleep, 33*(9), 1201–9.

Wheaton, A. G., Chapman, D. P., and Croft, J. B. (2016). School start times, sleep, behavioral, health, and academic outcomes: a review of the literature. *Journal of School Health, 86*(5), 363–81.

Wilhelm, I., Prehn-Kristensen, A., and Born, J. (2012). Sleep-dependent memory consolidation: what can be learnt from children? *Neuroscience and Biobehavioral Reviews, 36*(7), 1718–28.

Wilhelm, I., Rose, M., Imhof, K. I., et al. (2013). The sleeping child outplays the adult's capacity to convert implicit into explicit knowledge. *Nature Neuroscience, 16*(4), 391.

Gratitude, subjective well-being and prosociality: Implications for adolescence and education

Sarah A. Buckingham and Joseph O. L. Buckingham

As Cicero wrote, 'Gratitude is not only the greatest of the virtues, but the parent of all of the others' (see Wood et al., 2007). How many of us have been accused of not being grateful for what we have? Seneca, the Stoic philosopher, said that 'no other vice is so hostile to the harmony of the human race as ingratitude' (see Emmons, 2007, 148). When demanded and inauthentic, the concept of gratitude can seem punishing and negative, prompting resentment and anger. Thus, sermonizing may not produce the desired effect. The Latin derivative of gratitude is *gratia*, which primarily translates to 'the beauty of giving and receiving' (Pruyser, 1976, 69). We not only feel gratitude as an emotion but also acknowledge the gifts received from others who freely give to us and, in turn, we are able to reciprocate. Therefore, it has been found that the development of a habit of gratitude has the potential for people to feel happier, more motivated and more socially connected to others (Emmons, 2007).

Experiencing, expressing and receiving gratitude has been empirically linked with positive outcomes that benefit both individuals and their social environment. There is now a well-established link between gratitude and subjective well-being (Lavelock et al., 2016; Wood et al., 2010), and more recently, a meta-analysis has established that gratitude is positively linked with prosociality ($r = 0.374$; Ma et al., 2017).

Within this chapter, it is our aim to investigate in greater depth the mechanisms of gratitude in seven sections:

What is gratitude?

What does gratitude actually entail? Emmons (2004, 554) states that gratitude is 'a sense of thankfulness and joy in response to receiving a gift whether the gift is a tangible benefit from a specific other or a moment of peaceful bliss evoked by natural beauty'. Feelings of gratitude may be evoked when we receive gifts on our birthdays from loved ones or feel appreciation for what we contribute to others. We may stand in awe and feel gratitude when we perceive great beauty around us, for example, a beautiful sunset or a night sky with an abundance of stars.

The feeling of gratitude that we get from such experiences has been described as a mood and termed 'generalised gratitude' (see Lambert et al., 2009; McCullough et al., 2002). Areas of generalised gratitude include nature, beauty, the kindness of others and even the supernatural.

As such, gratitude has been described as a 'positively valenced emotion', a psychological term for describing the positive quality of an emotion (Algoe et al., 2016; Fredrickson et al., 2003). This is in contrast to a negatively valenced emotion, where the person views the world through a reductive lens, experiencing feelings of envy or resentment, for example. This concept of gratitude as an emotion can be extended further and perceived as a self-transcendental emotion (Stellar et al., 2017). This is not only positive but also allows individuals to extend their world beyond themselves. Gordon Stellar et al. (2017) highlight awe, compassion and gratitude as the significant self-transcendental emotions that help create the social glue that binds us through cooperation to our families and communities (see also Haidt, 2003; McCullough et al., 2001).

Therefore, gratitude can be seen as a virtuous personality trait and is therefore dispositional. It is potentially beneficial to the self and others; for example, 'Sam is a person who is appreciative and grateful' (McCullough et al., 2002; Wood et al., 2010). Paired with gratitude, a wider range of appreciative cues, acknowledged by a person, offers greater potential to build and expand on this positive and beneficial trait. We might even say that such characters are pillars of a strong, functioning society.

When triggered by kind acts (i.e. benefit-laden gratitude), gratitude is deemed as a cognitive affective state, that is, state-like (Watkins et al., 2009), which is temporary and linked to thoughts, actions and emotions. As such, the reciprocal expression of gratitude is perhaps best described as a moral motivator (e.g., to practise good deeds; Gilbert and Choden, 2015) that motivates people to approach others (Cacioppo et al., 1999). Therefore, gratitude has the potential to better the experience of others through voluntary generous reciprocal acts, thus promoting prosociality (Bartlett and DeSteno, 2006; Ma et al., 2017).

Further exploration into reciprocal acts leads to primitive reciprocal displays of gratitude, which have been observed in non-human primates – *I'll scratch your back if you scratch mine*. As such, this action has been described as symmetry-based reciprocity, practised among primates who live in close quarters (Bonnie and de Waal, 2014). Interestingly, having engaged in this reciprocal behaviour, chimpanzees were more likely to share food with their former grooming partner than other unknown chimps. This is described as a display of proto-gratitude (initial cognitive scaffolding), where the chimps appear to possess an ability to remember good deeds done and reciprocate a good deed at a later time (Bonnie and de Waal, 2014; Darwin, 1871/2004). Within symmetry-based reciprocity, non-verbal behaviours, such as touch (e.g. handshake), can potentially communicate with as much variance as verbal means in certain situations. We begin to see how gratitude might benefit others and also help to build and maintain bonds within certain communities, but do we see evidence of such positive outcomes in all cultures?

The ability to feel and express gratitude is universal but is mediated by cultural differences, cultural norms and other environmental factors. Cultures that express greater levels of gratitude are more likely to maintain reciprocity and group harmony (Kee et al., 2008; Naito et al., 2005). Furthermore, it has been found that the cultures that display greater levels of religiosity experience higher levels of gratitude (Emmons and Mishra, 2012), and more collectivist cultures that endorse and celebrate acts of thanks and appreciation report greater levels of subjective well-being and reduced levels of disease.

However, Robert Emmons and Charltes Shelton (2002) argue that although gratitude is universal, it is not innate. The development of gratitude as a moral virtue extends beyond proto-gratitude and instead changes throughout childhood, depending upon the influence of parents and caregivers, the wider cultural milieu and the psychological characteristics of the individuals involved. Research has even begun to report that these factors may predict the level of potential gratitude development (see Kağıtçıbaşı, 2007, 2012). Therefore, a supportive environment that encourages autonomy is a more fertile ground for gratitude development than one that is controlling and rule bound (see Carlo, 2014).

Differing forms of obligation may also mediate the development and response of gratitude. For example, with heteronomous obligation, gratitude may be dutifully expressed, whereas with autonomous obligation, gratitude may be more freely expressed and extend the bonds between self and others (see Mendonça and Palhares, 2018). A child's ability to move beyond the social norm response of 'thank you' to actually feeling grateful for a gift and additionally seeing the intention of the benefactor and willingly reciprocating requires some level of conscious awareness to be present. Indeed, the ability to recognize the intention of the benefactor is sophisticated and one that develops throughout childhood and adolescence. Significant figures such as Franziska Baumgarten-Tramer (1938) and Jean Piaget ([1932] 1997, [1965] 1995) have held that gratitude is a primary factor in a child's moral development.

In Baumgarten-Tamer's model, three developmental stages of verbal, concrete and connective gratitude are described. These stages emerged from a Swiss study (Baumgarten-Tramer, 1938) where Baumgarten-Tramer asked children aged 7–15 years ($\sim N$ = 1,000) to write down their greatest wish. The children were then asked to say what they would do for their benefactor if this wish were granted. The study found that children were roughly divided into the three categories of verbal, concrete and connective gratitude, ascending in levels of complexity. Verbal gratitude is a basic 'thank you', followed on by the more egocentric concrete gratitude where children tend to pay back their benefactor with gifts, such as toys or money, without the ability to think about the other person's wishes. Findings report that this stage generally diminishes from the ages of 7 to 15 years, with connective gratitude increasing in the same period. This more sophisticated stage of gratitude development acknowledges the 'other', taking into account their desires and wishes as a separate individual. The responsibility to return the favour (i.e. autonomous obligation) was not evidenced in children under age 11. This study has been elaborated and repeated by several research teams, which have found similar results (see Castro et al., 2011; Freitas et al., 2009, 2011; Tudge et al., 2015). Other work has focused on early adolescence (ages 11–13 years) and the impact gratitude has on their subjective well-being (Froh et al., 2009a, 2009b), which we will now explore further.

Gratitude and subjective well-being

What do we mean by subjective well-being? A helpful definition has been given by Ed Diener et al. (2002), who delineated three components: (1) a subjective life evaluation relating to experience of pleasant emotions, (2) a near absence of negative affect and (3) a satisfaction of experience in relation to a meaningful and rewarding life. Positive psychology has provided an initial platform for assessment (Linley et al., 2006) and an expansive and burgeoning literature (see McCullough et al., 2008). But perhaps a more integrative approach to health is worthy of consideration.

Many non-Western cultures have taken an approach to health that is more holistic, where mind, body and spirit are considered within the context of personal and collective well-being. In contrast, Western philosophy has tended to take a dualistic approach to physical and mental health, with the former still currently more dominant in the approach to well-being. As such, psychological health has previously been considered the underdog, and denial regarding its impact on the physical body is both prevalent and corrosive. In the West, we are beginning to re-evaluate the relationship between the mind and body and how they are intrinsically linked (see Naylor et al., 2016). The effects of stress on the physical body have been well documented (Yaribeygi et al., 2017). A 24/7 fast-paced contemporary lifestyle and the associated stresses have led medical practitioners to use more divergent approaches. With the advent and validation for mainstream use (e.g. to relieve stress among UK National Health Service staff) of more 'complementary' approaches to stress, such as mindfulness meditation and yoga, for example, we are nudged into considering a more integrated perspective (see Naylor et al., 2016).

It has been demonstrated that when such approaches are used, activation of the parasympathetic branch of the autonomic sympathetic nervous system (ANS) helps to reduce the sympathetic physiological response to stress (e.g., Pascoe and Bauer, 2015). Moreover, the regulatory action of the hypothalamic-pituitary-adrenal axis aids in restoring homeostatis. The experience and expression of gratitude may also act in a similar way and potentially stimulate a eudaimonic response (Kashdan et al., 2006; Wood et al., 2009).

For example, sleep hygiene has become big business with the acknowledgement that good-quality sleep is critical to both mental and physical health. Experiencing positive pre-sleep cognitions has been shown to improve quality and quantity of sleep (Nelson and Harvey, 2003). In a community sample ($N =$ 401) where 40% were suffering from sleep deprivation, a gratitude intervention demonstrated the positive impact of expressing gratitude pre-sleep and the resulting levels of refreshment and positivity on waking and more hours spent in slumber (see Wood et al., 2010).

Alongside increased quality of sleep, expression and experience of gratitude have been linked with lower blood pressure and better immune function (Emmons, 2015). Other studies have found that individuals who exhibited higher levels of gratitude consistently experienced lower levels of depression and stress (e.g. McCullough et al., 2004; Watkins et al., 2003). Gratitude would appear to act as a buffer to the more negative emotions.

To demonstrate this potential buffer further, two studies (Wood et al., 2008, 2009) compared gratitude with the thirty facets of the 'five factor model of personality' (Watson et al., 1994). Taken together, the findings demonstrated significant relationships with positive emotion, warmth, trust, altruism, tender mindedness, gregariousness, dutifulness, activity, competence, achievement striving, values and ideas. Significant negative relationships were found between gratitude and vulnerability, anger, hostility and depression. When the thirty facets of the five factor model were controlled, analysis demonstrated that gratitude predicted a unique variance of 8% ($r = 0.28$) in relationship to life satisfaction, the third component of the well-being definition.

Other studies have demonstrated relationships between gratitude and life satisfaction. For example, twenty-four personality strengths were linked with life satisfaction, where gratitude was found to be the third most significant factor, accounting for $r = 0.43$ variance (Park et al., 2004). In a sample of US participants ($N = 12,439$) where an online survey investigated links between life satisfaction, orientations to happiness and character strengths, gratitude was the most significant variable in relationship to life satisfaction (Peterson et al., 2007) but, interestingly, not to happiness. The same survey was conducted with pen and paper with a Swiss sample ($N = 445$) where gratitude was significantly related to the character strength of perseverance. These confounding results may be due to the differing mechanics of the study design or indeed to culture differences.

As such, it would appear that a significant proportion of life satisfaction is reliant on the amount of gratitude experienced. It has been described as a higher-order life orientation toward the positive and one that is adaptive, where the actor is more morally motivated to interact in an appreciative manner both personally and socially (Wood et al., 2009, 2010). Surrounding ourselves with beauty, for example, through studying the arts, poetry, prose or music or by being in nature extends our world views to encompass the positive and exhilarating aspects of life. We should not underestimate, however, the degree to which we are predominantly social beings, taking strength and gaining resilience from being among people similar to ourselves. Therefore, gratitude as a cognitive affective state may be a critical adaptive reflexive mechanism (Emmons and Crumpler, 2000; McCullough et al., 2008).

Within the mutual aid fellowship groups of Alcoholics Anonymous (AA), individuals are said to suffer from a threefold illness that is a physical, mental and spiritual 'dis-ease' (Alcoholics Anonymous, 2001). Frequently, many people who find themselves in this dilemma have lost everything, and they find themselves at 'rock bottom' and alone. As they enter the recovery stage and start to confront their unhelpful habits within a group setting, individuals are encouraged to express gratitude for what they do have. This seemingly simple process helps shift the perspective from self-pity, shame and remorse to a more positive one. The individual experience is less one of isolation and more one of a sense of belonging. The expression of gratitude on a daily basis provides an opportunity to focus on the positive benefits of staying sober and acts as a platform for expressing thanks to others within the group who aid in this process. Within this particular group, one approach is to encourage individuals to make a nightly gratitude list and to also notice elements of their day that could have gone better and to make amends to others, if appropriate. They are also encouraged to practise acts of kindness without getting found out. Stopping resentments when they arise alleviates the risk of gratitude being snagged by such corrosive emotions. As such, observation of this particular group's mechanisms is an excellent example of how acknowledging and expressing gratitude both impact subjective well-being and aid in prosociality. As a moral virtue, we can see how gratitude may act as a channel to individuals becoming more effective members of society.

Gratitude and prosociality

'Prosociality' has been defined as a broad spectrum of behaviours and intentions that benefit an individual or collective (see Ma et al., 2017). A three-part focused definition of gratitude delivered more recently by academics (philosophers and psychologists) for research purposes stresses the interpersonal quality of this cognitive construct. As such, (1) a benefactor (A) gives to beneficiary (B) with good intention; (2) the beneficiary (B) has knowledge of how the gift from the benefactor (A) was given, that is, in good spirit and freely gifted or in bad faith and under duress; and (3) the beneficiary (B) has a desire to repay the benefactor (A) freely and with something that (A) would value (see Fagley, 2016). Therefore, gratitude as a moral virtue is driven by intention; the ability to recognise the intention of the benefactor is sophisticated and one that develops through childhood and adolescence.

An act of gratitude towards a known benefactor not only benefits that person but may also benefit the known initiator. This is described as *direct* reciprocity. It makes one feel good about oneself and can trigger similar reciprocal acts of thanks and appreciation (McCullough et al., 2008). The benefactor is also more likely to extend such acts to unknown others (*indirect* reciprocity), and the effect of being in receipt of a gracious act through thought or deed may have a ripple effect, creating a cascade of *indirect upstream* reciprocal action (Sigmund, 2010). An act of gratitude by A to B leads B to an act of gratitude to C, and so on. *Indirect downstream* reciprocal action involves moral elevation through reputation of a group or individual but may ultimately bear group-laden benefits from third parties, that is, A to B and C to A (Nowak and Roch, 2007). For example, Joseph Rowntree of the confectionary family and also a Quaker, promoted good moral standards and social reform through generous acts towards his workers. He did this by considering their mental, moral and educational development, thus enabling recipients to enjoy benefits that previously would not have been in their grasp. In tandem, Rowntree's confectionary business was rewarding and successful (see Rowntree Society, www.rowntreesociety.org.uk). We see A giving to B, and C, through observation, reciprocates to A. Where direct and indirect reciprocal gratitude is the mechanism, we are more likely to observe the development of prosociality (Ma et al., 2017; Nowak, 2006; Nowak and Roch, 2007). In their meta-analysis, involving ninety-one studies and $N = 18,342$ participants, Ma et al. (2017) found that gratitude had the second largest effect size after general positive affect. These relationships were found to be over and above negative affect, shame, anger, happiness and empathy. Therefore, from this study, we can conclude that gratitude holds a special relationship with prosociality and is a key to the formation of social bonds and relationships.

Neuroscience and gratitude

So far, we have established that gratitude can be conceptualised as a positive emotion and that feelings of gratitude have been linked to both subjective well-being and prosociality. A cognitive neuroscience perspective may offer greater understanding of how gratitude is produced in the brain and help to explain the links to well-being and prosociality, possibly even helping to improve the design of gratitude interventions (see Fox et al., 2015; Huffman et al., 2016).

One of the first investigations to directly address the neural basis of gratitude asked participants to imagine themselves in the place of Holocaust survivors receiving crucial support and supplies from strangers (Fox et al., 2015). During these scripts, participants rated their feelings of gratitude for the gifts they received whilst functional magnetic resonance imaging (fMRI) was carried out. A type of brain imaging, fMRI indirectly measures neural activity by detecting changes in blood flow around the brain. A higher level of blood flow, as indicated by the blood oxygen level–dependent signal, implies a greater use of oxygen and, because of this, a greater use of energy by brain cells. This type of brain imaging has good spatial resolution and is capable of detecting changes on the scale of millimetres but is only able to capture an image every few seconds. The results of this study revealed that feelings of gratitude were correlated with increased activation in two different areas of the brain, the medial prefrontal cortex and the anterior cingulate cortex. Both these areas have been linked previously to reward and social cognitive processes. The medial prefrontal cortex is well established to play a role in theory of mind, empathy, social bonding and the calculation of subjective value, whilst both the anterior cingulate cortex and the medial prefrontal cortex have been associated with moral reasoning (Bzdok et al., 2012; Harris et al., 2007; Rameson et al., 2012; van den Bos et al., 2007). This led Glenn Fox et al. (2015) to propose that feelings of gratitude may involve the medial prefrontal cortex's processes of gauging subjective value and considering the mental states of other people. They additionally noted similarities between the pattern of activation they observed and those found in studies investigating empathy and pain (Jackson et al., 2006; Lamm et al., 2007; Singer et al., 2004). This led them to suggest that further investigations into possible links between gratitude, pain and empathy could help to establish means by which feelings of gratitude influence well-being or pro-sociality.

Another study investigating the neural correlates of gratitude examined the impact of a gratitude intervention on those who had begun receiving therapy for either anxiety or depression (Kini et al., 2016). In this study, the experimental group completed a gratitude writing exercise in addition to therapy, whilst the control group only completed therapy. After a period of three months, participants were then given a gift of money whilst being scanned in fMRI. They were then instructed to donate a proportion of their gift to charity if they felt grateful. Similar to the previous study, results of the fMRI again showed increased activation in the medial prefrontal cortex, as well as increased activity in occipital brain areas, even when feelings of guilt and desire to help were statistically accounted for. Additionally, participants who had completed the gratitude writing exercise three months earlier donated more money and showed an increased neural gratitude response, including more activation in the medial prefrontal cortex. These results extended those of Glenn Fox et al. (2015) by implying that expressing gratitude, even briefly, can have a lasting impact on behavior and brain function.

These findings were supported by a more recent investigation conducted by Hongbo Yu et al. (2017). Rather than use scripted situations, this study instead employed an interactive game in which participants received a painful shock during fMRI. In each round, an anonymous partner was able to share some of this painful stimulation with the participant. The results again showed that regions of the medial prefrontal cortex were most activated in response to the participant's partners sharing the painful stimulus. Additionally, sections of the septum and hypothalamus were also activated, areas associated with social bonding and positive feelings. Indeed, other research has shown that social bonding and the formation of attachment are both correlated with increased activation of these areas (Moll et al., 2012; Noriuchi et al., 2008; Strathearn et al., 2009). This is in line with the suggestion that feelings of gratitude are important to the formation of social relationships (e.g. Algoe, 2012) and further led the authors to suggest that receiving intentional help likely triggers feelings of attachment and may precipitate social bonding.

The work discussed so far has tended to focus on gratitude in terms of reciprocal exchange, but some recent research has instead begun to examine the impact that gratitude-based interventions have on the body and brain. A recent study conducted by Sunghyoun Kyeong et al. (2017) conducted fMRI brain scanning and heart rate measurement at baseline during a gratitude intervention and finally after the intervention. The intervention involved participants relaxing themselves with deep breaths before receiving instructions to spend a short period considering their gratitude, appreciation and love for their mothers. The data were then subjected to functional connectivity analysis, a method that spots coherent increases or decreases in activation in order to detect changes in the networks of the brain. The cardiovascular results showed that heart rate decreased whilst participants completed the gratitude meditation, implying a greater level of physical relaxation. The resting state of participants' brains was further shown to be influenced by the intervention, with changes in the functional connectivity of the amygdala, nucleus accumbens and a number of brain networks – all areas associated with emotion, motivation and reward. This led to the suggestion that interventions based on gratitude may influence well-being by changing the functional connectivity of these emotion-, reward- and motivation-related areas while the brain is in a resting state.

Other recent research similarly examined a written gratitude intervention and its influence on the brain (Karns et al., 2017). This involved participants completing a diary expressing their gratitude for a period of three weeks before observing gifts being given to a charity during fMRI scanning rather than to the participants themselves. The results showed that participants asked to keep the gratitude journal showed increased activation of altruism-associated signals in the ventromedial prefrontal cortex in response to observing the charitable donations. The researchers concluded that those asked to practice gratitude showed greater neural altruistic response, possibly implying a role for these kinds of gratitude interventions in increasing altruistic behavior, although more evidence will be needed to substantiate this further.

All this evidence suggests that feelings of gratitude are linked with activation in brain areas associated with thinking about other people, judging subjective value, emotion, motivation and reward (Fox et al., 2015; Karns et al., 2017; Kini et al., 2016; Kyeong et al., 2017; Yu et al., 2017). These changes occurred in response to a range of different manipulations and interventions, including scripted visualisations, gratitude writing exercises, tasks involving the charitable donation of money and even sharing painful stimuli. Of particular note is that a single gratitude writing exercise appears to have lasting neural effects on the brain after a period of three months. However, to our knowledge, there has yet to be investigations conducted on adolescents, an issue that limits the use of this research for educational contexts. Indeed, cognitive neuroscientific research conducted on adolescents suggests that neural processes relating to social cognition sometimes appear to operate differently to adults (see Blakemore, 2010). Of particular relevance is research suggesting that thinking about others mental states activates different systems in adolescents, which may imply that experiencing gratitude could similarly rely on alternative systems (e.g., Burnett and Blakemore, 2009). Despite these initial promising results, we conclude that more research is needed before strong claims can be made concerning the impact of gratitude in educational contexts from a cognitive neuroscience perspective.

Gratitude in children and adolescents in an educational setting

Interestingly, there are still only a limited number of studies that have investigated gratitude and adolescents/adolescence (~179; see Bausert et al., 2018). If gratitude is the *parent of all emotions* and we accept that it is a moral virtue that requires facilitation, we surely have a moral responsibility as parents and educators to explore, nurture and support this core emotion. Initially providing the scaffolding through the development of proto-gratitude, we can expose children and adolescents to situations where they can appreciate beauty through the arts or through study of the natural world, for example. We can also provide occasions for acts of giving and receiving gifts and to explore their feelings in connection with those interactions. The intention of the benefactor, the value of benefits and the roles that obligation, respect and trust play and the way they interact are critical areas of moral development that have been neglected until recently but are key points for consideration (see Morgan and Gulliford, 2018).

To provide adolescent students and members of staff with an opportunity to reflect on the role that gratitude played in their lives, a gratitude intervention entitled 'Nice November' was implemented by BrainCanDo at Queen Anne's School, Caversham, United Kingdom (2018). This month-long intervention was also designed to explore whether recording moments of daily gratitude within an educational setting would change levels of gratitude, subjective well-being and sense of belonging. All students and staff ($N = 665$) were invited to participate on an anonymous basis. Uptake for time 1 was $n = 384$ (57%) and for time 2 was $n = 225$ (34%). Online surveys designed on Survey Monkey recorded levels of gratitude, belonging and subjective well-being at Time 1 and 2. These surveys included a measurement of gratitude, that is, the 'Gratitude and Resentment Scale' (GRAT; Watkins et al., 2003); the measurement for subjective well-being, that is, the 'Satisfaction with Life Scale' (Diener et al., 1985); and a measurement of perceived school belonging and connectedness, that is, the 'Psychological Sense of School Membership Scale' (PSSM; Goodenow, 1992).

Each participant was given a gratitude journal that was designed with inspirational quotes for each day, for example, 'People will forget what you said, people will forget what you did, but people will never forget how you made them feel' (Angelou, 2004, 14). These quotes were also presented on white boards around the school environment as cues for gratitude during each particular November day. In the mornings, participants were invited to write messages of gratitude which were posted in collection points around the school. These anonymous messages were written on leaf-shaped paper and placed throughout the month on a gratitude tree so that it was fully blossomed at the end. Participants were invited to list areas of gratitude in their diaries at the end of each day, that is, 'I am thankful to/for', and then to record the reason for their gratitude, that is, 'because …'. Instruction given at the beginning of the journal asked participants to acknowledge areas of gratitude such as good turns done, gifts given (including opportunities), accolades won, moments of pleasure and so on. It was also stated that if the day had not gone as well as expected, it was suggested to participants to focus on acceptance of the situation and change perspective on the matter, thus taking responsibility for their own reaction.

Results demonstrated high levels of all variables both at the beginning and at the end of the month, although there was evidence of variability between all groups, that is, pupil year groups and staff members. It is noted that attrition rates were high, and therefore, it is difficult to draw conclusions from this initial study. Future work could include more interactive interventions, where, for example, a benefactor might be read the gratitude out loud, thus creating opportunity for reciprocity. As such, writing a thank-you note to someone who you feel gratitude for within the school environment may also prompt social closeness and deliver a more in vivo approach (Algoe et al., 2016; Seligman et al., 2005).

The online survey questionnaire may also need adjustment. For example, a criticism of the GRAT (Gulliford et al., 2013; Wang et al., 2015) used in this study suggests that the design of this particular gratitude measurement does not navigate the stages of development within differing age groups appropriately. Neither does it capture cultural differences within such an international educational establishment. Clarity and consistency of meaning may be better served with an assessment questionnaire where reciprocal gratitude is explored through assessing children's feelings toward their benefactor (see O'Brien et al., 2018). The use of vignettes is also proving useful in exploring this interaction and importantly may also deliver greater consistency for research purposes through coding (Freitas et al., 2009).

As November is a traditional month for giving thanks, it was anticipated that this particular intervention would be modified and potentially repeated within other educational settings, as it appeared to be a beneficial tool to highlight this important area of social and personal moral and emotional development within the school community. Interestingly, a couple of individuals who were struggling were able to voice their difficulties through this intervention and although anonymous were encouraged to seek guidance through the normal school channels.

Opportunities for exploration of gratitude interventions can be built around other international cultural festivals and celebrations and also invite a more integrative approach. This can be delivered through creative channels such as storytelling, spiritual/religious texts, inspirational films, dramatic enactment and other immersive gratitude activity such as Nice November.

Gratitude interventions

The most popular intervention has been the gratitude list (see Davis et al., 2016; Emmons and McCullough, 2003; Renshaw and Olinger Steeves, 2016; Wood et al., 2010). As already mentioned, asking people to keep a gratitude diary and listing three to six items before sleep have been beneficial and have been found to be just as effective or even superior to other clinical interventions in certain populations. These interventions have been extended up to periods of ten weeks with a weekly request for diary keeping. Other interventions have been shorter but requested a daily list. The effects of these interventions have been found to be sustained over longer periods and have also proved popular among participants, where many have continued the exercise over and above the study requirements (Seligman, 2005).

An alternative intervention has been gratitude focusing. This simple perceptual exercise asks people to divert their gaze to elements in their lives for which they feel gratitude and then to list them. This brief intervention of perhaps only five minutes has been found to elevate mood in a limited time frame (Koo et al., 2008).

Other interventions endorse behavioural expressions of gratitude, such as the 'gratitude visit', where individuals are encouraged to write a thank-you letter to a benefactor and then to take it to that person personally and to read it out aloud. Although effortful, this exercise appears to be successful, where greater levels of happiness and reduced levels of depression have been recorded (see Wood et al., 2010). The effects have been found to extend to two months after the intervention.

Gratitude interventions that promote social bonding directly and are *in vivo* have been shown to be more beneficial than those that are retrospective in nature. Lawrence Ma et al. (2017) suggest that as such, they are excellent vehicles to aid in subjective well-being. Interventions that 'broaden and build' affects and cognitions can potentially expand an individual's repertoire and aid in this process, benefitting both mental and physical health (Fredrickson, 2004). Taken further, the theory of find-remind-bind describes how this is operationalised through responsiveness to others, valuing those we have been helped by in the past and enhancing social bonds through reciprocal acts of kindness (see Algoe, 2012).

Conclusion

From this brief foray into the study of gratitude, it is evident that gratitude is intrinsic for both subjective well-being and pro-sociality. The ability to respond to nature and beauty with gratitude expands an individual's worldview in a positive way. The habitual practice of gratitude would appear to act as a buffer to negative emotions such as depression and resentment. The appreciation for the natural world instils a sense of awe, and in these days of climate change awareness, such feelings may be fundamental to move forward in the spirit of change.

Critically, if we are to continue effectively as a species, gratitude is among the character traits to which we should turn our gaze. History has shown us that we are more effective as a collective. It is the reciprocal action (both direct and indirect) of the act of gratitude that appears to support strengthening relationships through emotional exchanges of thanks. We become more flexible and adaptive, and gratitude allows us to appreciate nonkin others. Neuroscientific studies on gratitude endorse these findings, suggesting that this core emotion and moral virtue are fundamental if we are to feel a sense of belonging and engage in altruistic behaviour.

Critically, more research is needed in the area of gratitude and adolescence. This is especially true in the field of neuroscience. Interventions that promote reciprocity would aid in this work and deliver some much-needed research-based findings to explore the roles of empathy, motivation and reward in relation to gratitude.

In the spirit of this chapter, we would like to extend our thanks to the editors for the opportunity to deliver our research into gratitude and contribute to this worthy volume. Finally, it is, we suggest, our responsibility to practise gratitude in all areas of our lives, to act as mentors to our children and as facilitators of reciprocal actions that benefit both ourselves and our communities.

References

Alcoholics Anonymous. (2001). *Alcoholics Anonymous: The Story of How Thousands of Men and Women Have Recovered from Alcoholism*. New York: Alcoholics Anonymous World Services.

Algoe, S. B. (2012). Find, remind, and bind: the functions of gratitude in everyday relationships. *Social and Personality Psychology Compass, 6,* 455–69.

Algoe, S. B., Kurtz, L. E., and Hilaire, N. M. (2016). Putting the 'you' in 'thank you': examining other-praising behavior as the active relational ingredient in expressed gratitude. *Social Psychological and Personality Science, 7,* 658–66.

Angelou, M. (2004). They may forget what you said, but they will never forget how you made them feel.. In D. Booth and M. Hachiya (Eds.), *The Arts Go to School: Classroom-based Activities that Focus on Music, Painting, Drama, Movement, Media, and More*(p. 14). Markham, ON: Pembroke Publishers. Available at https://quoteinvestigator.com/2014/04/06/they-feel/#note-8611-1.

Bartlett, M. Y., and DeSteno, D. (2006). Gratitude and prosocial behavior. *Psychological Science, 17,* 319–25.

Baumgarten-Tramer, F. (1938). 'Gratefulness' in children and young people. *Journal of Genetic Psychology, 53,* 53–66.

Bausert, S., Froh, J. J., Bono, G., et al., (2018). Gratitude in adolescence: determinants and effects on development, prosocial behaviour, and well-being. In J. R. H. Tudge and L. B. L. Freitas (Eds.), *Developing Gratitude in Children and Adolescents* (pp. 89–110). Cambridge, UK: Cambridge University Press.

Blakemore, S. J. (2010). The developing social brain: implications for education. *Neuron, 65,* 744–47.

Bonnie, K. E., and de Waal, F. B. M. (2014). Primate social reciprocity and the origin of gratitude. In R. A. Emmons and M. E. McCullough (Eds.), *The Psychology of Gratitude* (pp. 213–29). New York: Oxford University Press.

Burnett, S., and Blakemore, S. J. (2009). Functional connectivity during a social emotion task in adolescents and in adults. *European Journal of Neuroscience, 29,* 1294–301.

Bzdok, D., Schilbach, L., Vogeley, K., et al. (2012). Parsing the neural correlates of moral cognition: ALE meta-analysis on morality, theory of mind, and empathy. *Brain Structure and Function, 217*, 783–96.

Cacioppo, J. T., Gardner, W. L., and Berntson, G. G. (1999). The affect system has parallel and integrative processing components: form follows function. *Journal of Personality and Social Psychology, 76*, 839–55.

Carlo, G. (2014). The development and correlates of prosocial moral behaviors. In M. Killen and J. G. Smetana (Eds.), *Handbook of Moral Development* (2nd ed., pp. 208–34). New York: Psychology Press.

Castro, F. M. P., Rava, P. G. S., Hoefelmann, T. B., et al. (2011). Deve-se retribuir? Gratidão e dívida simbólica na infância [Should one return a favor? Gratitude and symbolic debt in childhood]. *Estudos de Psicologia, 16*, 75–82.

Darwin, C. ([1871] 2004). *The Descent of Man and Selection in Relation to Sex.* London: Penguin Books.

Davis, D. E., Choe, E., Meyers, J., et al. (2016). Thankful for the little things: a meta-analysis of gratitude interventions. *Journal of Counseling Psychology, 63*, 20–31.

Diener, E., Emmons, R. A., Larsen, R. J., and Griffin, S. (1985). The satisfaction with life scale. *Journal of Personality Assessment, 49*, 71–75.

Diener, E., Lucas, R. E., and Oishi, S. (2002). Subjective well-being: the science of happiness and life satisfaction. In C. R. Snyder and S. J. Lopez (Eds.), *The Handbook of Positive Psychology* (pp. 213–29). New York: Oxford University Press.

Emmons, R. A. (2004). The psychology of gratitude: an introduction. In R. A. Emmons and M. E. McCullough (Eds.), *Series in Affective Science. The Psychology of Gratitude* (pp. 3–16). New York: Oxford University Press.

Emmons, R. A. (2007). *Thanks! How Practicing Gratitude Can Make You Happier.* Boston: Houghton Mifflin Company.

Emmons, R. A. (2015). Gratitude is good medicine. Available at https://health.ucdavis.edu/medicalcenter/features/2015-2016/11/20151125_gratitude.html.

Emmons, R. A., and Crumpler, C. A. (2000). Gratitude as a human strength: appraising the evidence. *Journal of Social and Clinical Psychology, 19*, 56–69.

Emmons, R. A., and McCullough, M. E. (2003). Counting blessings versus burdens: an experimental investigation of gratitude and subjective well-being in daily life. *Journal of Personality and Social Psychology, 84*, 377–89.

Emmons, R. A., and Mishra, A. (2012). Why gratitude enhances well-being: what we know, what we need to know. In K. M. Sheldon, T. B. Kashdan, and M. F. Steger (Eds.), *Designing Positive Psychology: Taking Stock and Moving Forward* (pp. 248–62). New York: Oxford University Press.

Emmons, R. A., and Shelton, C. M. (2002). Gratitude and the science of positive psychology. In C. R. Snyder and S. J. Lopez (Eds.), *Handbook of Positive Psychology* (pp. 459–71). New York: Oxford University Press.

Fagley, N. S. (2016). The construct of appreciation: it is so much more than gratitude. In D. Carr (Ed.), *Perspectives on Gratitude: An Interdisciplinary Approach* (pp. 70–84). New York: Routledge.

Fox, G. R., Kaplan, J., Damasio, H., and Damasio, A. (2015). Neural correlates of gratitude. *Frontiers in Psychology*, 6(1491). doi:10.3389/fpsyg.2015.01491.

Fredrickson, B. L. (2004). Gratitude, like other positive emotions, broadens and builds. In R. A. Emmons and M. E. McCullough (Eds.), *The Psychology of Gratitude* (pp. 145–66). New York: Oxford University Press.

Fredrickson, B. L., Tugade, M. M., Waugh, C. E., and Larkin, G. R. (2003). What good are positive emotions in crises? A prospective study of resilience and emotions following the terrorist attacks on the United States on September 11th, 2001. *Journal of Personality and Social Psychology*, *84*, 365–76.

Freitas, L. B. L., Pieta, M. A. M., and Tudge, J. R. H. (2011). Beyond politeness: the expression of gratitude in children and adolescents. *Psicologia: Reflexão E Crítica*, *24*, 757–64.

Freitas, L. B. L., Silveira, P. G., and Pieta, M. A. M. (2009). The feeling of gratitude in 5- to 12-year-old children. *Studying Psychology*, *14*, 243–50.

Froh, J. J., Kashdan, T. B., Ozimkowski, K. M., and Miller, N. (2009a). Who benefits the most from a gratitude intervention in children and adolescents? Examining positive affect as a moderator. *Journal of Positive Psychology*, *4*, 408–22.

Froh, J. J., Yurkewicz, C., and Kashdan, T. B. (2009b). Gratitude and subjective well-being in early adolescence: examining gender differences. *Journal of Adolescence*, *32*, 633–50.

Gilbert, P., and Choden. (2015). *Mindful Compassion: Using the Power of Mindfulness and Compassion to Transform Our Lives*. London: Constable & Robinson.

Goodenow, C. (1992). The psychological sense of school membership among adolescents: scale development and educational correlates. *Psychology in the Schools*, *30*, 79–90.

Gulliford, L., Morgan, B., and Kristjánsson, K. (2013). Recent work on the concept of gratitude in philosophy and psychology. *Journal of Value Inquiry*, *47*, 285–317.

Haidt, J. (2003). The moral emotions. In R. J. Davidson, K. R. Scherer, and H. H. Goldsmith (Eds.), *Handbook of Affective Sciences* (pp. 852–70). Oxford, UK: Oxford University Press.

Harris, L. T., McClure, S. M., van den Bos, W., et al. (2007). Regions of the MPFC differentially tuned to social and nonsocial affective evaluation. *Cognitive, Affective and Behavioral Neuroscience*, 7, 309–16.

Huffman, J. C., DuBois, C. M., Mastromauro, C. A., et al. (2016). Positive psychological states and health behaviors in acute coronary syndrome patients: a qualitative study. *Journal of Health Psychology*, *21*, 1026–36.

Jackson, P., Brunet, E., Meltzoff, A., and Decety, J. (2006). Empathy examined through the neural mechanisms involved in imagining how I feel versus how you feel pain. *Neuropsychologia*, *44*, 752–61.

Kağıtçıbaşı, C. (2007). *Family, Self, and Human Development Across Cultures: Theory and Applications*. New York: Psychology Press.

Kağıtçıbaşı, C. (2012). Sociocultural change and integrative syntheses in human development: autonomous-related self and social-cognitive competence. *Child Development Perspectives*, *6*, 5–11.

Karns, C. M., Moore, W. E., III, and Mayr, U. (2017). The cultivation of pure altruism via gratitude: a functional MRI study of change with gratitude practice. *Frontiers in Human Neuroscience*, *11*(599). doi:10.3389/fnhum.2017.00599.

Kashdan, T. B., Uswatte, G., and Julian, T. (2006). Gratitude and hedonic and eudaimonic well-being in Vietnam war veterans. *Behaviour Research and Therapy*, *44*, 177–99.

Kee, Y. H., Tsai, Y.-M., and Chen, L. H. (2008). Relationships between being traditional and sense of gratitude among Taiwanese high school athletes. *Psychological Reports*, *102*, 920–26.

Kini, P., Wong, J., McInnis, S., et al. (2016). The effects of gratitude expression on neural activity. *NeuroImage*, *128*, 1–10.

Koo, M., Algoe, S. B., Wilson, T. D., and Gilbert, D. T. (2008). It's a wonderful life: mentally subtracting positive events improves people's affective states, contrary to their affective forecasts. *Journal of Personality and Social Psychology*, *95*, 1217–24.

Kyeong, S., Kim, J., Kim, D. J., et al. (2017). Effects of gratitude meditation on neural network functional connectivity and brain-heart coupling. *Scientific Reports*, *7*, 432–57.

Lambert, N. M., Graham, S. M., and Fincham, F. D. (2009). A prototype analysis of gratitude: varieties of gratitude experiences. *Personality and Social Psychology Bulletin*, *35*, 1193–207.

Lamm, C., Nusbaum, H., Meltzoff, A., and Decety, J. (2007). What are you feeling? Using functional magnetic resonance imaging to assess the modulation of sensory and affective responses during empathy for pain. *PLoS One*, *2*, e1292. doi:10.1371/journal.pone.0001292.

Lavelock, C. R., Griffin, B. J., Worthington, E. L., et al. (2016). A qualitative review and integrative model of gratitude and physical health. *Journal of Psychology and Theology*, *44*, 55–86.

Linley, P. A., Joseph, S., Harrington, S., and Wood, A. M. (2006). Positive psychology: past, present, and (possible) future. *Journal of Positive Psychology*, *1*, 3–16.

Ma, L. K., Tunney, R., and Ferguson, E. (2017). Does gratitude enhance prosociality? A meta-analytic review. *Psychological Bulletin*, *143*, 601–35.

McCullough, M. E., Emmons, R. A., and Tsang, J.-A. (2002). The grateful disposition: A conceptual and empirical topography. *Journal of Personality and Social Psychology*, *82*, 112–27.

McCullough, M. E., Kilpatrick, S. D., Emmons, R. A., and Larson, D. B. (2001). Is gratitude a moral affect? *Psychological Bulletin*, *127*, 249–66.

McCullough, M. E., Kimeldorf, M. B., and Cohen, A. D. (2008). An adaptation for altruism? The social causes, social effects, and social evolution of gratitude. *Current Directions in Psychological Science*, *17*, 281–85.

McCullough, M. E., Tsang, J., and Emmons, R. A. (2004). Gratitude in inter-mediate affective terrain: links of grateful moods with individual differences and daily emotional experience. *Journal of Personality and Social Psychology, 86,* 295–309.

Mendonça, S. E., and Palhares, F. (2018). Gratitude and moral obligation. In J. R. H. Tudge and L. B. L. Freitas (Eds.), *Developing Gratitude in Children and Adolescents* (pp. 89–110). Cambridge, UK: Cambridge University Press.

Moll, J., Bado, P., de Oliveira-Souza, R., et al. (2012). A neural signature of affiliative emotion in the human septohypothalamic area. *Journal of Neuroscience, 32,* 12499–505.

Morgan, B., and Gulliford, L. (2018). Assessing influences on gratitude experi-ence: age-related differences in how gratitude is understood and experienced. In J. R. H. Tudge and L. B. L. Freitas (Eds.), *Developing Gratitude in Children and Adolescents* (pp. 65–88). Cambridge, UK: Cambridge University Press.

Naito, T., Wangwan, J., and Tani, M. (2005). Gratitude in university students in Japan and Thailand. *Journal of Cross-Cultural Psychology, 36,* 247–63.

Naylor, C., Das, P., Ross, S., Honeyman, M., et al. (2016). *Bringing Together Physical and Mental Health: A New Frontier for Integrated Care.* London: The Kings Fund. Available at www.kingsfund.org.uk/sites/default/files/field/field_publication_file/Bringing-together-Kings-Fund-March-2016_1.pdf.

Nelson, J., and Harvey, A. G. (2003). An exploration of pre-sleep cognitive activ-ity in insomnia: imagery and verbal thought. *British Journal of Clinical Psychology, 42,* 271–88.

Noriuchi, M., Kikuchi, Y., and Senoo, A. (2008). The functional neuroanatomy of maternal love: mother's response to infant's attachment behaviors. *Biological Psychiatry, 63,* 415–23.

Nowak, M., and Roch, S. (2007). Upstream reciprocity and the evolution of gratitude. *Proceedings of the Royal Society of London, Series B: Biological Sciences, 274,* 605–10.

Nowak, M. A. (2006). Five rules for the evolution of cooperation. *Science, 314,* 1560–63.

O'Brien, L., Liang, Y., Merçon-Vargas, E. A., Price, U. S., and Leon, E. D. (2018). Relations between parents' and childrens's gratitude. In J. R. H. Tudge and L. B. L. Freitas (Eds.), *Developing Gratitude in Children and Adolescents* (pp. 65–88). Cambridge, UK: Cambridge University Press.

Park, N., Peterson, C., and Seligman, M. E. P. (2004). Strengths of character and well-being. *Journal of Social and Clinical Psychology, 23,* 603–19.

Pascoe, M. C., and Bauer, I. E. (2015). A systematic review of randomised con-trol trials on the effects of yoga on stress measures and mood. *Journal of Psychi-atric Research, 68,* 270–82. doi:10.1016/j.jpsychires.2015.07.013.

Peterson, C., Ruch, W., Beerman, U., et al. (2007). Strengths of character, orien-tations to happiness, and life satisfaction. *Journal of Positive Psychology, 2,* 149–56.

Piaget, J. ([1932] 1997). *The Moral Judgment of the Child.* New York: Free Press.

Piaget, J. ([1965] 1995). *Sociological Studies.* New York: Routledge.

Pruyser, P. W. (1976). *The Minister as Diagnostician: Personal Problems in Pastoral Perspective*. Oxford, UK: Westminster.

Rameson, L. T., Morelli, S. A., and Lieberman, M. D. (2012). The neural correlates of empathy: experience, automaticity, and prosocial behavior. *Journal of Cognitive Neuroscience*, *24*, 235–45.

Renshaw, T. L., and Olinger Steeves, R. M. (2016). What good is gratitude in youth and schools? A systematic review and meta-analysis of correlates and intervention outcomes. *Psychology in the Schools*, *53*, 286–305.

Seligman, M. E. P. (2005). Positive interventions. Paper presented at the Fourth International Positive Psychology Summit, Washington, DC.

Seligman, M. E. P., Steen, T. A., Park, N., and Peterson, C. (2005). Positive psychology progress: empirical validation of interventions. *American Psychologist*, *60*, 410–21.

Sigmund, K. (2010). *The Calculus of Selfishness*. Princeton, NJ: Princeton University Press.

Singer, T., Seymour, B., O'Doherty, J., et al. (2004). Empathy for pain involves the affective but not sensory components of pain. *Science*, *303*, 1157–62.

Stellar, J. E., Gordon, A. M., Piff, P. K., et al. (2017). Self-transcendent emotions and their social functions: compassion, gratitude, and awe bind us to others through pro-sociality. *Emotion Review*, *9*(3), 200–7. doi:10.1177/754039166 84557.

Strathearn, L., Fonagy, P., Amico, J., and Montague, P. R. (2009). Adult attachment predicts maternal brain and oxytocin response to infant cues. *Neuropsychopharmacology*, *34*, 2655–66.

Tudge, J. R. H., Freitas, L. B. L., Mokrova, I. L., et al. (2015). Children's wishes and their expression of gratitude. *Paidéia*, *25*, 281–88.

van den Bos, W., McClure, S. M., Harris, L. T., et al. (2007). Dissociating affective evaluation and social cognitive processes in the ventral medial prefrontal cortex. *Cognitive, Affective and Behavioral Neuroscience*, *7*, 337–46.

Wang, D., Wang, Y. C., and Tudge, J. R. H. (2015). Expressions of gratitude in children and adolescents: insights from China and the United States. *Journal of Cross-Cultural Psychology*, *46*, 1039–158.

Watkins, P. C., Gelder, M. V., and Frias, A. (2009). Furthering the science of gratitude. In S. J. Lopez and C. R. Snyder (Eds.), *The Oxford Handbook of Positive Psychology* (2nd ed., pp. 437–46). Oxford, UK: Oxford University Press.

Watkins, P. C., Woodward, K., Stone, T., and Kolts, R. L. (2003). Gratitude and happiness: development of a measure of gratitude, and relationships with subjective well-being. *Social Behavior and Personality*, *31*, 431–52.

Watson, D., Clark, L. A., and Harkness, A. R. (1994). Structures of personality and their relevance to psychopathology. *Journal of Abnormal Psychology*, *103*, 18–31.

Wood, A., Joseph, S., and Linley, A. (2007). Gratitude: parent of all virtues. *The Psychologist*, *20*, 18–21.

Wood, A. M., Froh, J. J., and Geraghty, A. W. A. (2010). Gratitude and well-being: a review and theoretical integration. *Clinical Psychology Review*, *30*, 890–905.

Wood, A. M., Joseph, S., and Maltby, J. (2008). Gratitude uniquely predicts satisfaction with life: incremental validity above the domains and facets of the five-factor model. *Personality and Individual Differences, 45,* 49–54.

Wood, A. M., Joseph, S., and Maltby, J. (2009). Gratitude predicts psychological well-being above the big five facets. *Personality and Individual Differences, 46,* 443–47.

Yaribeygi, H., Panahi, Y., Sahraei, H., et al. (2017). The impact of stress on body function: a review. *EXCLI Journal, 16,* 1057–72.

Yu, H., Cai, Q., Shen, B., et al. (2017). Neural substrates and social consequences of interpersonal gratitude: intention matters. *Emotion, 17,* 589–601.

Subject-specific research

10

Brain and cognitive development during adolescence: Implications for science and mathematics education

Annie Brookman-Byrne and Iroise Dumontheil

Introduction

Adolescence is a period of development that begins at the onset of puberty and ends when an individual achieves a stable, independent role in society. While there is a great deal of variation in the rate of development and the manifestation of changes in behaviour between individuals during this time, there are many aspects of development that are common. In this chapter we first explore the neural changes occurring during adolescence and how these support the maturation of cognitive functions and behaviours. We then examine the development of science and mathematics skills during adolescence, with a particular focus on misconceptions in these disciplines. Finally, we consider what this evidence suggests teachers can do to help remedy science and mathematics misconceptions during this important period of development, as students work towards compulsory exams.

Defining adolescence

The term 'adolescence' does not only encompass the teenage years. It is defined as starting when puberty begins and ending when a position of responsibility within society has been achieved. This clearly varies widely among individuals and across cultures (Duell et al., 2018) and history. The World Health Organization (WHO) defines adolescence as the period between 10 and 19 years of age (WHO, 2014), but researchers often extend their focus to 'young people', a composite of adolescents and young adults aged 10- to 24-years (Sawyer et al., 2012). Adolescence is marked by substantial changes in the brain and accompanying changes in cognition and behaviour and is often associated with a number of negative stereotypes, such as moodiness, risk-taking and irresponsibility (Qu et al., 2018). Adolescence is not just a human phenomenon; periods of adolescence have been noted in other mammalian species (Brenhouse and Anderson, 2011), demonstrating that adolescence is not a new or concocted stage of life.

It is crucial to keep in mind that although much of this chapter is devoted to describing the typical adolescent, there are huge differences between individuals, with no one single pattern of behaviour that applies to everyone. Nonetheless, the special state of the brain during this time of change has important implications for teaching and learning, which we are just starting to understand as the evidence base grows.

Neural changes during adolescence

Post-mortem brain studies in the 1970s and 1980s had shown that synaptic density, which corresponds to the number of connections ('synapses') between neurons observed per unit of neuronal surface, increases drastically in the first few months and years of life and then progressively decreases during childhood in the visual and auditory cortex and during adolescence in the prefrontal cortex (Huttenlocher, 1979; Huttenlocher and Dabholkar, 1997; see also Petanjek et al. (2011) for more recent data). This process of synaptic pruning, where infrequently used connections between neurons are eliminated, allows the developing brain to fine-tune to the individual's experiences and environment (Petanjek et al., 2011). Despite this evidence for early dendritic arborisation and later prolonged pruning of synaptic connections, it was until recently widely held that the brain was anatomically mature by the end of childhood and that changes in behaviour during the teen years were a result of hormones, social experience and the changing social environment. These factors are likely to play a major role, but neuro-anatomical development may also play a role. In the last couple of decades, results from large magnetic resonance imaging (MRI) studies investigating the development of the brain have provided further evidence that the structure of the brain continues to change during adolescence (Dumontheil, 2016).

Structural MRI data have shown that the thickness of the cortex, or the amount of grey matter in the cortex, decreases during childhood, adolescence and early adulthood and that the timing of this decrease is region specific. The cortex is the outer surface of the brain, comprised of grey matter (cell bodies).

Notably, the frontal lobes, which support cognitive control, and the temporal lobes, which support social cognition, undergo the most protracted development, with significant changes occurring during adolescence (Giedd et al., 1999; Gogtay et al., 2004; Mills et al., 2014, 2016; Shaw et al., 2008; Sowell et al., 1999). One study has shown that cortical thinning is accelerated during adolescence compared to childhood and adulthood, highlighting this developmental period as unique in the neural changes taking place (Zhou et al., 2015). Whilst cortical thinning is thought to be adaptive, leading to more efficient brain functioning, anomalies in this neural developmental process may underlie developmental disorders such as attention deficit/hyperactivity disorder (ADHD), where delayed cortical thinning is observed, especially in the frontal lobes (Shaw et al., 2007), and schizophrenia, which is associated with accelerated cortical thinning during adolescence and early adulthood (Fraguas et al., 2016; Penzes et al., 2011).

Alongside this reduction in grey matter volume and cortical thickness, there is an increase in white matter volume (Lebel and Beaulieu, 2011; Mills et al., 2016). White matter consists of axons – long arms that allow neurons to reach other neurons in different parts of the brain or the body. Axons are covered in a fatty substance called 'myelin', which insulates the axons and allows signals to travel faster. The increase in white matter during development is thought to reflect increased axon diameter and increased myelination, allowing faster exchange of information across brain networks with increasing age. Like grey matter changes, white matter changes in structure are region or tract specific. Some tracts show more prolonged increases in myelination, into the twenties, than other tracts, which stabilise earlier (Lebel and Beaulieu, 2011). Importantly, both grey matter and white matter developmental structural changes show significant variation between individuals (Lebel and Beaulieu, 2011; Mills et al., 2014). Whilst there is some evidence that greater changes, possibly reflecting greater brain plasticity, are associated with a higher intelligence quotient (IQ; Shaw et al., 2006), it is not clear at this point what the characteristics of 'optimal' brain development would be. In any case, more work is needed to understand individual differences in adolescent brain development (Foulkes and Blakemore, 2018).

A third structural component of the brain consists of subcortical regions, which are located deep in the brain. Some of these subcortical regions are linked to the stereotypical behaviours associated with adolescence, such as emotional volatility, risk-taking, novelty seeking and susceptibility to peer influence. The subcortical regions include the amygdala and the hippocampus, which are involved in emotion and mood regulation, and the striatum and its substructures, which are involved in decision making and reward seeking (Goddings et al., 2014). Structural MRI analyses indicate that the amygdala and hippocampus increase in volume during adolescence, whilst regions of the striatum show decreases in volume during adolescence. Importantly, these developmental changes have been found to be driven by a combination of age and pubertal stage, suggesting that the hormonal changes associated with puberty impact the development of subcortical structures (Goddings et al., 2014). Further research indicates that subcortical regions, namely the amygdala and nucleus accumbens (part of the striatum), show relatively earlier maturation than the prefrontal cortex (Mills et al., 2014). These results align with the 'dual systems hypothesis'. This proposes a developmental mismatch in brain maturation, with subcortical regions maturing during adolescence and development of the prefrontal cortex into adulthood, leading to greater social and emotional influences on behaviours (e.g. peer influence or interference from strong emotions) during adolescence than in childhood or adulthood (Casey et al., 2008; Somerville and Casey, 2010). This may account for stereotypical adolescent risk-taking, including risky driving, unprotected sex or taking drugs – but also positive risks such as trying a new hobby.

Cognitive and behavioural changes during adolescence

The maturation of the brain is key to understanding adolescent patterns of behaviour. Two aspects of cognition have been focused on in adolescent cognitive neuroscience research: cognitive control and sensitivity to the social and emotional contexts of cognition. Executive functions are a set of cognitive skills that develop alongside the maturation of the prefrontal cortex and enable higher-order thinking skills, including planning ahead, reasoning effectively and problem solving – a host of skills essential for school success (Diamond, 2013). Executive functions (also referred to as 'cognitive control') are typically conceptualised as encompassing three separate but related functions (Miyake et al., 2000). The first is inhibitory control, which is the ability to inhibit (or stop) an automatic response or desirable action. The second is shifting, sometimes called 'flexibility', which is the ability to switch between different tasks or mental states. The final executive function is working memory, which is the ability to update, monitor and manipulate information in the mind (on working memory, see Chapter 4 of this volume). Executive functions show prolonged development during adolescence, which is accompanied by changes in functional brain activity (Crone and Dahl, 2012). The lateral parietal cortex tends to show increases in activation over the course of development, whilst in the prefrontal cortex the results are more varied and suggest that over development particular aspects of the prefrontal cortex become more specialised for specific executive functions (Crone and Dahl, 2012; Dumontheil, 2016). In a large cross-cultural study of 5,404 individuals aged between 10 and 30 years, a composite measure of cognitive control (or 'self-regulation') was taken through combined performance on an inhibitory control task, a planning task and a questionnaire on planning abilities. The study found that cognitive control improved steeply throughout adolescence, before reaching a plateau in the mid-twenties (23–26 years of age; Steinberg et al., 2018). Executive function skills work together to help the formation and achievement of short- and long-term goals and are particularly important when thoughts or behaviours need to be adjusted and adapted in response to the environment (Crone and Dahl, 2012). The fact that executive functions are still developing through adolescence means that students may find it difficult to inhibit certain behaviours in class, switch effectively between tasks or hold instructions in their minds. At a more complex level, adolescents also show improving 'metacognition'; this is the ability to think about thinking or to reflect on one's own ability and performance (Weil et al., 2013). Whilst students may sometimes use metacognition in their work without explicit instruction, evidence suggests that teaching metacognitive strategies improves performance (Education Endowment Foundation, 2019). One way in which teachers can do this is to model how to plan, monitor and evaluate learning.

The relatively earlier structural and functional maturation of subcortical regions is thought to make adolescence a time of heightened emotional reactivity and sensitivity to reward. For example, compared with children and adults, adolescents show increased activity in the amygdala, a brain region sensitive to threat and salient information in the environment, when they are presented with pictures of emotional (happy or fearful) faces (Hare et al., 2008). Similarly, adolescents show greater activity in the striatum when receiving a reward (Crone and Dahl, 2012; Dumontheil, 2016). This increased emotional reactivity and sensitivity to reward is thought to lead to greater social and emotional influences on goals and decision making (Crone and Dahl, 2012; Somerville and Casey, 2010). Adolescents also exhibit relatively high levels of risk-taking in comparison to children or adults. Risk-taking behaviours peak around the mid-twenties and then gradually decrease through adulthood (Willoughby et al., 2013), although the precise age of peak risk-taking depends on the type of risk considered. For example, there is an earlier peak in antisocial risk-taking, such as ringing a doorbell before running away, than in health-related risk-taking, such as smoking (Duell et al., 2018). Sensation-seeking, a related concept, studied as a composite measure of risky driving in a laboratory driving game, gambling task and via a questionnaire (e.g., 'I like doing things just for the thrill of it'), was found to peak at 19 years of age in a cross-cultural study of 5,404 individuals (Steinberg et al., 2018).

An informative study using a laboratory driving game showed that adolescents took more driving risks than adults when in the presence of their peers, but not when they were alone, suggesting that adolescent decision making is particularly susceptible to the social context (Gardner and Steinberg, 2005). In a neuroimaging study using the same driving simulation game, adolescents showed heightened activity in reward-related brain regions when in the presence of peers compared to on their own. This was not observed in adults, who instead showed greater activation of the lateral prefrontal cortex during the test across both the peer and alone conditions (Chein et al., 2011). These results were interpreted as showing that adolescents experience greater reward when they take risks in front of their friends than when they are alone. These findings highlight that adolescence is a period of substantial social development, where individuals seek to find their place in society independently of their families but

209

also to develop culturally appropriate social skills. For example, the ability to mentalise, or to see things from someone else's point of view (perspective taking), also develops through adolescence (Dumontheil et al., 2010). Peers are particularly important during adolescence, and it has been proposed that avoiding social risk, that is, social exclusion, is a key driver of adolescent decision making (Blakemore, 2018a). Research has also shown that when ostracised by other players in a virtual ball game, adolescents feel greater anxiety and lower mood than adults (Sebastian et al., 2010), as well as lower recruitment of the ventrolateral prefrontal cortex than adults, thought to reflect poorer regulation of the emotions elicited by the social rejection (Sebastian et al., 2011). Ensuring that adolescent students feel socially included in the classroom, which could reduce anxiety and improve mood, could therefore lead to better learning.

While the preceding is not an exhaustive coverage of the cognitive and behavioural developments during adolescence, it demonstrates the breadth of changes that occur at this time.

Science and mathematics skills during adolescence

This chapter considers science and mathematics skills together for a number of reasons. Thinking scientifically and mathematically enables individuals to understand the world around them, to make informed decisions about current issues (e.g. relating to health or the environment) and to have a positive contribution to wealth in society (Royal Society, 2014). They are core compulsory components of the school curriculum with associated national exams that can help determine future career paths. Science and mathematics are also considered difficult disciplines to learn (Lortie-Forgues et al., 2015; Zaitchik et al., 2014), making the investigation of underlying skills particularly important in supporting teaching and learning. Finally, the mechanisms driving success in science and mathematics appear to be similar, and this seems to especially be the case in the context of counterintuitive reasoning, where specific skills may be required to overcome misconceptions (Mareschal, 2016).

Counterintuitive concepts are those that do not accord with our intuitions – that is, concepts about which our intuitive responses are incorrect. Successful counterintuitive reasoning requires, therefore, being able to go beyond our intuitive or automatic responses. Failure to do this may result in misconceptions in both science and mathematics. A wide body of research has shown that misconceptions are prevalent in science and mathematics across all learners (not just those who struggle) and that they persist into adulthood (e.g. Brault Foisy et al., 2015; Masson et al., 2014). These misconceptions persist despite individuals having been taught the correct response at school (Brookman-Byrne et al., 2018). A classic example of a common misconception resulting from our intuitions is that a rubber ball filled with lead will fall to the ground faster than a rubber ball filled with feathers. Students are taught at school that both balls would reach the ground at the same time, yet it feels intuitive that the heavy item would reach the ground first. There are many counterintuitive concepts like this across science and mathematics curricula for England, and likely across the world.

Counterintuitive concepts often appear to conform to one of three rules proposed by Ruth Stavy and Dina Tirosh (2000). These three rules seem to be common to science and mathematics, leading to misconceptions that persist into adulthood. Rule 1 is called 'More A – More B' and refers to the intuition that more of one substance or dimension corresponds to more of the other. In the rubber ball example, the (incorrect) intuition would be that more weight corresponds to more speed. A further example is shown in Figure 10.1a, where the intuitive response to the stimulus is that angle x is larger than angle w, when in fact they are the same size. In this case, the intuition is that greater arc length is related to greater angle size. Rule 2, 'Same A – Same B', is the intuition that when two quantities are the same in one dimension, they are the same in the other. Figure 10.1b exemplifies this rule, where the intuition is that since the shapes have the same area, they must have the same perimeter. In fact, shape y has a larger perimeter. Rule 3, 'Everything Can Be Divided', is the incorrect application of infinity, leading to the intuition that all substances can be infinitely divided, such as a piece of paper in the example given in Figure 10.1c. These rules provide a useful framework for thinking about misconceptions in science and mathematics and show that they arise from intuitions that everyone experiences.

The origins of these intuitive rules may lie in previous encounters with the world. For example, it may be that misconceptions arise through misleading perceptual information, experiences that appear to contradict scientific reality or simplified ideas that are taught at an early age but are later superseded by more detailed concepts (Dunbar et al., 2007; Houdé, 2000; Mareschal, 2016). Figures 10.1a and 10.1b are examples of misleading

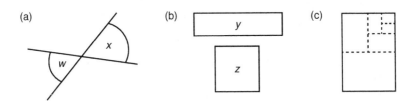

Figure 10.1 Example intuitive rules leading to misconceptions (adapted from Stavy and Tirosh, 2000). (a) 'More A – More B'. An intuitive reasoning is that angle **x** is larger than angle **w** because angle **x**'s arc is longer. (b) 'Same A – Same B'. An intuitive reasoning is that shapes **y** and **z** have equal perimeters because their areas are equal. (c) 'Everything Can Be Divided'. An intuitive reasoning is that a piece of paper can be cut in half infinitely.

perceptual cues, where the visual information provided gives an impression that is contrary to reality, or non-veridical. Experiences that appear to contradict scientific theories about the nature of reality include the fact that it appears as though the Sun revolves around the Earth, and we speak of and conceptualise the Sun as 'rising' and 'setting' every day, yet in reality the Earth revolves around the Sun. In other cases, students may be taught a simplified theory that constitutes an early introduction to a challenging and complicated topic. A few years later, a more accurate version may be taught, perhaps contradicting the original information. One example is that at an early age, we are taught that the number 2 is smaller than the number 4. However, when we start learning about fractions, ½ is larger than ¼; now the number containing a 4 is smaller than the number that contains a 2. All these factors can make reasoning and learning new concepts in science and mathematics challenging and counterintuitive.

A number of studies have shown an association between inhibitory control (the executive function that allows the suppression of an unwanted response) and the ability to reason effectively about counterintuitive concepts (Brookman-Byrne et al., 2018; Gilmore et al., 2015; Khng and Lee, 2009). These studies provide support for the theory that inhibitory control enables the suppression of the incorrect response in order to reason effectively about a counterintuitive concept (Dunbar et al., 2007; Houdé, 2000; Mareschal, 2016). According to this theory, students need to use their inhibitory control in order to inhibit any misleading or incorrect information that may interfere with the correct reasoning. This means that prior knowledge can be a barrier to learning, since it may conflict with newly presented information (Heit, 1994).

Conceiving of learning in this manner differs from a more traditional understanding of knowledge acquisition, which refers to the replacement, reorganisation or restructuring of previous knowledge when something new is learnt (Posner et al., 1982). According to traditional ways of thinking about learning, prior knowledge does not pose a problem when it comes to learning new information. In fact, the latest evidence suggests that we all keep hold of our old theories and use our executive function skills to suppress them (Mareschal, 2016). As seen earlier, executive functions, and the neural mechanisms that support them, are continuing to develop throughout adolescence. This means that students in this age range need support in using their executive functions and specifically their inhibitory control when approaching counterintuitive problems.

What can teachers do?

This theory of learning has implications for teaching and learning of science and mathematics material in school. While key stage 3 curricula for science and mathematics in England (for 11- to 14-year-olds) acknowledge the presence of misconceptions in students, they provide little information regarding the source of misconceptions and no examples of commonly held misconceptions (Department for Education, 2013a, 2013b). This makes it especially challenging for teachers who may be unaware of the incorrect theories that students hold. Both curricula encourage teachers to use discussion to probe and remedy misconceptions, but there is no reference to the best way to tackle them. Teachers therefore need to recognise misconceptions, try to remedy them and all the while build on students' correct prior knowledge (Klahr et al., 2011).

The scientific literature on this topic has led to a number of concrete recommendations for teachers. The first suggestion is to encourage students not to give their first answer to a problem, instead spending more time reasoning about the problem presented. This idea was suggested in the context of science education by Mary Rowe (1986), alongside evidence from a range of studies suggesting that both comprehension and attitude improved through introducing 'wait time'. A current study, from the Centre for Educational Neuroscience in London, is investigating whether this strategy can encourage learners (primary school aged in this sample) to use their inhibitory control in the context of science and mathematics (for more on this study, see unlocke.org). The idea is that encouraging students to 'stop and think' before answering counterintuitive problems in science and mathematics may enable them to engage their inhibitory control. This strategy may help students to take their time thinking about a problem, which, in turn, could lead to more right answers. After a promising pilot study (Wilkinson et al., 2019), the 'Stop and Think' intervention was assessed in a large randomised, controlled trial. Children in the intervention group made, on average, the equivalent of one additional month of progress in mathematics and two additional months of progress in science (an effect that reached significance), both assessed using standardised tests, compared to control children (Roy et al., 2019).

In mathematics, often in relation to mental mathematics, fast answers are sometimes seen as important, or indicative of mathematical ability. It might be that requiring fast responses means that students are sometimes not able to demonstrate their mathematical skills (if they cannot calculate the answer in the time limit) and that not allowing time for inhibitory control engagement leads to reduced accuracy (if they end up responding according to their intuition). Allowing students to take their time may therefore be beneficial, especially in individuals with poorer inhibitory control, such as those with ADHD. These students may require extra support in suppressing their first intuitive answer.

It is important to be clear that training inhibitory control in isolation is not anticipated to have any impact on suppressing incorrect responses in science and mathematics. Early efforts to improve executive functions through training were promising (Diamond and Lee, 2011), but these programmes (where a particular skill is trained through computer games) have seen limited success (Melby-Lervåg and Hulme, 2013) and have very little impact on learning. The key in the 'Stop and Think' programme is to encourage inhibition within the context of science and mathematics problem solving and lessons. Given that adolescents are particularly sensitive to their peers and do not want to risk social exclusion, it may be that giving students extra time to think about their responses has social benefits. Specifically, students may be less reluctant to raise their hands in class if they are given more time to think about their answers, as they may be more confident of being right (and thus less likely to risk embarrassment in front of their peers). Finally, to help students arrive at the correct answer, and to take their time to do so, examination times should perhaps be longer for all students. This would allow students to carefully check their responses and take their time to think before writing their answer, which might particularly benefit those with ADHD or poor inhibitory control. There is little that individual teachers can do about this, but nonetheless, this may be something that could be built into end-of-topic tests, even if not in national exams.

The second suggestion for teachers is to raise students' awareness of misconceptions, telling them explicitly about incorrect answers and why they may be appealing but wrong. This may increase students' awareness of the skills involved in effective scientific and mathematical reasoning, helping them to apply such reasoning more effectively. If students know that there are counterintuitive concepts that need to be understood and overcome, they may become better placed to look out for them and suppress their initial response. This suggestion is consistent with recommendations to use refutation texts, which explicitly address misconceptions and explain why they are wrong in detail (Ecker et al., 2014). Here the idea is to go further than simply saying the information or response is wrong (a plain retraction) and to include supporting evidence explaining why it is wrong and, if possible, where the misconception came from. As long as the refutation text is clear, well constructed and the students engage fully in the material (as opposed to skim reading), this is more effective than a plain retraction (Ecker et al., 2014).

Julie Ryan and Julian Williams (2007) also argued that simply correcting errors is unproductive and suggested a 'dialogic pedagogy' approach in mathematics. The starting point for this approach is when there is some kind of disagreement between students about something mathematical. This should be followed by the teacher encouraging argument in discussion. It is vital that students are encouraged to listen to each other and to be open to other points of view. Students first articulate their point of view, then ideally reformulate their ideas based on what others have said, reflect on why their initial reasoning was incorrect and conclude by reaching a resolution. While this approach was proposed in the context of mathematics (Ryan and Williams, 2007), the same strategy could be used in science when disagreements occur. Indeed, Rosalind Driver et al. (2015) highlight the importance of peer discussions in science, showing that such conversations help students to clarify their own thoughts and build on their collective understanding. Considering the importance of social interactions with peers during adolescence, this type of peer discussion may also be beneficial as a result of raising the engagement of pupils in the lesson. Although not mentioned by the authors, as in mathematics, the presence of a teacher would help to ensure that misconceptions are not propagated when discussions relate to counterintuitive concepts.

Ruth Stavy and Dina Tirosh (2000) suggested the 'conflict teaching' approach as a way to help students overcome misconceptions. In this approach, students are presented with a problem known to elicit an incorrect (intuitive) response, triggering a misconception, followed by a second problem that contradicts their first response. There is some evidence that this approach is effective and that performance in counterintuitive reasoning tasks following this approach improves (Stavy and Tirosh, 2000). It is likely that this would highlight students' own tendencies to answer intuitively, thus raising awareness of the need to go beyond initial responses. As cognitive control and metacognitive skills develop during adolescence, adolescents may become more able over the course of secondary school to reflect on their tendencies to answer intuitively and to develop appropriate strategies to combat them.

These suggestions for teachers are based on the best available evidence concerning misconceptions and are intended to be additional tools that can be tried in the classroom. Different approaches may be appropriate with different groups of students and with different ages. As yet, there is no evidence about which strategy is best at which time, and it is likely that future research will develop new and more effective tools for overcoming misconceptions that draw on our increasing understanding of adolescent development.

Beyond misconceptions

Inhibitory control is considered to be one of the cognitive skills that enable students to overcome misconceptions and reason correctly about counterintuitive concepts. But overcoming misconceptions is just one aspect of successful science and mathematics, and inhibitory control is just one of many skills involved in adolescent scientific and mathematical reasoning. A host of other factors supports science and mathematics, each of which varies between individuals. The two other executive functions described earlier, working memory and shifting, also have a role in scientific and mathematical reasoning (Cragg and Gilmore, 2014; Donati et al., 2019; Rhodes et al., 2014, 2016). These enable students to hold the problem in mind, manipulate relevant information and switch between different ways of thinking or types of problems. Spatial ability allows students to mentally rotate objects or consider spatial relations (Gilligan et al., 2018; Hodgkiss et al., 2018), whilst processing speed may allow for fast problem solving (Donati et al., 2019). Vocabulary, and language skills more broadly, enable students to read and understand the problems presented (Donati et al., 2019). Relational reasoning, the ability to detect meaningful patterns (Alexander et al., 2016), also plays a key role in problem solving, with analogical reasoning in particular helping students to understand concepts through analogy – that is, through comparing a new concept to a previously learnt concept (Miller Singley and Bunge, 2014; Vendetti et al., 2015). Nonverbal relational reasoning, requiring the detection of meaningful patterns visuo-spatially, is also linked to science and mathematics performance (Brookman-Byrne et al., 2019). In addition to these cognitive skills, science- and mathematics-specific factual knowledge, procedural skills and conceptual understanding all support performance in these disciplines (Cragg and Gilmore, 2014; Zimmerman, 2000). For all these skills, there will be variation in ability across students, particularly during this period of prolonged development and maturation in adolescence.

Science and mathematics teachers seeking to take advantage of the developing adolescent brain face the considerable challenge of recognising and addressing misconceptions in their students. Understanding that the brain and the cognitive systems it supports are undergoing profound change and that there are huge differences in many abilities between students may help teachers to adapt classroom materials to enhance learning opportunities. An understanding of the importance of these wide-ranging cognitive skills appears to be beneficial for teachers (Gilmore and Cragg, 2014), and researchers are continuing to uncover more about the link between adolescent development and scientific and mathematical skills. In time, this will lead to more trials of evidence-based practices, more recommendations for teachers and the development of more resources to help educators to teach and students to learn.

Recommended resources

Researchers from the Centre for Educational Neuroscience have created a professional film for teachers that summarises the adolescent brain in just three minutes. This resource is intended to provide a brief introduction to the key changes during adolescence and is hosted on a website full of further information about the adolescent brain. The researchers are crowdsourcing ideas and strategies from teachers who are using this science in their classrooms. Please visit the website, watch the film, share with fellow teachers and leave your feedback: tinyurl.com/brain-teach.

Professor Sarah-Jayne Blakemore from University College London is an expert in the adolescent brain and has a popular science book called *Inventing Ourselves: The Secret Life of the Teenage Brain* (Blakemore, 2018).

References

Alexander, P. A., Dumas, D., Grossnickle, E. M., et al. (2016). Measuring relational reasoning. *Journal of Experimental Education, 84*(1), 119–51.

Blakemore, S.-J. (2018a). *Inventing ourselves: The secret life of the teenage brain.* London: Doubleday.

Blakemore, S.-J. (2018b). Avoiding social risk in adolescence. *Current Directions in Psychological Science, 27*(2), 116–22.

Brault Foisy, L.-M., Potvin, P., Riopel, M., and Masson, S. (2015). Is inhibition involved in overcoming a common physics misconception in mechanics? *Trends in Neuroscience and Education, 4,* 26–36.

Brenhouse, H. C., and Anderson, S. L. (2011). Developmental trajectories during adolescence in males and females: a cross-species understanding of underlying brain changes. *Neuroscience & Biobehavioral Reviews, 35*(8), 1687–1703.

Brookman-Byrne, A., Mareschal, D., Tolmie, A., and Dumontheil, I. (2018). Inhibitory control and counterintuitive science and maths reasoning in adolescence. *PLoS ONE, 13*(6), e019873.

Brookman-Byrne, A., Mareschal, D., Tolmie, A., and Dumontheil, I. (2019). The unique contributions of verbal analogical reasoning and nonverbal matrix reasoning to science and maths problem-solving in adolescence. *Mind, Brain, and Education, 13*(3), 211–23.

Casey, B. J., Getz, S., and Galvan, A. (2008). The adolescent brain. *Developmental Review, 28,* 62–77.

Chein, J., Albert, D., O'Brien, L., et al. (2011). Peers increase adolescent risk taking by enhancing activity in the brain's reward circuitry. *Developmental Science, 14*(2), F1–10.

Cragg, L., and Gilmore, C. (2014). Skills underlying mathematics: the role of executive function in the development of mathematics proficiency. *Trends in Neuroscience and Education, 3*(2), 63–8.

Crone, E. A., and Dahl, R. E. (2012). Understanding adolescence as a period of social-affective engagement and goal flexibility. *Nature Reviews Neuroscience, 13,* 636–50.

Department for Education. (2013a). *Mathematics Programmes of Study: Key Stage 3* (DFE-00179-2013). Available at https://assets.publishing.service.gov.uk/govern ment/uploads/system/uploads/attachment_data/file/239058/SECONDARY_ national_curriculum_-_Mathematics.pdf.

Department for Education. (2013b). *Science Programmes of Study: Key Stage 3* (DFE-00185-2013). Available at https://assets.publishing.service.gov.uk/government/ uploads/system/uploads/attachment_data/file/335174/SECONDARY_natio nal_curriculum_-_Science_220714.pdf.

Diamond, A. (2013). Executive functions. *Annual Review of Psychology, 64,* 135–68.

Diamond, A., and Lee, K. (2011). Interventions shown to aid executive function development in children 4 to 12 years old. *Science, 333*(6045), 959–64.

Donati, G., Meaburn, E. L., and Dumontheil, I. (2019). The specificity of associations between cognition and attainment in English, maths and science during adolescence. *Learning and Individual Differences, 69,* 84–93.

Driver, R., Squires, A., Rushworth, P., and Wood-Robinson, V. (2015). *Making Sense of Secondary Science: Research into Children's Ideas* (Classic). New York: Routledge.

Duell, N., Steinberg, L., Icenogle, G., et al. (2018). Age patterns in risk taking across the world. *Journal of Youth and Adolescence*, 47(5), 1052–72.

Dumontheil, I. (2016). Adolescent brain development. *Current Opinion in Behavioural Sciences*, 10, 39–44.

Dumontheil, I., Apperly, I. A., and Blakemore, S.-J. (2010). Online usage of theory of mind continues to develop in late adolescence. *Developmental Science*, 13(2), 331–38.

Dunbar, K. N., Fugelsang, J. A., and Stein, C. (2007). Do naïve theories ever go away? Using brain and behavior to understand changes in concepts. In M. Lovett and P. Shah (Eds.), *Thinking with Data* (pp. 193–205). Mahwah, NJ: Lawrence Erlbaum Associates.

Ecker, U. K. H., Swire, B., and Lewandowsky, S. (2014). Correcting misinformation. In D. N. Rapp and J. L. G. Braasch (Eds.), *Processing Inaccurate Information: Theoretical and Applied Perspectives from Cognitive Science and the Educational Sciences* (pp. 13–37). Cambridge, MA: MIT Press.

Education Endowment Foundation. (2019). Metacognition and self-regulated learning. Available at https://educationendowmentfoundation.org.uk/public/files/Presentations/Publications/Metacognition/EEF_Metacognition_and_self-regulated_learning.pdf.

Foulkes, L., and Blakemore, S.-J. (2018). Studying individual differences in human adolescent brain development. *Nature Neuroscience*, 21(3), 315–23.

Fraguas, D., Díaz-Caneja, C. M., Pina-Camacho, et al. (2016). Progressive brain changes in children and adolescents with early-onset psychosis: a meta-analysis of longitudinal MRI studies. *Schizophrenia Research*, 173(3), 132–9.

Gardner, M., and Steinberg, L. (2005). Peer influence on risk taking, risk preference, and risky decision making in adolescence and adulthood: an experimental study. *Developmental Psychology*, 41(4), 625–35.

Giedd, J. N., Blumenthal, J., Jeffries, N. O., et al. (1999). Brain development during childhood and adolescence: a longitudinal MRI study. *Nature Neuroscience*, 2, 861–3.

Gilligan, K., Hodgkiss, A., Thomas, M. S. C., and Farran, E. K. (2018). The developmental relations between spatial cognition and mathematics in primary school children. *Developmental Science*, 22(4), e12786.

Gilmore, C., and Cragg, L. (2014). Teachers' understanding of the role of executive functions in mathematics learning. *Mind, Brain, and Education*, 8(3), 132–36.

Gilmore, C., Keeble, S., Richardson, S., and Cragg, L. (2015). The role of cognitive inhibition in different components of arithmetic. *ZDM Mathematics Education*, 47, 771–82.

Goddings, A.-L., Mills, K. L., Clasen, L. S., et al. (2014). The influence of puberty on subcortical brain development. *NeuroImage*, 88, 242–51.

Gogtay, N., Giedd, J. N., Lusk, L., et al.(2004). Dynamic mapping of human cortical development during childhood through early adulthood. *PNAS*, 101(21), 8174–9.

Hare, T. A., Tottenham, N., Galvan, A., et al. (2008). Biological substrates of emotional reactivity and regulation in adolescence during an emotional go-nogo task. *Biological Psychiatry*, *63*(10), 927–34.

Heit, E. (1994). Models of the effects of prior knowledge on category learning. *Journal of Experimental Psychology: Learning, Memory, and Cognition*, *20*(6), 1264–82.

Hodgkiss, A., Gilligan, K. A., Tolmie, A. K., et al. (2018). Spatial cognition and science achievement: the contribution of intrinsic and extrinsic spatial skills from 7 to 11 years. *British Journal of Educational Psychology*, *88*(4), 675–97.

Houdé, O. (2000). Inhibition and cognitive development: object, number, categorization, and reasoning. *Cognitive Development*, *15*, 63–73.

Huttenlocher, P. R. (1978). Synaptic density in human frontal cortex – developmental changes and effects of aging. *Brain Research*, *163*(2), 195–205.

Huttenlocher, P. R. and Dabholkar, A. S. (1997). Regional differences in synaptogenesis in human cerebral cortex. *Journal of Comparative Neurology*, *387*(2), 167–78.

Khng, K. H., and Lee, K. (2009). Inhibiting interference from prior knowledge: arithmetic intrusions in algebra word problem solving. *Learning and Individual Differences*, *19*(2), 262–68.

Klahr, D., Zimmerman, C., and Jirout, J. (2011). Educational interventions to advance children's scientific thinking. *Science*, *333*(6045), 971–75.

Lebel, C., and Beaulieu, C. (2011). Longitudinal development of human brain wiring continues from childhood into adulthood. *Journal of Neuroscience*, *31*(30), 10937–47.

Lortie-Forgues, H., Tian, J., and Siegler, R. S. (2015). Why is learning fraction and decimal arithmetic so difficult? *Developmental Review*, *38*, 201–21.

Mareschal, D. (2016). The neuroscience of conceptual learning in science and mathematics. *Current Opinion in Behavioral Sciences*, *10*, 114–18.

Masson, S., Potvin, P., Riopel, M., and Brault Foisy, L.-M. (2014). Differences in brain activation between novices and experts in science during a task involving a common misconception in electricity. *Mind, Brain, and Education*, *8*(1), 44–55.

Melby-Lervåg, M., and Hulme, C. (2013). Is working memory training effective? A meta-analytic review. *Developmental Psychology*, *49*(2), 270–91.

Miller Singley, A. T., and Bunge, S. A. (2014). Neurodevelopment of relational reasoning: implications for mathematical pedagogy. *Trends in Neuroscience and Education*, *3*(2), 33–37.

Mills, K. L., Goddings, A.-L., Clasen, L. S., et al. (2014). The developmental mismatch in structural brain maturation during adolescence. *Developmental Neuroscience*, *36*(3–4), 147–60.

Mills, K. L., Goddings, A.-L., Herting, M. M., et al. (2016). Structural brain development between childhood and adulthood: convergence across four longitudinal samples. *NeuroImage*, *141*, 273–81.

Miyake, A., Friedman, N. P., Emerson, M. J., et al. (2000). The unity and diversity of executive functions and their contributions to complex 'frontal lobe' tasks: a latent variable analysis. *Cognitive Psychology*, *41*(1), 49–100.

Penzes, P., Cahill, M. E., Jones, K. A., et al. (2011). Dendritic spine pathology in neuropsychiatric disorders. *Nature Neuroscience*, *14*(3), 285–93.

Petanjek, Z., Judaš, M., Šimi⬛, G., et al. (2011). Extraordinary neoteny of synaptic spines in the human prefrontal cortex. *PNAS*, *108*(32), 13281–6.

Posner, G. J., Strike, K. A., Hewson, P. W., and Gertzog, W. A. (1982). Accommodation of a scientific conception: toward a theory of conceptual change. *Science Education*, *66*(2), 211–27.

Qu, Y., Pomerantz, E. M., McCormick, E., and Telzer, E. H. (2018). Youth's conceptions of adolescence predict longitudinal changes in prefrontal cortex activation and risk taking during adolescence. *Child Development*, *89*(3), 773–83.

Rhodes, S. M., Booth, J. N., Campbell, L. E., et al. (2014). Evidence for a role of executive functions in learning biology. *Infant and Child Development*, *23*(1), 67–83.

Rhodes, S. M., Booth, J. N., Palmer, L. E., et al. (2016). Executive functions predict conceptual learning of science. *British Journal of Developmental Psychology*, *34*(2), 261–75.

Rowe, M. B. (1986). Wait time: slowing down may be a way of speeding up! *Journal of Teacher Education*, *37*, 43–50.

Roy, P., Rutt, S., Easton, C., et al. (2019). Stop and think: learning counterintuitive concepts. Education Endowment Foundation, London. Available at https://educationendowmentfoundation.org.uk/projects-and-evaluation/projects/learning-counterintuitive-concepts/.

Ryan, J., and Williams, J. (2007). *Children's Mathematics 4–15: Learning from Errors and Misconceptions*. Maidenhead, UK: Open University Press.

Sebastian, C., Viding, E., Williams, K. D., and Blakemore, S.-J. (2010). Social brain development and the affective consequences of ostracism in adolescence. *Brain and Cognition*, *72*(1), 134–45.

Sebastian, C. L., Tan, G. C. Y., Roiser, J. P., et al. (2011). Developmental influences on the neural bases of responses to social rejection: Implications of social neuroscience for education. *NeuroImage*, *57*(3), 686–94.

Sawyer, S. M., Afifi, R. A., Bearinger, L. H. et al. (2012). Adolescence: a foundation for future health. *The Lancet*, *397*(9826), 1630–40.

Shaw, P., Eckstrand, K., Sharp, W., et al. (2007). Attention-deficit/hyperactivity disorder is characterized by a delay in cortical maturation. *PNAS*, *104*(49), 19649–54.

Shaw, P., Greenstein, D., Lerch, J., et al. (2006). Intellectual ability and cortical development in children and adolescents. *Nature*, *440*(7084), 676–9.

Shaw, P., Kabani, N.J., Lerch, J.P., et al.(2008). Neurodevelopmental trajectories of the human cerebral cortex. *Journal of Neuroscience*, *28*, 3586–94.

Somerville, L. H., and Casey, B. (2010). Developmental neurobiology of cognitive control and motivational systems. *Current Opinion in Neurobiology*, *20*(2), 236–41.

Sowell, E. R., Thompson, P. M., Holmes, C. J., et al. (1999). In vivo evidence for post-adolescent brain maturation in frontal and striatal regions. *Nature Neuroscience*, *2*, 859–61.

Stavy, R., and Tirosh, D. (2000). *How Students (Mis-) Understand Science and Mathematics: Intuitive Rules.* New York: Teachers College Press.

Steinberg, L., Icenogle, G., Shulman, E. P., et al. (2018). Around the world, adolescence is a time of heightened sensation seeking and immature self-regulation. *Developmental Science, 21*(2), e12532.

The Royal Society. (2014). *Vision for Science and Mathematics Education.* London: Royal Society.

Vendetti, M. S., Matlen, B. J., Richland, L. E., and Bunge, S. A. (2015). Analogical reasoning in the classroom: insights from cognitive science. *Mind, Brain, and Education, 9*(2), 100–6.

Weil, L. G., Fleming, S. M., Dumontheil, I., et al. (2013). The development of metacognitive ability in adolescence. *Consciousness and Cognition, 22*, 264–71.

Wilkinson, H. R., Smid, C., Morris, S., et al. (2019). Domain-specific inhibitory control training to improve children's learning of counterintuitive concepts in mathematics and science. *Journal of Cognitive Enhancement.* doi.org/10.1007/s41465-019-00161-4.

Willoughby, T., Good, M., Adachi, P. J. C., et al. (2013). Examining the link between adolescent brain development and risk taking from a social-developmental perspective. *Brain and Cognition, 83*(3), 315–23.

World Health Organization. (2014). Recognizing adolescence. Available at https://apps.who.int/adolescent/second-decade/section2/page1/recognizing-adolescence.html.

Zaitchik, D., Iqbal, Y., and Carey, S. (2014). The effect of executive function on biological reasoning in young children: an individual differences study. *Child Development, 85*(1), 160–75.

Zhsou, D., Lebel, C., Treit, S., et al. (2015). Accelerated longitudinal cortical thinning in adolescence. *NeuroImage, 104*, 138–45.

Zimmerman, C. (2000). The development of scientific reasoning skills. *Developmental Review, 20*(1), 99–149.

11

The impact of music on adolescents' cognitive and socio-emotional learning

Daniel Müllensiefen and Peter Harrison

Music relates to many aspects of human development. Firstly, music involves the perception of auditory sensory input as well as the understanding and mental manipulation of abstract structures. In this cognitive perspective, music is similar to the languages that we learn to understand and speak. Secondly, music has an important social dimension. It is often played together with others or for others, and one of music's main functions is to convey emotions in social contexts or by simulating social contexts (Schäfer et al., 2013). Thirdly, music making also has a physical side, requiring sensorimotor coordination and – for many instruments including the voice – physical strength and good body control. This combination of several important aspects of human nature makes music unique and distinguishes it from other activities such as sports, literature and purely cognitive games such as chess.

The adolescent period is characterised by fundamental changes in the physical socio-emotional and cognitive development of young people (Slater and Bremner, 2017). At the same time, adolescence is the period where music often becomes part of an individual's identity (North et al., 2000). This goes along with deliberate and self-determined choices to invest time, money, effort and other resources into music as opposed to other possible activities. During adolescence, these choices are made with increasing independence and are less influenced by parents or teachers compared to the preteen years. Thus, because of the growing importance of music during adolescence, it becomes an obvious question of whether and how the broad range of opportunities that music provides can be harnessed to improve learning and development in general during this period.

To answer this question, this chapter first provides an overview of music and its relationship with important psychological factors. We then show how longitudinal research can provide a sound empirical basis for understanding the causes and effects of musical engagement and describe the LongGold project as an example of this type of research. Following important insights from this research, we show how a teaching unit focusing on the cognitive neuroscience of musicality could serve as a potential intervention for acquiring positive learning attitudes not only for music learning but also for learning in general.

Music and relationships with important psychological factors

Music, cognitive skills, academic performance and psycho-social development

There is plenty of evidence that music has close relationships with a range of important domains, including general cognitive ability (e.g. intelligence, memory, attention), academic achievement, personality, and pro-social attitudes (Hargreaves and Lamont, 2017). Often these relationships are discussed under the term 'musical transfer effects' (Schellenberg, 2005). This terminology already implies a specific directionality of the effects (i.e. musical engagement being the cause for a change in a different domain). But recent discussions (Schellenberg, 2019) question this a priori assumption that music is always the cause for development in other domains and argues that the reverse could be true. Glenn Schellenberg (2019) as well as Miriam Mosing and Frederik Ullén (Butkovic et al., 2015; Mosing et al., 2014) have argued that the engagement with music, as well as musical skills and achievements, could be caused by other factors (e.g. personality and genetic makeup). With the debate on the directionality of music effects still ongoing, it is important to keep an open mind to the question of causality.

Among cognitive transfer effects, verbal memory (Chan et al., 1998; Ho et al., 2003) and general intelligence (Ruthsatz et al., 2008; Schellenberg, 2004) are often named as the primary faculties that benefit from music training. However, at least in younger children, phonological awareness and later reading abilities have also been shown to be influenced positively by music training (Degé and Schwarzer, 2011). In addition to increases in cognitive abilities, academic achievements also go along with higher musical activity during adolescence. Using data from a large panel study, Adrian Hille and Jürgen Schupp (2014) have shown how learning a musical instrument during adolescence is generally associated with higher grades towards the end of students' school careers. Their results have been supported by evidence from a large cohort study with more than 100,000 Canadian secondary school students. In this study, Martin Guhn et al. (2020) showed that participation in music courses at school had a positive effect on grades in unrelated subjects (i.e. mathematics and English). The effect was strongest for students who were highly engaged with learning an instrument, and for this subgroup, the effect of music was similar in size to the annual academic gains of students without music training. Or, to phrase it differently, these students who actively engaged in learning an instrument were 'on average academically over 1 year ahead of their peers' (Guhn et al., 2020, 308).

Musical activity is not only related to cognitive abilities and academic achievement, but the effect of music is also thought to extend to psycho-social skills as well. Here, coping and emotion regulation are two key areas where engagement with music appears to be connected to the use of more effective strategies to regulate emotions and cope with stressful events (Lonsdale and North, 2011; Miranda and Claes, 2009; Roden et al., 2016). Similarly, pro-social behaviour has been shown to increase with musical engagement (Kirschner and Tomasello, 2010; Williams et al., 2015). More generally, in his comprehensive literature review, Dave Miranda (2013) finds that music is closely related to the psycho-social development of adolescents and also acts as a protective factor against externalising and internalising problem behaviours. This conclusion is supported by the empirical evidence from a large intervention study by Xiomara Aleman et al. (2017) demonstrating how musical opportunities can enhance self-control and reduce behaviour problems, specifically among students from disadvantaged backgrounds. In line with these associations between musical activity and psycho-social skills, several studies have also pointed to the positive links with young people's mental health and well-being (Farahmand et al., 2011; Papinczak et al., 2015).

Music: the magic bullet for adolescent development?

Given the large amount of evidence for the positive associations of musical activity with many important psychological factors during adolescence, it is tempting to regard music as a 'magic bullet' that comes along with 'free' and automatic transfer effects to almost all relevant psychological domains during adolescence. However, it is very easy to overstate or over-interpret this evidence and overlook the problems that go along with parts of the literature.

One pervasive problem in many studies that *look for the effects of music* is that they assume from the outset, a priori, the causal direction of the effect caused by music onto another factor. For example, it might be assumed that taking additional music instruction made students smarter, when it might have actually been that the smarter students in fact chose to take more music instruction. Assuming a specific causal direction in this way is certainly justified in experimental studies where participants are assigned to different conditions of an experiment at random, for example, receiving additional music instruction versus additional instruction in science or art. This random assignment ensures that the effects of additional music instruction are not confounded with any other factors. But many studies on transfer effects of music do not use random assignment to experimental conditions but instead are observational in nature; that is, they record the amount of musical activity of individuals as well as their achievements and relate the two to each other. Hence, the data collected by these studies are correlational. But correlations do not necessarily imply a specific causal direction. Hence, even from the data of a very large study such as the one by Guhn et al. (2020), it is not possible to infer whether the additional music instruction children took made them smarter or whether the smarter kids chose to take more music instructions. In correlational studies, children are not assigned to a music versua a control group randomly, making it difficult to eliminate confounding variables that may drive differences in the outcome variables. For example, children from families with a higher socio-economic status may be more likely to have had a positive experience with music instruction earlier in their life. This might make them more likely to volunteer for a music intervention group if they are given the choice. Then the benefits of music training that we can measure in a self-selected music intervention group might at least partly arise from the higher socio-economic background of participants in this group. In sum, it is important for observational studies to take pre-existing differences between participants into account.

Finally, most studies on the general benefits of music training use very different kinds of music instruction programmes (e.g. traditional individual or group lessons, ensemble training, the Kodaly method, the El Sistema programme), and it is not yet entirely clear whether all these instruction methods deliver roughly the same kind of positive effects or whether there is a 'magic formula' of music teaching that would achieve maximal effects, for example, in terms of gains in cognitive abilities. Moreover, it remains unclear how the instruction methods employed in research studies compare to alternative ways of music learning that are prevalent in the real world, including informal music learning and self-teaching.

These issues and questions suggest that it might not be easy to generalise transfer effects of music across different psychological domains and types of studies. This difficulty, of establishing what the general effect of music is, is reflected in the small effect size ($d = 0.17$) that Giovanna Sala and Fernand Gobet (2017) find in their large meta-analysis of thirty-eight studies, which includes forty independent samples and 118 reported effect sizes (Sala and Gobet, 2017). However, they also report that the effects of music training are considerably stronger for some cognitive domains (e.g. general intelligence and memory) than for others (e.g. literacy and spatial processing). Thus, music instruction certainly appears not to serve as a magic booster across the board, and even for those cognitive aspects where music seems to have a consistent positive effect (i.e. intelligence and memory), the effect size still needs to be considered as very moderate ($d = 0.35$).

By contrast, brain plasticity has been established as a cognitive mechanism by which music learning can affect changes in the brain's anatomy and physiology. These music-induced changes are then assumed to serve other cognitive functions as well. Among the changes induced by music training is an increase in grey matter volume in the superior parietal and inferior temporal cortex – areas that are strongly engaged in audio-motor processing during music making (Gaser and Schlaug, 2003). Similarly, Annemarie Seither-Preisler et al. (2014) found in a controlled study with school children that those who take additional music lessons develop a larger Heschl's gyrus over time. Heschl's gyrus is the area in the brain where auditory information arrives from the ears and where it is initially analysed. That the effect of music training on the brain is even visible when the genetic makeup of the participants is identical has been shown by Örjan De Manzano and Frederick Ullén (2017), with a sample of monozygotic twins that differed strongly in the degree to which they had received musical training in their life.

Hence, we know that engaging with music changes the brain and that music-induced brain plasticity may underly these positive psychological effects. Yet, there remain several unanswered questions concerning how the engagement with music can affect adolescent development.

Open questions

A very simple way to identify whether music training has any effect on an individual is to measure its primary intended effect, that is, the gain in musical skills and abilities. Such a near-transfer effect could manifest in terms of the progress with learning an instrument or increased musical listening abilities. But hardly any studies investigating far-transfer effects of music (e.g. on intelligence or school grades) include any measures of near-transfer effects. Hence, it is largely an open question of how near- and far-transfer effects of music are related. If a child does not develop his or her musical skills despite engaging in regular music training, could there still be effects on intelligence and memory? Or, phrased differently, are the cognitive benefits of music training only received by those who are also good musical learners? Finally, it is hitherto unclear how musical, cognitive and social abilities develop together over adolescence. Does development in one domain always precede development in another domain, or do musical skills, cognitive abilities and socio-emotional characteristics of young people co-develop in parallel?

It is difficult to answer these questions from the current published literature because of the lack of virtually any studies that document musical development across the teenage years in a quantitative way.

LongGold: a study on the development of musical, cognitive and socio-emotional skills during adolescence

Motivation and study design

The lack of empirical quantitative literature concerning the role of music in adolescent development led us to design and implement a new longitudinal study with the support of BrainCanDo. The LongGold study aims to track the development of musical abilities together with cognitive and socio-emotional skills across adolescence. The study aims to describe how musicality develops through maturation, musical training and other activities as different potential causes for musical development. Furthermore, it aims to identify pre-existing individual differences that might affect musical development causally. Because the study gathers data from the same individuals over several years, it will be possible to analyse how later engagement with music may be predicted from measurements at earlier stages, thereby answering questions such as, 'Who will take up music seriously during their teenage years?' and 'Who will give it up again, despite good opportunities to learn music?'. In addition, the longitudinal nature of the study will allow us to test the causal directions of hypothetical transfer effects between music and other psychological domains by examining temporal precedence (e.g. 'Does a major development in cognitive or social skills follow an earlier increase in musical training, or is the reverse true?'). Finally, the LongGold study considers musical activity alongside sports and theatre activities that serve as control domains. This will help us to address the question of whether music has a special capacity to generate transfer effects, or whether similar effects can also be achieved through analogous training in other domains.

The LongGold project started with a pilot year of data collection at Queen Anne's School, Caversham, in 2015 and has grown substantially since. So far, four UK schools have participated in the project, with eight schools from across Germany joining the project in recent years. As part of the yearly data collection, pupils go through a battery of musical listening tests, take brief tests on their general intelligence and working memory and answer questions about their growth mindset, their personal strengths and difficulties, their social and academic self-concepts, their personality, their musical activities and their other leisure-time activities. Academic achievement is monitored through the children's school grades. The annual testing session takes about ninety minutes, with pupils being tested in groups in a classroom environment. All tests and questionnaires are implemented via an online platform, and students can go through the battery individually using a browser interface and headphones. All questionnaires and tests are designed to be short and maximally efficient, using computerised adaptive procedures that adapt the difficulty of subsequent items to the ability of the individual participant, as estimated from their performance on previous test items (for details, see Harrison et al., 2017; Harrison and Müllensiefen, 2018; Larrouy-Maestri et al., 2019). None of the tests requires formal musical knowledge, and the resulting test scores are comparable across age groups such that individual growth can be expressed in terms of score gains on the same metric.

It is important to note that unlike previous projects investigating the effects of music training, the LongGold project does not include a specific music intervention, and there is no focus on a specific music or style. Instead, the focus is on monitoring and recording the type and intensity of musical activities as they occur in the real world. Hence, results from the project will generalise more easily to a wider range of real-world scenarios of musical opportunities provided to

227

secondary school students. While data collection on the project is still ongoing, with insights from preliminary longitudinal analysis to be published soon, a cross-sectional analysis from the first year of data collection already provides highly interesting insights into the relationships between musical variables, learning attitudes, self-concepts and academic achievements. The full results from the first year of data collection have been published as an open-access journal article (Müllensiefen et al., 2015) but are summarised in the following section to provide the basis for the developing ideas around teaching interventions that use the topic of music and brain plasticity to influence student attitudes towards their own learning capacities.

How music relates to learning attitudes and academic achievement

The data collection of the first year of the LongGold project included 312 girls between 10 and 18 years of age at Queen Anne's School, Caversham, United Kingdom. Whilst the girls each went through a full battery of twenty tests and questionnaires, we focus here only on the relationship between musical variables, learning attitudes and academic achievement. We used the brief 'theory of intelligence' and 'academic goals choice' questionnaires developed by Carol Dweck et al. (Dweck, 2000) to assess learning attitudes that are widely known as 'growth mindsets'. Broadly speaking, a growth mindset is characterised by the subjective belief that one's own cognitive capacity can change and grow over time. In Dweck's conceptualisation, this incremental belief is the opposite of a 'static' or 'entity' view, where the child regards mental capacities as fixed and unchangeable. Several empirical studies demonstrate that growth mindset attitudes are generally independent of the actual intelligence level of participants (e.g. Dweck et al., 1995) but are positively related to a range of important achievement measures, for example, school performance (Robins and Pals, 2002). This pattern of results suggests that a positive growth mindset helps individuals to reach good results in achievement domains and that this is true regardless of the individual's cognitive ability level (Dweck and Sorich, 1999). In addition to Dweck's brief questionnaires asking for subjective opinions on the incremental versus static nature of intelligence, we also included newly adapted versions asking questions regarding subjective views on the nature of musicality. In analogy, we termed these questionnaires 'theory of musicality' and 'musical goals'. The main results are summarised in Figure 11.1.

The numbered dots represent individual variables (i.e. scores from tests or questionnaires) from the test battery. The figure shows a network graph that indicates the relationship between any two variables of the test battery, after taking into account the influence of all other measured variables. A line (mathematically speaking, an 'edge') between two variables means that these variables are significantly related, even after accounting for the influence from all other variables. A missing line between two variables means that these variables are not directly related, though they might be indirectly

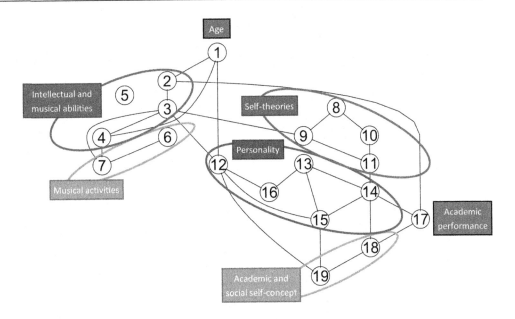

Figure 11.1 Relationships between the nineteen psychological factors assessed in the first year of the LongGold study. The nodes represent 1, age; 2, intelligence; 3, melodic memory; 4, beat perception; 5, sound similarity perception; 6, concurrent musical activities; 7, musical training; 8, musical goals; 9, theory of musicality; 10, academic goals; 11, theory of intelligence; 12, extraversion; 13, agreeableness; 14, conscientiousness; 15, emotional stability; 16, openness; 17, academic achievement; 18, academic self-concept; and 19, social self-concept. (Reproduced with permission from Müllensiefen et al., 2015.)

related through other variables. Clusters of variables are highlighted and labelled by ovals for easier understanding. Figure 11.1 shows a large number of edges between variables, but here we restrict discussion to those which are central to the debate concerning musical expertise, growth mindset and academic performance. As expected, intelligence (2) is connected to musical skills, as represented by melodic memory (3), and melodic memory is also connected to concurrent musical activities (6), which include music practice, music playing time and other types of active musical engagement. Then melodic memory (3) connects to theory of musicality (9), which further connects to theory of intelligence (11). This has a direct connection with conscientiousness (14), a personality trait. Finally, conscientiousness is connected to academic achievement (17) and academic self-concept (18). The edges between variables in Figure 11.1 are not directed, and from the data alone, we cannot tell which way the depicted effects work. Under the assumption that the chain from theory of musicality to conscientiousness to academic achievement is causal and effects are going in this direction, then changing the self-beliefs about one own's musicality would have a positive effect on academic performance.

This assumption seems plausible. In many cases, the first phases of learning to play an instrument are characterised by relatively quick progress. If learning is structured well, early learners can achieve initial successes, which go along with the awareness that they have acquired a skill that is completely new for them (e.g. producing sounds on a new instrument or being able to play along with other people). This learning can take place in the span of a few weeks and in a way that learners become aware of the apparent relation between the time spent playing the instrument and the degree of musical achievement. Hence, the opportunity to consciously experience the causal effect of training on the development of new skills is a feature that makes music a good experiential domain for influencing an individual's growth mindset. Realising that one has acquired a new skill through learning might be an earlier effect than effects stemming from music-induced neuroplasticity. Thus, it is possible that the initial effects of music training that some studies report are driven rather by a change in learning attitude than by changes at neuro-anatomical or neuro-physiological levels.

The neuro-psychology of musicality as an intervention for positive learning attitudes

The rationale

The network graph in Figure 11.1 shows that musical training and abilities are not directly related to conscientiousness and academic achievement, but the path goes through growth mindset variables (theory of musicality and theory of intelligence). Phrased differently, musical training and skills are independent of academic achievement, conditional on musical self-theories. This implies that changing one's self-theory about one's own musicality could be sufficient to bring about the desired positive changes towards an incremental growth mindset, which, in turn, can then have positive effects on academic achievement. Therefore, teaching a classroom intervention on the neuropsychology of music, including the development of musicality, brain plasticity and the effects of musical learning, could serve as an effective way to improve adolescents' attitudes towards learning. Compared with actual instrumental training, a teaching intervention on the neuropsychology of musical learning is also cheaper and has a number of practical advantages because it can be delivered as part of the normal curriculum in music or psychology.

Generally, music appears to be a suitable domain for interventions that target learning attitudes and the growth mindset. Music is personally and emotionally very important for many adolescents and is therefore a domain that many care about. Many adolescents would also have their own first-hand experience of musical learning, and teaching concepts can take into account prior skill acquisition and contributions that pupils can make to a teaching unit. Finally, music seems ideal for discussing topical talent versus practice perspectives. Views on musical achievement due to hard work or mere talent are pervasive in most musical discourses, ranging from art music to the depths of commercial popular music culture, as perpetuated in the mass media. Hence, statements on the role of talent or practice from music critics, classical performers, rock stars or hip-hop producers can be included as content materials in any musical growth mindset intervention.

Elements of an intervention teaching the neuropsychology of musical learning

To our knowledge, there is no intervention to influence learning attitudes and growth mindsets in the published literature that addresses musical learning and the development of musicality. This short chapter does not aim to provide a comprehensive description of such an intervention or provide a teaching protocol. Instead, we collate some elements and ideas from which a successful teaching intervention could be constructed by practitioners engaged in teaching or curriculum development. The implementation of a concrete intervention programme would then need to consider the frame and context in which this intervention ought to take place. Points to consider are, first of all, whether and how topics around musicality are usually taught at the target schools. Would the teaching of musical learning and music-induced brain plasticity be best taught within the music, psychology or even biology curricula? A second question to answer concerns the age groups that should be targeted by the intervention. Teaching for older age groups can possibly take advantage of prior knowledge and include a more detailed description of the brain's anatomy and physiology. For younger age groups, gaming elements and a more playful teaching style might be more appropriate. In addition to age, the socio-economic, educational and cultural background of pupils should be taken into account. Their background will matter not only in terms of prior knowledge acquisition but also in terms of preferences for musical genres, styles and artists that children can relate to and that can increase their interest and engagement. Luckily, the notion of musical mastery and the evaluative distinction between musical achievements and success either due to raw musical talent or due to effortful work is as common in most popular music styles as it is in Western art music. Therefore, introducing these opposing causal explanations for how exceptional musical skills come about can serve as an engaging starting point of an intervention illustrating how talent and hard practice work are fundamental concepts for understanding success in music, regardless of the musical style. A final point to consider concerns the concrete elements of the teaching intervention, for example, whether children should experience successful musical learning themselves, what the balance between the active creation and the teaching of knowledge is and if the intervention should be taught as a single-event workshop or be spread across several normal school lessons.

Fortunately, over the last two decades, a large number of suggestions for general interventions for positive self-theories and growth mindset have been published (e.g., Aronson et al., 2002; Bedford, 2017; Blackwell et al., 2007; Burnette et al., 2018; Donohoe et al., 2012; Paunesku et al., 2015; Schmidt et al., 2017; Zeng et al., 2016). These suggestions, together with empirical evaluations of their effectiveness and practicality, serve as very helpful examples that can guide the design of a music-based intervention.

In this respect, a recent meta-analysis of the conditions under which growth mindset interventions can affect academic achievements is particularly helpful. Overall, Jennifer Sisk et al. (2018) find in their meta-analysis of twenty-nine growth mindset intervention studies that only five of the forty-three reported effect sizes were significantly different from zero. This overall weak effect demonstrates that the specific design and delivery of growth mindset interventions hugely matter for their effectiveness, and careful thought needs to be put into selecting the target group of the intervention, the contents of that intervention and its mode of delivery.

Sisk et al. (2018) show that growth mindset interventions have their largest effects with students from low socio-economic backgrounds and students who are academically at risk. However, the type and length of the interventions were not related to their effectiveness. The authors also report that interventions were more effective when students read paper materials on growth mindset topics as opposed to interventions that were administered through a computer in an interactive way or combined different presentation modes. However, the combining of different media in an interactive computer-based presentation to deliver the intervention might not be a disadvantage, as a recent large study has shown. Using a rigorous methodological design, Yeager et al. (2019) found moderate to large effect sizes for their growth mindset intervention that was delivered online. Their intervention specifically aimed to reduce the credibility of negative effort beliefs (i.e. the belief that trying hard is an indicator of lacking ability), fixed-trait attributions (i.e. the belief that failure is caused by low ability) and performance avoidance goals (i.e. avoiding to fail and appear stupid when performing a task). The intervention used a series of guided and engaging exercises, via an online interface, to reduce the credibility of these beliefs. It comprised stories from older students and adults accepted as role models on the benefits of a growth mindset as well as interactive parts for students to reflect on in their own learning attitudes. The intervention also included an exercise where pupils were required to take a different perspective and reflect how a positive growth mindset could help a younger student who is struggling at school. The intervention contents and protocol are described in more detail in Yeager et al. (2016), but it is noteworthy that this effective intervention shares several elements with earlier successful growth mindset interventions. Perspective taking and an exercise that involved giving advice to younger at-risk children were also elements of the intervention programme employed by Joshua Aronson et al. (2002). In addition, the growth mindset intervention for science subjects by Susannah Bedford (2017) included units that encouraged students to reflect on the personal value of science and how science can help them to achieve personal goals in life.

From the synopsis of these general growth mindset intervention programmes, several elements can be adapted for an intervention programme with a focus on music learning. Potential elements of such a teaching and learning unit could be

- A workshop and lessons on the general principles of brain plasticity and how learning is manifest through physiological and anatomical changes in the brain.
- A workshop and lessons on the specific effects of musical learning and how the brains of musicians brains differ from those of non-musicians.
- A workshop and lessons on transfer effects of music and how musical learning can have effects in other domains.
- Case studies of musicians and music producers representing different musical styles that can serve as examples of how learning music transformed their attitudes and lives. Similarly, case studies can easily demonstrate how famously talented musicians also worked very hard (e.g. Mozart and Beethoven) and how talent and practice are not contradictory concepts but reciprocally depend on each other.
- Teaching and learning a new and potentially practical auditory skill. This should be a skill that is different to instrumental playing or music notation reading where backgrounds in the pupil group might differ widely already. Instead, a listening skill where preexisting differences are small and where the effects of learning become visible quickly would be more suitable (e.g. fine- pitch discrimination; Micheyl et al., 2006).
- Reflective exercises on the students' own music learning or acquisition of new skills.
- An exercise that requires answering (a fictitious) letter from a younger student describing his or her difficulties in school. Pupils can be encouraged to make use of learned contents regarding brain plasticity, the malleable nature of intelligence and music as a domain where the positive effects of (effortful) learning are visible and can contribute to success in life.
- An exercise that requires preparing a speech to younger pupils or pupils at risk on the malleability of their own cognitive capacities using music as an example.

Obviously, the outcomes of such a musical growth mindset intervention will largely depend on its exact focus and contents. Nonetheless, a likely outcome of any such intervention would be that students attribute a greater importance to music and musical learning in their lives; given that lifelong engagement with music is generally associated with greater life satisfaction (Gembris, 2012; Hallam and Creech, 2016), this would surely count as a positive effect.

Furthermore, the retention rate and degree of active contribution to school music programmes would surely benefit from such musical growth mindset interventions. Beyond these fairly direct effects in the musical domain, a number of further non-musical effects are to be expected as well. Primarily, the programme might change self-theories towards incremental beliefs about one own's cognitive capacities and better strategies for coping with failure. These can lead to greater academic efforts and ultimately to better academic performance, especially for low-performing students, students from disadvantaged backgrounds or at-risk students. It is an open question whether growth mindset interventions can or should also affect personality dimensions such as conscientiousness. But, in any case, the studies by Aronson et al. (2002), Bedford (2017), Blackwell et al. (2007), and Yeager et al. (2019) have shown that they can affect attitudes towards learning across a broad range of demographics. Hence, it seems like the time is ripe for the development of a musical growth mindset intervention and to evaluate how its potential benefits compare to the non-musical interventions that are already described in the literature.

Conclusion

This chapter has given a brief overview of the many areas where associations between musical training and engagement and positive development are reported. Music has been shown to be related to better memory, higher IQ and better academic performance but is also positively associated with pro-social behaviour, coping and emotion regulation and psycho-social skills in general.

The rich literature on these fields strongly implies that creating opportunities for musical development should be a primary item on the school agenda. However, the mechanisms by which music interacts with other psychological factors need to be understood better. It is by no means clear that the positive associations with music reported in the psychological literature can always be interpreted such that musical engagement and training are the primary causes and positive development in a different area is the consequence.

One principled way to investigate these causal questions is to conduct longitudinal studies in which the development of musical and non-musical abilities are recorded in parallel, and any observations of temporal precedence provide evidence for the direction of causality. Empirical evidence from longitudinal studies, such as the LongGold study described in this chapter, will not only make substantial contributions to fundamental psychological research but also will provide the necessary evidence base for designing effective educational interventions, be they music centred or not. In this sense, we subscribe to Kurt Lewin's aphorism that 'there is nothing as practical as a good theory' (Lewin, 1943, 118).

Of course, it is unrealistic to suppose that opportunities for high-quality musical learning and instruction could be provided to all students across all school types and demographic backgrounds. Nonetheless, a theoretical model supported by the data gathered in the first year of the LongGold study suggests that learning an instrument might not be necessary for the development of a positive growth mindset. Instead, it could be sufficient to understand how practice and musical learning can contribute to the development of new musical skills. This gives rise to a plausible hypothesis: learning about the effects of music can possibly have tangible benefits for learning attitudes as well – without the need to become a music virtuoso first. This hypothesis forms the basis for a growth mindset intervention around musical learning for which we have sketched out possible frameworks and elements in this chapter.

The actual design and implementation of such an intervention will require careful experimentation and close collaboration between teaching practitioners and psychologists. This may appear to be a huge task, but certainly it is an endeavour worth starting, as it may well produce a new learning and teaching tool with a broad range of benefits.

References

Alemán, X., Duryea, S., Guerra, N. G., et al. (2017). The effects of musical training on child development: a randomized trial of El Sistema in Venezuela. *Prevention Science*, *18*(7), 865–78. doi:10.1007/s11121-016-0727-3.

Aronson, J., Fried, C. B., and Good, C. (2002). Reducing the effects of stereotype threat on African American college students by shaping theories of intelligence. *Journal of Experimental Social Psychology*, *38*(2), 113–25. doi:10.1006/jesp.2001.1491.

Bedford, S. (2017). Growth mindset and motivation: a study into secondary school science learning. *Research Papers in Education*, *32*(4), 424–43. doi:10.1080/02671522.2017.1318809.

Blackwell, L. S., Trzesniewski, K. H., and Dweck, C. S. (2007). Implicit theories of intelligence predict achievement across an adolescent transition: a longitudinal study and an intervention. *Child Development*, *78*(1), 246–63. doi:10.1111/j.1467-8624.2007.00995.x.

Burnette, J. L., Russell, M. V., Hoyt, C. L., et al. (2018). An online growth mindset intervention in a sample of rural adolescent girls. *British Journal of Educational Psychology*, *88*(3), 428–45. doi:10.1111/bjep.12192.

Butkovic, A., Ullén, F., and Mosing, M. A. (2015). Personality related traits as predictors of music practice: underlying environmental and genetic influences. *Personality and Individual Differences*, *74*, 133–38. doi:10.1016/j.paid.2014.10.006.

Chan, A. S., Ho, Y.-C., and Cheung, M.-C. (1998). Music training improves verbal memory. *Nature*, *396*(6707), 128. doi:10.2307/1165285.

de Manzano, Ö., and Ullén, F. (2017). Same genes, different brains: neuroanatomical differences between monozygotic twins discordant for musical training. *Cerebral Cortex*, *28*(1), 387–94. doi:10.1093/cercor/bhx299.

Degé, F., and Schwarzer, G. (2011). The effect of a music program on phonological awareness in preschoolers. *Frontiers in Psychology*, *2*, 124. doi:10.3389/fpsyg.2011.00124.

Donohoe, C., Topping, K., and Hannah, E. (2012). The impact of an online intervention (brainology) on the mindset and resiliency of secondary school pupils: a preliminary mixed methods study. *Educational Psychology*, *32*(5), 641–55. doi:10.1080/01443410.2012.675646.

Dweck, C. S. (2000). *Self-theories: Their Role in Motivation, Personality, and Development*. Philadelphia: Psychology Press.

Dweck, C. S., Chiu, C. Y., and Hong, Y. Y. (1995). Implicit theories and their role in judgments and reactions: a word from two perspectives. *Psychological Inquiry*, *6*(4), 267–85. doi:10.1207/s15327965pli0604_1.

Dweck, C. S., and Sorich, L. A. (1999). Mastery-orientated thinking. In C. R. Snyder (Ed.), *Coping: The Psychology of What Works* (pp. 232–78). New York: Oxford University Press.

Farahmand, F. K., Grant, K. E., Polo, A. J., and Duffy, S. N. (2011). School-based mental health and behavioral programs for low-income, urban youth: a systematic and meta-analytic review. *Clinical Psychology: Science and Practice*, *18*(4), 372–90. doi:10.1111/j.1468-2850.2011.01265.x.

Gaser, C., and Schlaug, G. (2003). Brain structures differ between musicians and non-musicians. *Journal of Neuroscience*, *23*(27), 9240–45. doi:10.1523/JNEUROSCI.23-27-09240.2003.

Gembris, H. (2012). Music-making as a lifelong development and resource for health. In R. MacDonald, G. Kreutz, and L. Mitchell (Eds.), *Music, Health, and Wellbeing* (pp. 367–82). New York: Oxford University Press.

Guhn, M., Emerson, S. D., and Gouzouasis, P. (2020). A population-level analysis of associations between school music participation and academic achievement. *Journal of Educational Psychology*, *112*(2). doi:10.1037/edu0000376.

Hallam, S., and Creech, A. (2016). Can active music making promote health and well-being in older citizens? Findings of the music for life project. *London Journal of Primary Care*, *8*(2), 21–25. doi:10.1080/17571472.2016.1152099.

Hargreaves, D., and Lamont, A. (2017). *The Psychology of Musical Development*. New York: Cambridge University Press.

Harrison, P. M., Collins, T., and Müllensiefen, D. (2017). Applying modern psychometric techniques to melodic discrimination testing: item response theory, computerised adaptive testing, and automatic item generation. *Scientific Reports*, *7*(1), 3618. doi:10.1038/s41598-017-03586-z.

Harrison, P. M., and Müllensiefen, D. (2018). Development and validation of the Computerised Adaptive Beat Alignment Test (CA-BAT). *Scientific Reports, 8* (1), 12395. doi:10.1038/s41598-018-30318-8.

Hille, A., and Schupp, J. (2014). How learning a musical instrument affects the development of skills. *Economics of Education Review, 44,* 56–82. doi:10.1016/j. econedurev.2014.10.007.

Ho, Y.-C., Cheung, M.-C., and Chan, A. S. (2003). Music training improves verbal but not visual memory: cross-sectional and longitudinal explorations in children. *Neuropsychology, 17*(3), 439–50. doi:10.1037/0894-4105.17.3.439.

Kirschner, S., and Tomasello, M. (2010). Joint music making promotes prosocial behavior in 4-year-old children. *Evolution and Human Behavior, 31*(5), 354–64. doi:10.1016/j.evolhumbehav.2010.04.004.

Larrouy-Maestri, P., Harrison, P. M., and Müllensiefen, D. (2019). The mistuning perception test: a new measurement instrument. *Behavior Research Methods, 51*(2), 663–75. doi:10.3758/s13428-019-01225-1.

Lewin, K. (1943). Psychology and the process of group living. *Journal of Social Psychology, 17*(1), 113–31. (Reprinted in *The Complete Social Scientist: A Kurt Lewin reader,* pp. 333–45, by M. Gold, Ed., 1999, Washington, DC: American Psychological Association).

Lonsdale, A. J., and North, A. C. (2011). Why do we listen to music? A uses and gratifications analysis. *British Journal of Psychology, 102*(1), 108–34. doi:10.1348/ 000712610X506831.

Micheyl, C., Delhommeau, K., Perrot, X., and Oxenham, A. J. (2006). Influence of musical and psychoacoustical training on pitch discrimination. *Hearing Research, 219*(1–2), 36–47. doi:10.1016/j.heares.2006.05.004.

Miranda, D. (2013). The role of music in adolescent development: much more than the same old song. *International Journal of Adolescence and Youth, 18*(1), 5–22. doi:10.1080/02673843.2011.650182.

Miranda, D., and Claes, M. (2009). Music listening, coping, peer affiliation and depression in adolescence. *Psychology of Music, 37*(2), 215–33. doi:10.1177/ 0305735608097245.

Mosing, M. A., Pedersen, N. L., Madison, G., and Ullén, F. (2014). Genetic pleiotropy explains associations between musical auditory discrimination and intelligence. *PloS One, 9*(11), e113874. doi:10.1371/journal.pone.0113874.

Müllensiefen, D., Harrison, P., Caprini, F., and Fancourt, A. (2015). Investigating the importance of self-theories of intelligence and musicality for students' academic and musical achievement. *Frontiers in Psychology, 6,* 1702. doi:10.3389/ fpsyg.2015.01702.

North, A. C., Hargreaves, D. J., and O'Neill, S. A. (2000). The importance of music to adolescents. *British Journal of Educational Psychology, 70*(2), 255–72. doi:10.1348/000709900158083.

Papinczak, Z. E., Dingle, G. A., Stoyanov, S. R., et al. (2015). Young people's uses of music for well-being. *Journal of Youth Studies, 18*(9), 1119–34. doi:10.1080/13676261.2015.1020935.

Paunesku, D., Walton, G. M., Romero, C., et al. (2015). Mind-set interventions are a scalable treatment for academic underachievement. *Psychological Science, 26* (6), 784–93. doi:10.1177/0956797615571017.

Robins, R. W., and Pals, J. L. (2002). Implicit self-theories in the academic domain: implications for goal orientation, attributions, affect, and self-esteem change. *Self and Identity, 1*(4), 313–36. doi:10.1080/15298860290106805.

Roden, I., Zepf, F. D., Kreutz, G., et al. (2016). Effects of music and natural science training on aggressive behavior. *Learning and Instruction, 45,* 85–92. doi:10.1016/j.learninstruc.2016.07.002.

Ruthsatz, J., Detterman, D., Griscom, W. S., and Cirullo, B. A. (2008). Becoming an expert in the musical domain: it takes more than just practice. *Intelligence, 36*(4), 330–38. doi:10.1016/j.intell.2007.08.003.

Sala, G., and Gobet, F. (2017). When the music's over: does music skill transfer to children's and young adolescents' cognitive and academic skills? A meta-analysis. *Educational Research Review, 20,* 55–67. doi:10.1016/j.edurev.2016.11.005.

Schäfer, T., Sedlmeier, P., Städtler, C., and Huron, D. (2013). The psychological functions of music listening. *Frontiers in Psychology, 4,* 511. doi:10.3389/fpsyg.2013.00511.

Schellenberg, E. G. (2004). Music lessons enhance IQ. *Psychological Science, 15*(8), 511–14. doi:10.1111/j.0956-7976.2004.00711.x.

Schellenberg, E. G. (2005). Music and cognitive abilities. *Current Directions in Psychological Science, 14*(6), 317–20. doi:10.1111/j.0963-7214.2005.00389.x.

Schellenberg, E. G. (2019). Correlation = causation? Music training, psychology, and neuroscience. *Psychology of Aesthetics, Creativity, and the Arts.* advance online publication. doi:10.1037/aca0000263.

Schmidt, J. A., Shumow, L., and Kackar-Cam, H. Z. (2017). Does mindset intervention predict students' daily experience in classrooms? A comparison of seventh and ninth graders' trajectories. *Journal of Youth and Adolescence, 46*(3), 582–602. doi:10.1007/s10964-016-0489-z.

Seither-Preisler, A., Parncutt, R., and Schneider, P. (2014). Size and synchronization of auditory cortex promotes musical, literacy, and attentional skills in children. *Journal of Neuroscience, 34*(33), 10937–49. doi:10.1523/JNEUROSCI.5315-13.2014.

Sisk, V. F., Burgoyne, A. P., Sun, J., et al. (2018). To what extent and under which circumstances are growth mind-sets important to academic achievement? Two meta-analyses. *Prevention Science, 29*(4), 549–71. doi:10.1177/0956797617739704.

Slater, A., and Bremner, J. G. (Eds.). (2017). *An Introduction to Developmental Psychology.* Hoboken, NJ: John Wiley and Sons.

Williams, K. E., Barrett, M. S., Welch, G. F., et al. (2015). Associations between early shared music activities in the home and later child outcomes: findings from the longitudinal study of Australian children. *Early Childhood Research Quarterly, 31,* 113–24. doi:10.1016/j.ecresq.2015.01.004.

Yeager, D. S., Hanselman, P., Walton, G. M., et al. (2019). A national experiment reveals where a growth mindset improves achievement. *Nature, 573* (7774), 364–69. doi:10.1038/s41586-019-1466-y.

Yeager, D. S., Romero, C., Paunesku, D., et al. (2016). Using design thinking to improve psychological interventions: the case of the growth mindset during the transition to high school. *Journal of Educational Psychology, 108*(3), 374–91. doi:10.1037/edu0000098.

Zeng, G., Hou, H., and Peng, K. (2016). Effect of growth mindset on school engagement and psychological well-being of Chinese primary and middle school students: the mediating role of resilience. *Frontiers in Psychology, 7*, 1873. doi:10.3389/fpsyg.2016.01873.

Index

Page numbers in *italics* refer to Figures, and page numbers in **bold** refer to Tables.

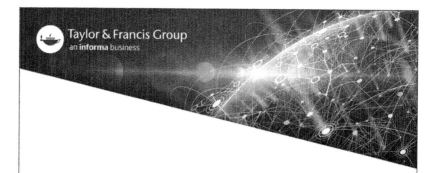